~ DISNEY KINGDOMS ~

BIG THUNDER MOUNTAIN RAILROAD

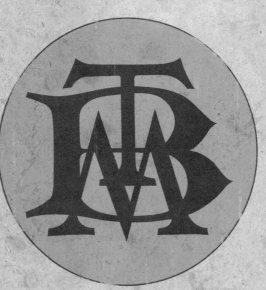

Collection Editor MARK D. BEAZLEY
Assistant Editor SARAH BRUNSTAD
Associate Managing Editor ALEX STARBUCK
Editor, Special Projects JENNIFER GRÜNWALD
Senior Editor, Special Projects JEFF YOUNGQUIST
Book Design ADAM DEL RE

SVP Print, Sales & Marketing DAVID GABRIEL
Editor in Chief AXEL ALONSO
Chief Creative Officer JOE QUESADA
Publisher DAN BUCKLEY

Special Thanks to DAVID GABRIEL, MARK PANICCIA & VANESSA HUNT

BIG THUNDER MOUNTAIN RAILROAD. Contains material originally published in magazine form as BIG THUNDER MOUNTAIN RAILROAD #1-5. First printing 2015. ISBN# 978-0-7851-9701-0. Published by MARVEL WORLDWIDE, INC., a subsidiary of MARVEL ENTERTAINMENT, LLC. OFFICE OF PUBLICATION: 135 West 50th Street, New York, NY 10020. **Printed in the U.S.A.** ALAN FINE, President, Marvel Entertainment; DAN BUCKLEY, President, TV, Publishing and Brand Management; JOE QUESADA, Chief Creative Officer; TOM BREVOORT, SVP of Publishing; DAVID BOGART, SVP of Operations & Procurement, Publishing; C.B. CEBULSKI, VP of International Development & Brand Management; DAVID GABRIEL, SVP Print, Sales & Marketing; JIM O'KEEFE, VP of Operations & Logistics; DAN CARR, Executive Director of Publishing Technology; SUSAN CRESPI, Editorial Operations Manager; ALEX MORALES, Publishing Operations Manager; STAN LEE, Chairman Emeritus. For information regarding advertising in Marvel Comics or on Marvel.com, please contact Jonathan Rheingold, VP of Custom Solutions & Ad Sales, at jrheingold@marvel.com. For Marvel subscription inquiries, please call 800-217-9158. **Manufactured between 7/3/2015 and 8/10/2015 by R.R. DONNELLEY, INC., SALEM, VA, USA.**

10 9 8 7 6 5 4 3 2 1

BIG THUNDER MOUNTAIN RAILROAD

Writer
DENNIS HOPELESS

Artists
TIGH WALKER (#1-2, #4-5)
& FELIX RUIZ (#3)
with GUILLERMO MOGORRON (#4; #5 FINISHES)

~

Colorist
JEAN-FRANCOIS BEAULIEU

Letterer
VC's JOE CARAMAGNA

~

Walt Disney Imagineers
BRIAN CROSBY, ANDY DIGENOVA,
TOM MORRIS & JOSH SHIPLEY

Editors
BILL ROSEMANN, MARK BASSO & EMILY SHAW

Cover Artists
PASQUAL FERRY (#1-3),
MARCIO TAKARA & ESTHER SANZ (#4-5)

BIG THUNDER STRIKES

When Walt Disney World opened back in 1971, it was without Pirates of the Caribbean, the flagship attraction in California's Disneyland. Legendary Imagineer Marc Davis had plans for Western River Expedition, an equally exciting attraction featuring rowdy cowboys and Indians within a massive Frontierland structure called Thunder Mesa. Under pressure from initial visitors, Walt Disney World began moving forward with Pirates, which would delay Thunder Mesa and put its similar Western River ride into limbo.

I had just finished a year working initial construction on Florida's Magic Kingdom, and needed a new project. From these two situations, the idea for Big Thunder Mountain would take flight.

A mine train ride crisscrossing the face of Thunder Mesa had been proposed. I figured if the track could be detached from the rock facade, the train ride could "go forward," even if there was no decision yet for the Western River. To explain this new idea for the mine train and freestanding rock formations, I made a small model and sketches for the scenes and grottos. To this I added a fearful "curse" to protect the mine's legendary gold from ever being claimed. Management was intrigued with the project's flexibility, and I landed a dream role as creative designer!

Years before, while in college, I drove mine trains through Nature's Wonderland at Disneyland. Nature's Wonderland featured a mountain with several waterfalls, the first being… "Big Thunder, the largest waterfall in Disneyland!" I heard this line every eight minutes, so it sort of stuck in my head. I pushed that name forward as work continued on a larger model with scenery reminiscent of Utah's Monument Valley.

The design challenge was to show just enough train track to make the ride look enticing, while disguising major sections to avoid revealing the jumble of "spaghetti-like" steel coaster rails. For realism, the man-made rock formations had to convince visitors that they existed way before the trains. Big Thunder Railroad had to look like it "travels where it travels" out of geological necessity, rather than following a precisely engineered "ride" layout.

When Disneyland saw the Florida model, a surprise decision was made to build it in California first. This required a mirror image redesign to fit on the opposite side of Frontierland and next to Fantasyland. With this new location, I recalled a National Geographic article about Bryce Canyon, describing it as something more from the fantasies of Walt Disney than of nature itself. I also remembered standing on the rim of Bryce, imagining the exhilaration of falling down in a coaster car towards the dark narrow canyons below!

In the end, "spectacular" Monument Valley continued to inspire the Walt Disney World version, but the more fanciful Bryce Canyon would complement the "charm" of Disneyland. This emotional distinction would continue to guide me in devising other attractions for these distinctly different Disney destinations, but to this day I wonder how Marc Davis may have felt about the plans that ultimately led to "Thunder" without "Mesa."

Tony Baxter

Disney Legend and Creative Advisor,
Walt Disney Imagineering

Working in the WED [later renamed Walt Disney Imagineering] Model Shop in the '70s, I got to know Tony Baxter and was able to watch him develop the quarter-inch-scale design model for his Big Thunder concept for Walt Disney World. Tony was working out a "falling rock" effect for the third lift and needed a larger scale model to see if it would really work, so one day he asked me if I could carve rocks. I did have a degree in sculpture but I had never carved a rock before so I, of course, said yes. That started a veritable career of carving not only small-scale models of rocks and mountains, but also as the FAD (Field Art Director) on all four of the full-sized Big Thunders that were eventually built around the world.

Although I was trained as a sculptor, I had no idea about building construction; and that is basically what all the BigTs are—just much more complicated. Very detailed half-inch-scale models are dissected and blown up to full-scale drawings that iron workers bend rebar to match. These bars are then welded together and covered with metal lath which is then covered with cement plaster, which is then detail carved to emulate all the various textures, cracks, offsets, nooks and crannies of real rocks and mountains. Being very large projects with aggressive schedules, we had to hire crews of iron workers and plaster carvers. They were not artists but craftsmen who built office buildings, hospitals and the like, not organic, aesthetically pleasing rocks. We usually got two or three art directors to teach four to six construction crews how to carve art. I've always said that it is "much easier to teach an artist about basic building construction than it is to teach a union plasterer to be an artist." After struggling through the first three BTs, we were finally able to hire many more artists to carve the majority of the Paris BT and use the union workers to support them. Not to say that the first three aren't as impressive as the Paris BT but if you look closely, it has more realistic nuances overall.

Even with more artists, Big Thunder Paris was probably the most challenging for many reasons. There was the language barrier, of course, but there were also large cultural differences which made for interesting confrontations; one that nearly started a war. As the steel is being erected, it of course gets higher and higher, and the trip down to the bottom to use a port-a-potty gets to be more and more of a chore. One day one of the workers near the top decided it was too much of a hassle and relieved himself from on high. As it was a rare dry day in Paris, the precipitation was noticed immediately down below and, especially being a crew of a different culture, they were understandably quite upset.

A little known fact about Big T Paris is that is that, at 110 feet, it is three meters (or about ten feet) taller than all the others. This was not deliberate but, in my eyes, a nice happenstance. As I mentioned earlier, the half-inch-scale model is used for bending the rebar, and it is also what the engineers designing the steel use for their calculations. In the field, the steel goes up first, and then we hang or set the cages onto it, stacking from the bottom up. However, to expedite the construction we build the topmost 30 feet or so of the steel and cages on the ground and then crane it up to the waiting base steel for the "topping-off party." Well, when that was done in Paris, there was a naked "collar" which had no cages to cover it; a gap. After some finger-pointing and discussion about cutting the main steel to lower the top 30 feet to fit, a very big and time-consuming task, it was decided to let us artists "arm wave" new shapes and cages to fill in the gap without making it look like we had merely "stretched" the shapes. It worked quite well from an artistic point of view, did not break the bank and we got a taller Big T. And we all know that bigger is better!

The "fearful curse" that Tony mentioned did seem to be real during the construction of the Big T at WDW. While building the cages away from the site in a large section of a commandeered parking lot, lightning struck one of those booster boxes which was hanging on a telephone pole right above our drawing shack and next to the layout area on the blacktop. The incredibly loud "boom" along with huge sparks and smoke (it was just like the movies!) brought us all to our knees; it was literally grown men crying. Then during the last stages of completing the main steel, with iron men on several levels with welders, lightning struck again at the very top! I had just left the office, where I was informed that a storm was coming our way. On my way out to the mountain I saw the strike hit and travel dancing down the large steel columns to the ground; quite a sight indeed! Luckily no one got hurt, but you have never seen hardened macho iron workers scramble down steel so fast in your life.

One quick little story about Tokyo's BT is that, during their "topping off" ceremony, there was a tiny glitch that got a laugh out of the mostly stoic Japanese. In Japan they really put together quite a ceremony of salt and sake poured over the steel base plates by a priest, and then gold and silver bolts used for the final tightening down. All the men in the various crews were in their cleanest uniforms and standing at attention facing the mountain as the top was slowly being raised into position. As it was being lowered into place, I noticed that it was backwards, front facing back. After waiting a few seconds to see if they would notice it, I finally decided I had to do something without causing a big stir and embarrassing anyone. But there was no way of getting anyone's attention because they were all watching the ceremony and I was in the back. Whisperering, I explained to my interpreter what was wrong and she was able to get the steel foreman to turn around and look at me. Without saying a word, I moved my hand in a twisting motion and pointed up at the topping which was beginning to be tightened down. He did a double take, grabbed his radio from its holster and suddenly many people were whispering "ah so" while other excited-sounding instructions could be heard. They began unbolting the steel and lifting the mountain top back up to turn it around. As the crowd began to understand what was happening, stifled laughter trickled all about and the head guy, Abe-san, gave me a sly smile.

Back to Paris for one last happening—and an example of the dedication the sculpting crews came to embrace. As the schedule began to press us more and more, I was told that a certain area that we had been working on for a while HAD to be done by the next morning, or the painters were going to paint over incomplete rockwork—as well as any carver working on it! So, after putting in a ten-hour day of our normal work, I collected the best carvers from around the park and asked them to stay until this section was complete. After bribing them with a pizza dinner, they agreed. Well, it took longer than expected, of course, and it began to get dark. No one else was on site so we had to fend for ourselves. I found one of those large gas-powered lights, but it was chained which is no problem when working with iron workers. After using a pair of huge bolt cutters, we were able to drag it over to our site. No gas was our next hurdle, which took more exploring and bolt cutters and we were in business again. As it got later and the memory of pizza wore off, I had to make a beer run—which gave everyone a final push to get us out of there at around 12:30 or so. And, it looked great. I even thought that some of the best work was done after the beer run!

One last comment on this little fiasco. A week or so later, Mickey Steinberg, the president of WDI at the time, came over for one of his park walkthroughs and general fact-gathering visits. During the design and budget phase of the project, he was not a fan of the little project that we stayed most of the night to finish. It was a natural arch-bridge formation that was part of but not attached to Big T, and thus could be cut without impacting anything else—with a big savings as the result. I was aware of his opinion, but left the U.S. for the site before a decision was made. To be honest, I was surprised to see the natural arch package show up at the site, but figured he had changed his mind; I mean there it was to be built. Well, back to the walkthrough. After viewing Big T from across the river and making very nice comments about how great it looked, we turned around and started to walk back along the shoreline. I thought I had dodged a bullet. Suddenly he stopped, turned around, looked at the arch again, then swung around again and looked me right in the eye. "I thought we took that arch out," he said in a heated sort of way. I stammered a little but then said that no one told me not to build it and it was part of the package that was sent to us. After a pause, to break the tension, I said without thinking, "Would you like us to take it down?" It's still there and I did not lose my job.

Fond Memories,

Skip Lange

Executive Production Designer Vice President,
Walt Disney Imagineering

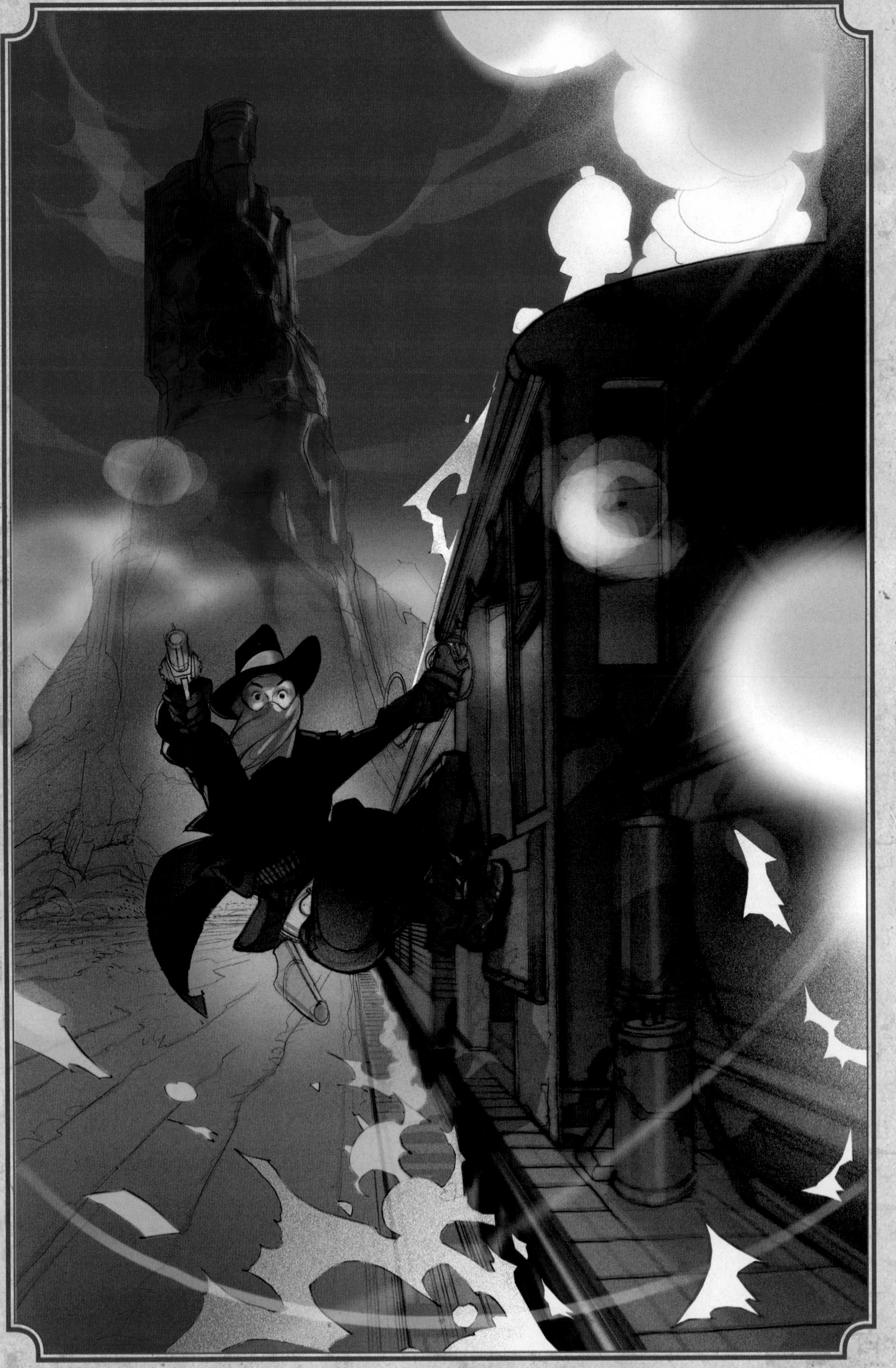

~ 1 ~

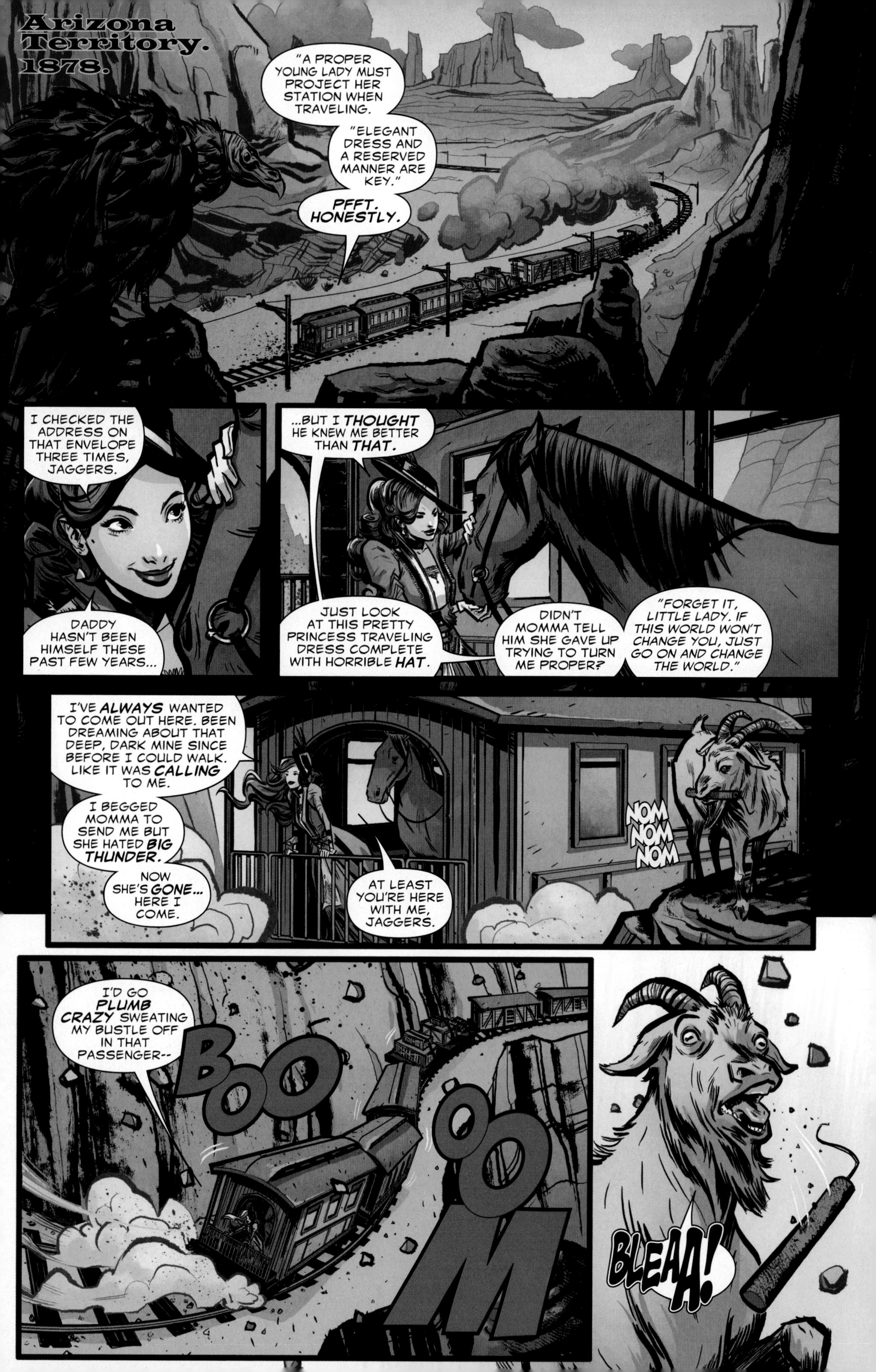
Arizona Territory. 1878.
"A PROPER YOUNG LADY MUST PROJECT HER STATION WHEN TRAVELING.
"ELEGANT DRESS AND A RESERVED MANNER ARE KEY."
PFFT. HONESTLY.
I CHECKED THE ADDRESS ON THAT ENVELOPE THREE TIMES, JAGGERS.
DADDY HASN'T BEEN HIMSELF THESE PAST FEW YEARS...
...BUT I THOUGHT HE KNEW ME BETTER THAN THAT.
JUST LOOK AT THIS PRETTY PRINCESS TRAVELING DRESS COMPLETE WITH HORRIBLE HAT.
DIDN'T MOMMA TELL HIM SHE GAVE UP TRYING TO TURN ME PROPER?
"FORGET IT, LITTLE LADY. IF THIS WORLD WON'T CHANGE YOU, JUST GO ON AND CHANGE THE WORLD."
I'VE ALWAYS WANTED TO COME OUT HERE. BEEN DREAMING ABOUT THAT DEEP, DARK MINE SINCE BEFORE I COULD WALK. LIKE IT WAS CALLING TO ME.
I BEGGED MOMMA TO SEND ME BUT SHE HATED BIG THUNDER.
NOW SHE'S GONE... HERE I COME.
AT LEAST YOU'RE HERE WITH ME, JAGGERS.
NOM NOM NOM
I'D GO PLUMB CRAZY SWEATING MY BUSTLE OFF IN THAT PASSENGER--
BOOOOM
BLEAA!

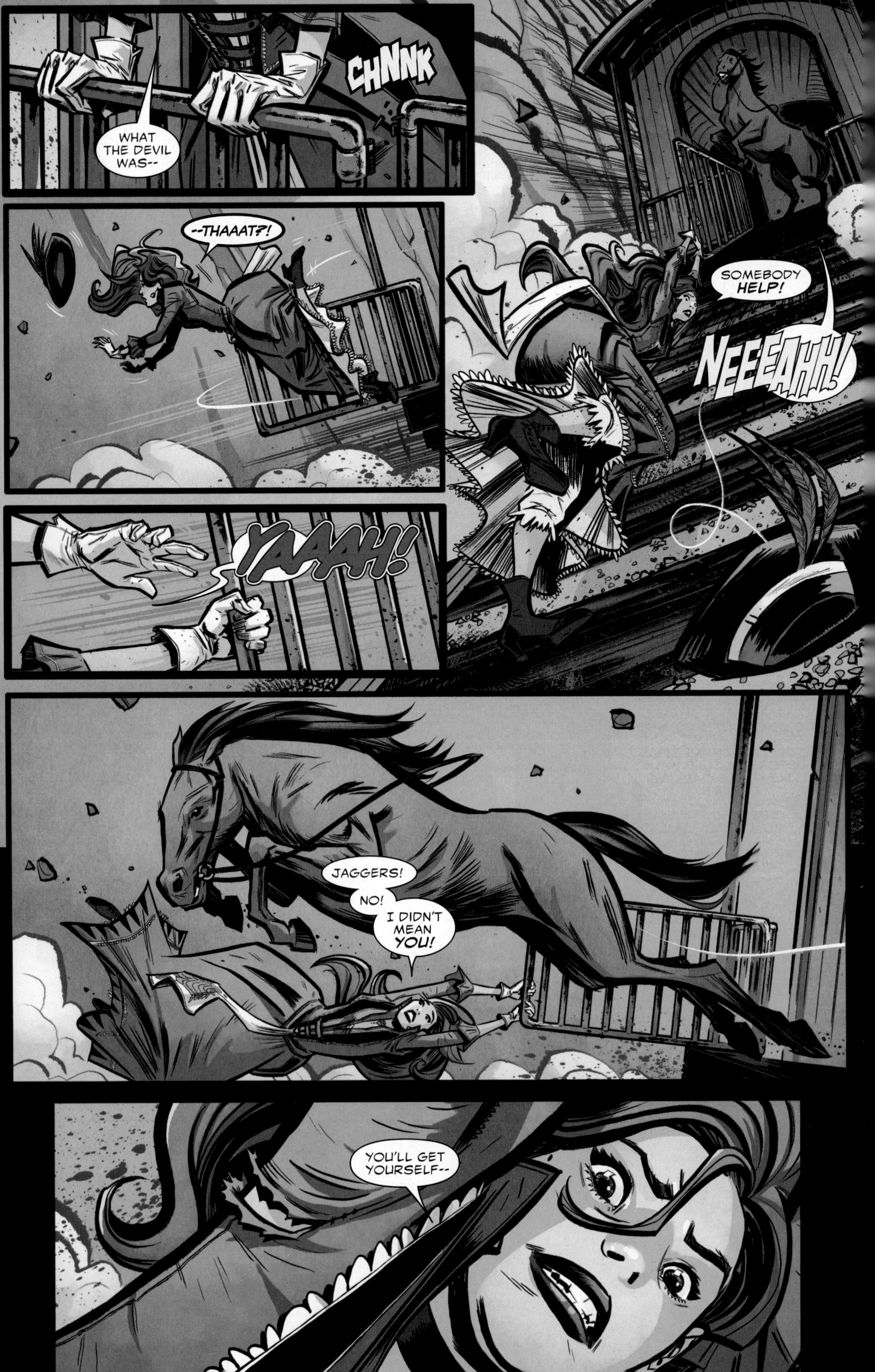
CHNNK
WHAT THE DEVIL WAS--
--THAAAT?!
YAAAH!
SOMEBODY HELP!
NEEEAHH!
JAGGERS!
NO!
I DIDN'T MEAN YOU!
YOU'LL GET YOURSELF--

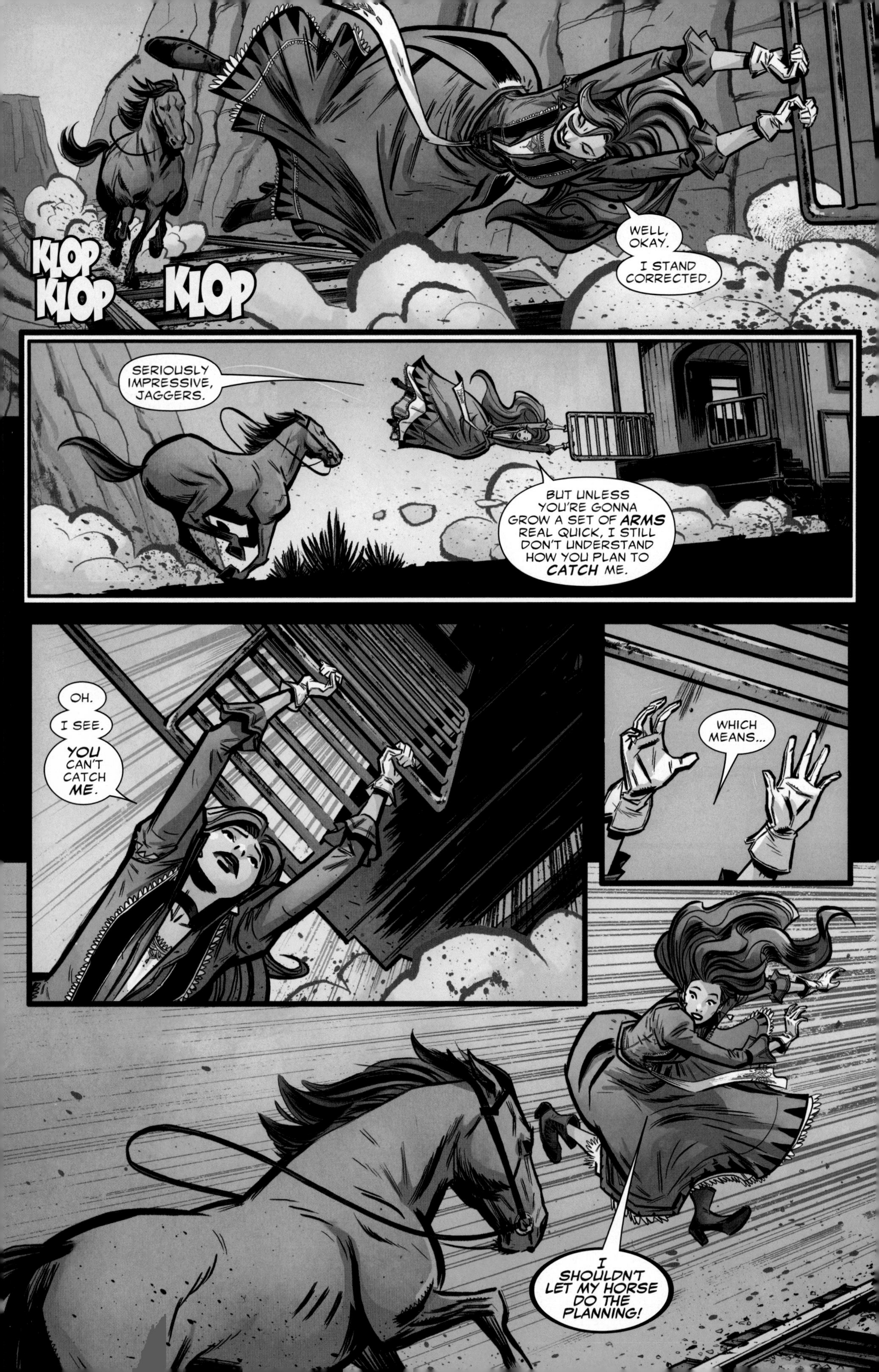
KLOP KLOP KLOP
WELL, OKAY.
I STAND CORRECTED.
SERIOUSLY IMPRESSIVE, JAGGERS.
BUT UNLESS YOU'RE GONNA GROW A SET OF ARMS REAL QUICK, I STILL DON'T UNDERSTAND HOW YOU PLAN TO CATCH ME.
OH.
I SEE.
YOU CAN'T CATCH ME.
WHICH MEANS...
I SHOULDN'T LET MY HORSE DO THE PLANNING!

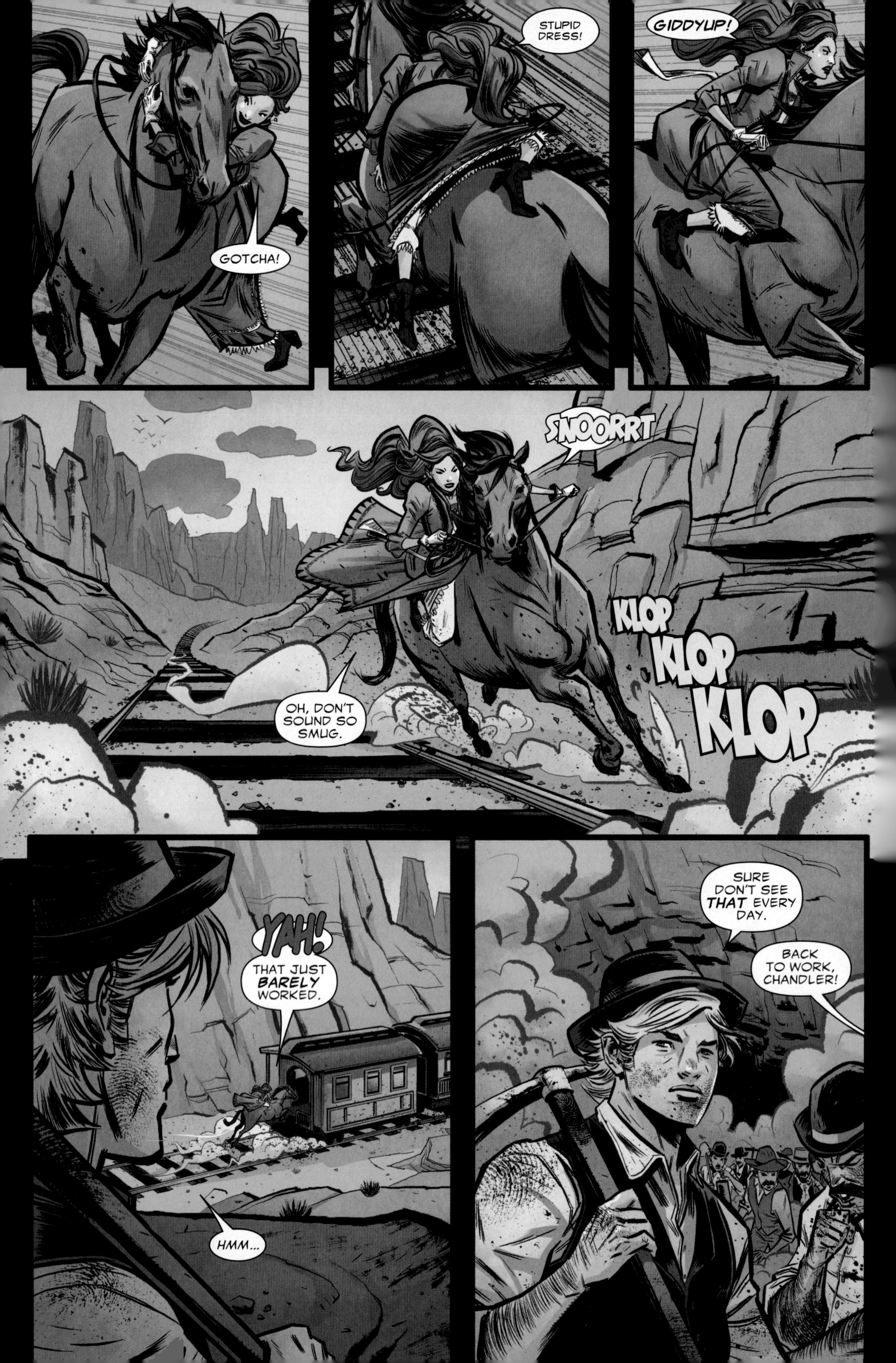
GOTCHA!
STUPID DRESS!
GIDDYUP!
SNOORRT
OH, DON'T SOUND SO SMUG.
KLOP KLOP KLOP
YAH!
THAT JUST BARELY WORKED.
HMM...
SURE DON'T SEE THAT EVERY DAY.
BACK TO WORK, CHANDLER!

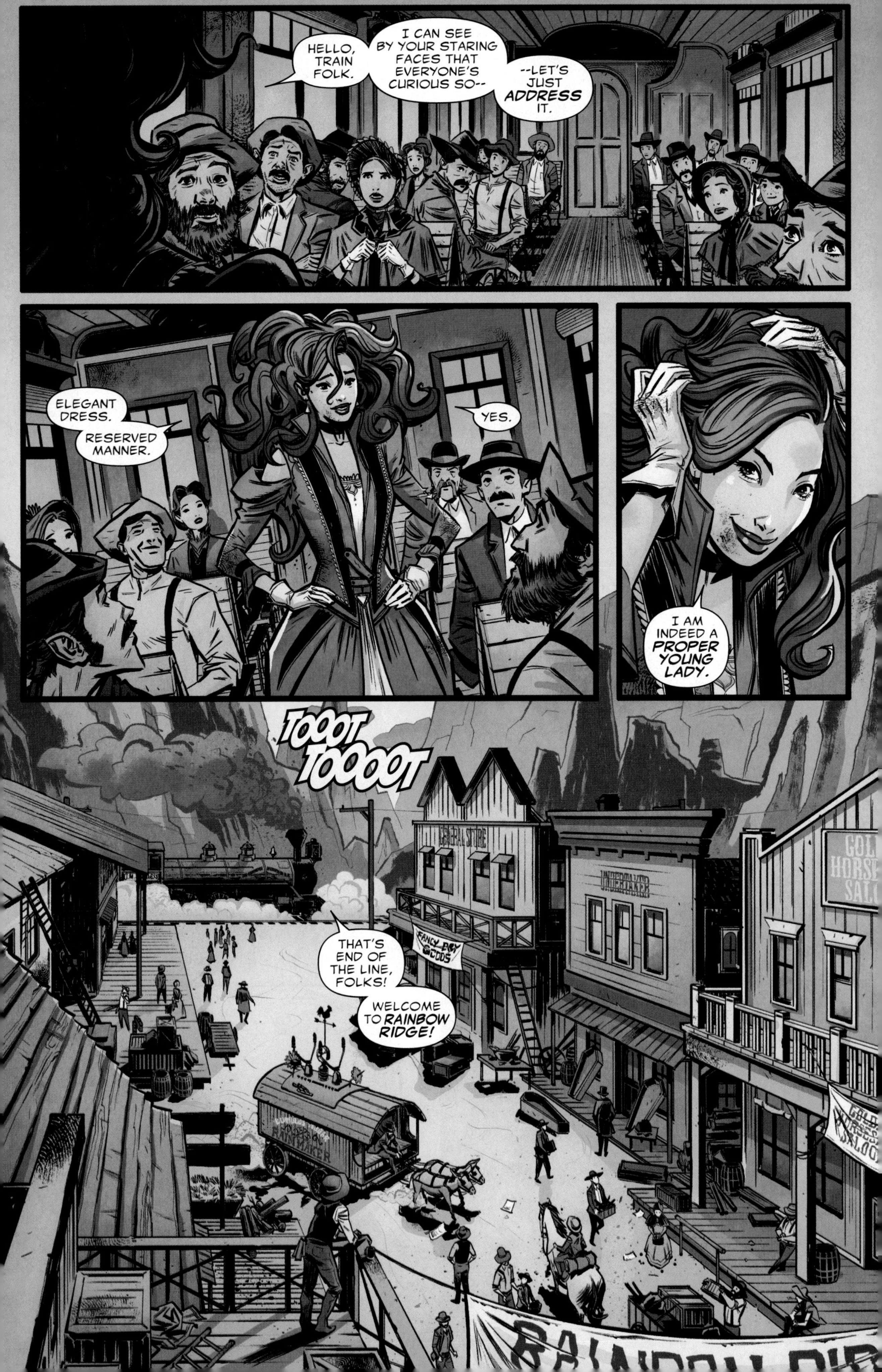

HELLO, TRAIN FOLK.
I CAN SEE BY YOUR STARING FACES THAT EVERYONE'S CURIOUS SO--
--LET'S JUST ADDRESS IT.
ELEGANT DRESS.
RESERVED MANNER.
YES.
I AM INDEED A PROPER YOUNG LADY.
TOOOT TOOOOT
GENERAL STORE
UNDERTAKER
THAT'S END OF THE LINE, FOLKS!
WELCOME TO RAINBOW RIDGE!

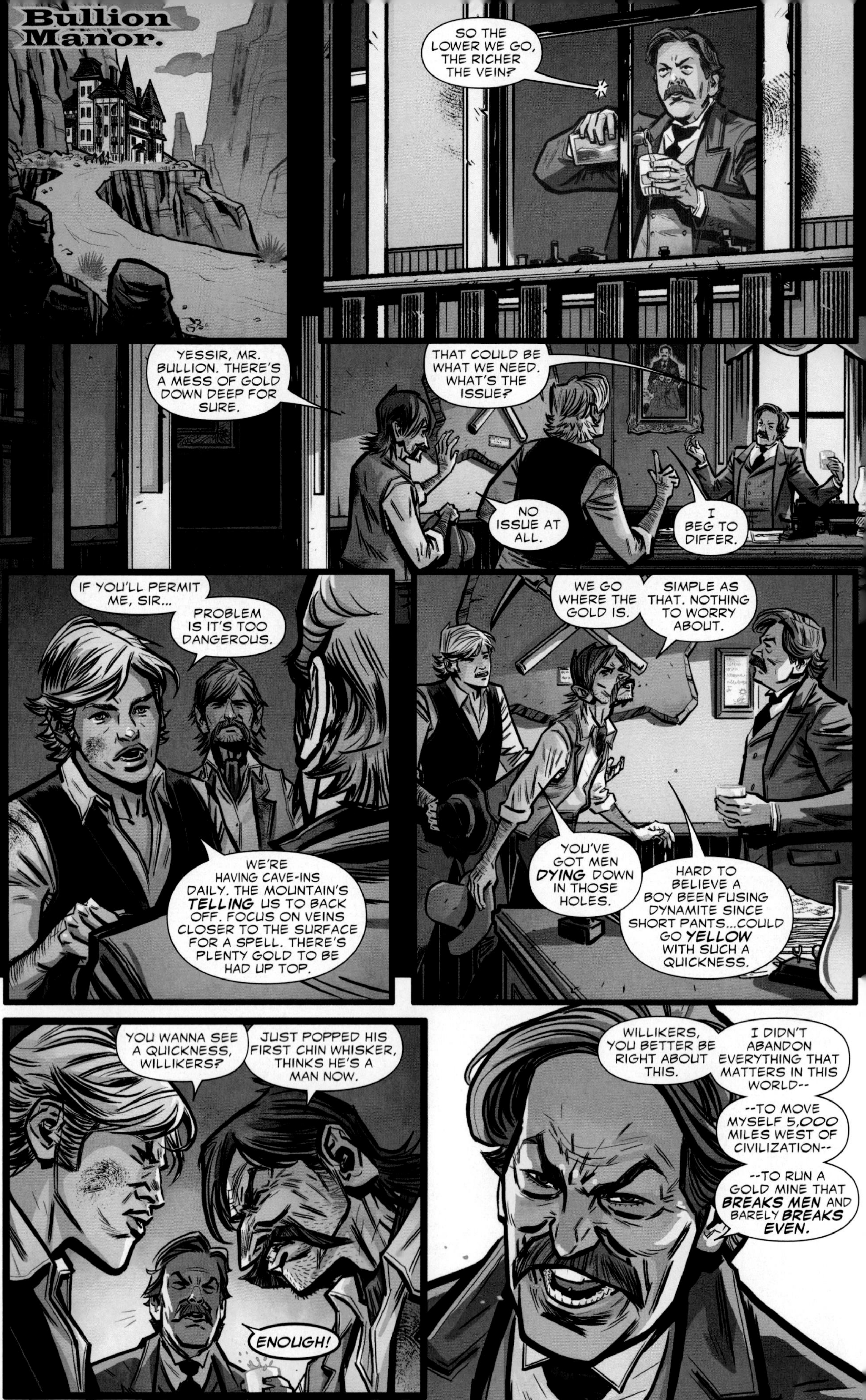
Bullion Manor.
SO THE LOWER WE GO, THE RICHER THE VEIN?
YESSIR, MR. BULLION. THERE'S A MESS OF GOLD DOWN DEEP FOR SURE.
THAT COULD BE WHAT WE NEED. WHAT'S THE ISSUE?
NO ISSUE AT ALL.
I BEG TO DIFFER.
IF YOU'LL PERMIT ME, SIR...
PROBLEM IS IT'S TOO DANGEROUS.
WE'RE HAVING CAVE-INS DAILY. THE MOUNTAIN'S TELLING US TO BACK OFF. FOCUS ON VEINS CLOSER TO THE SURFACE FOR A SPELL. THERE'S PLENTY GOLD TO BE HAD UP TOP.
WE GO WHERE THE GOLD IS.
SIMPLE AS THAT. NOTHING TO WORRY ABOUT.
YOU'VE GOT MEN DYING DOWN IN THOSE HOLES.
HARD TO BELIEVE A BOY BEEN FUSING DYNAMITE SINCE SHORT PANTS...COULD GO YELLOW WITH SUCH A QUICKNESS.
YOU WANNA SEE A QUICKNESS, WILLIKERS?
JUST POPPED HIS FIRST CHIN WHISKER, THINKS HE'S A MAN NOW.
ENOUGH!
WILLIKERS, YOU BETTER BE RIGHT ABOUT THIS.
I DIDN'T ABANDON EVERYTHING THAT MATTERS IN THIS WORLD--
--TO MOVE MYSELF 5,000 MILES WEST OF CIVILIZATION--
--TO RUN A GOLD MINE THAT BREAKS MEN AND BARELY BREAKS EVEN.

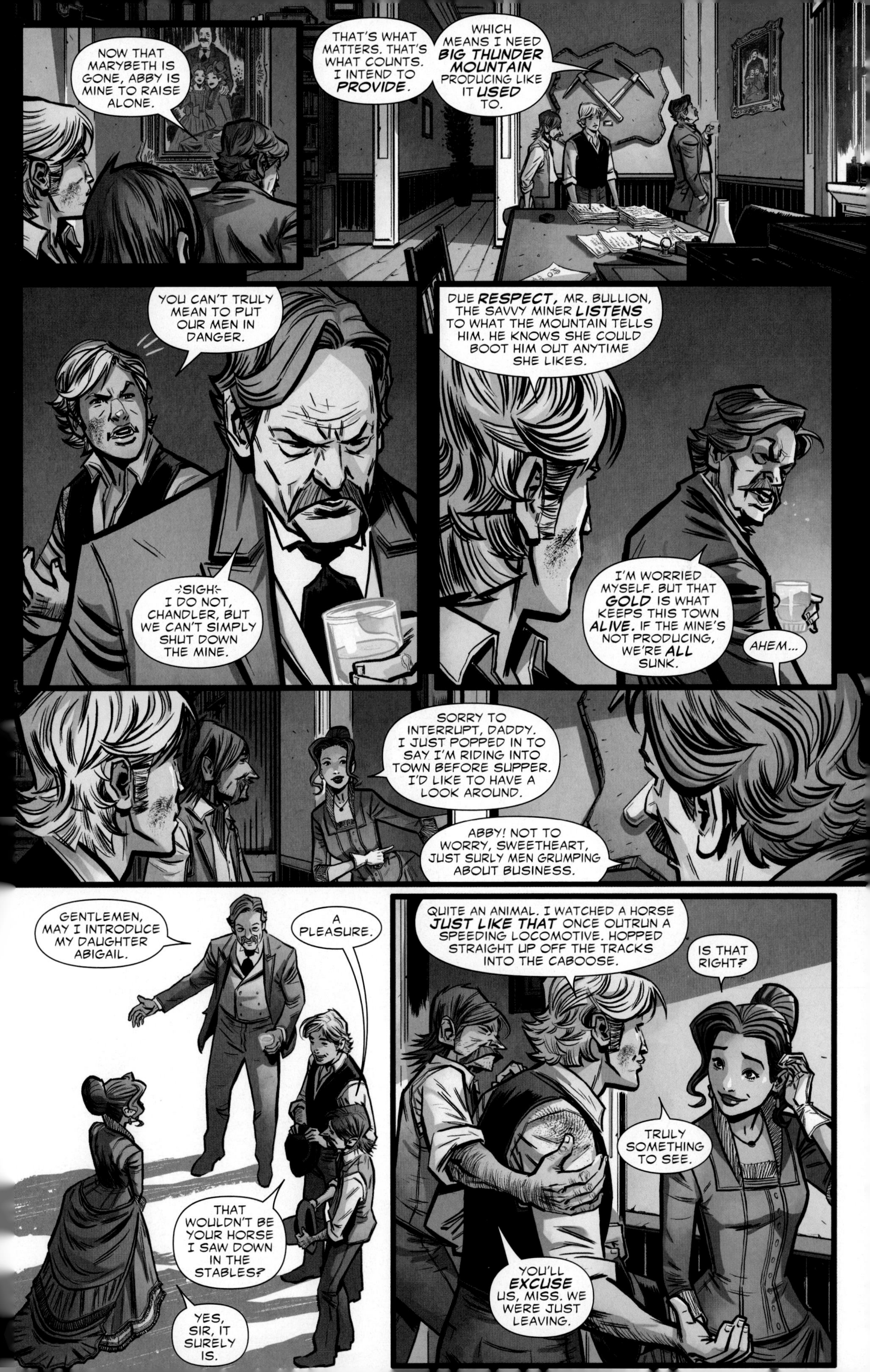
NOW THAT MARYBETH IS GONE, ABBY IS MINE TO RAISE ALONE.
THAT'S WHAT MATTERS. THAT'S WHAT COUNTS. I INTEND TO PROVIDE.
WHICH MEANS I NEED BIG THUNDER MOUNTAIN PRODUCING LIKE IT USED TO.
YOU CAN'T TRULY MEAN TO PUT OUR MEN IN DANGER.
SIGH
I DO NOT, CHANDLER, BUT WE CAN'T SIMPLY SHUT DOWN THE MINE.
DUE RESPECT, MR. BULLION, THE SAVVY MINER LISTENS TO WHAT THE MOUNTAIN TELLS HIM. HE KNOWS SHE COULD BOOT HIM OUT ANYTIME SHE LIKES.
I'M WORRIED MYSELF. BUT THAT GOLD IS WHAT KEEPS THIS TOWN ALIVE. IF THE MINE'S NOT PRODUCING, WE'RE ALL SUNK.
AHEM...
SORRY TO INTERRUPT, DADDY. I JUST POPPED IN TO SAY I'M RIDING INTO TOWN BEFORE SUPPER. I'D LIKE TO HAVE A LOOK AROUND.
ABBY! NOT TO WORRY, SWEETHEART, JUST SURLY MEN GRUMPING ABOUT BUSINESS.
GENTLEMEN, MAY I INTRODUCE MY DAUGHTER ABIGAIL.
A PLEASURE.
THAT WOULDN'T BE YOUR HORSE I SAW DOWN IN THE STABLES?
YES, SIR, IT SURELY IS.
QUITE AN ANIMAL. I WATCHED A HORSE JUST LIKE THAT ONCE OUTRUN A SPEEDING LOCOMOTIVE. HOPPED STRAIGHT UP OFF THE TRACKS INTO THE CABOOSE.
IS THAT RIGHT?
TRULY SOMETHING TO SEE.
YOU'LL EXCUSE US, MISS. WE WERE JUST LEAVING.

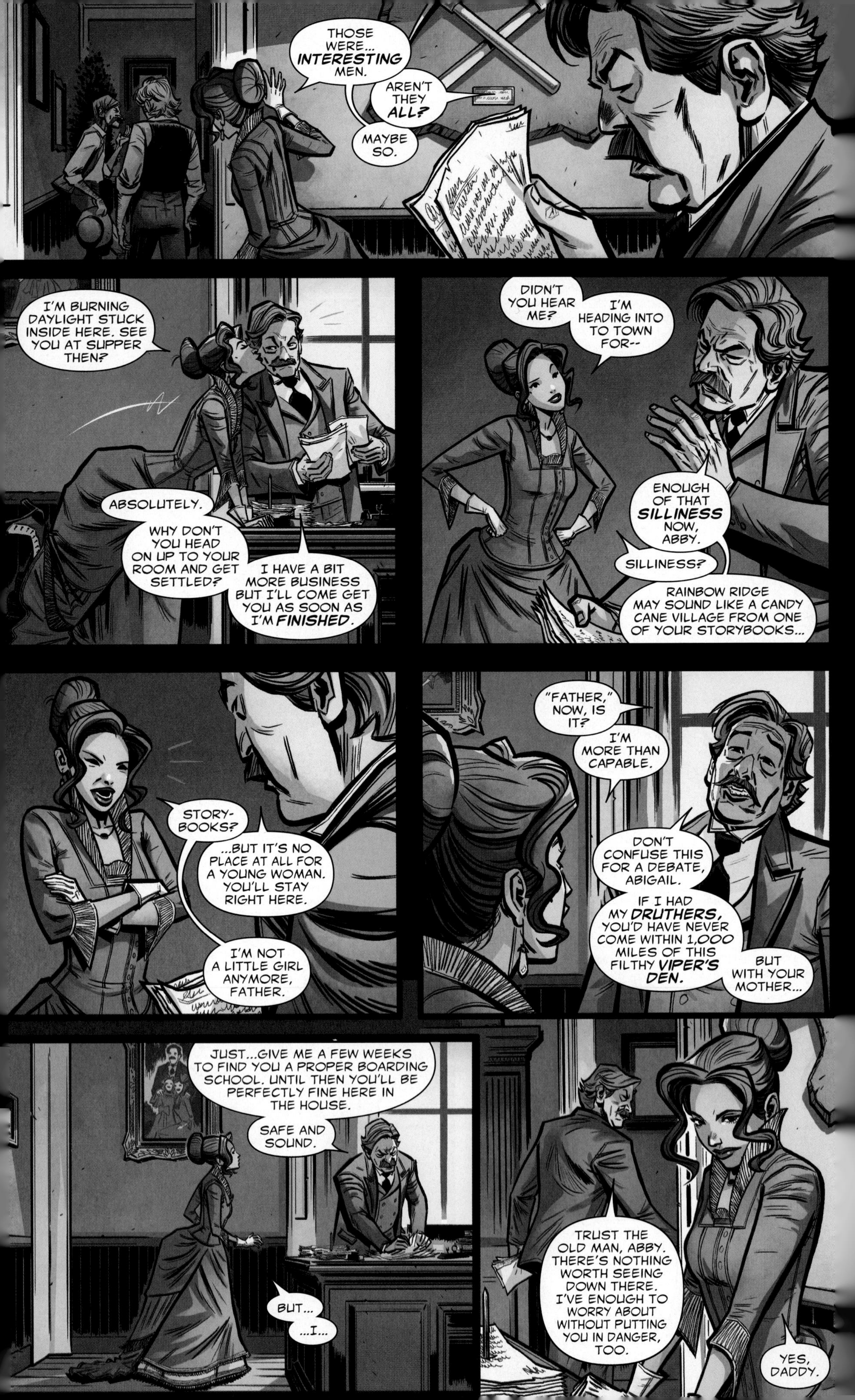
THOSE WERE... INTERESTING MEN.
AREN'T THEY ALL?
MAYBE SO.
I'M BURNING DAYLIGHT STUCK INSIDE HERE. SEE YOU AT SUPPER THEN?
ABSOLUTELY.
WHY DON'T YOU HEAD ON UP TO YOUR ROOM AND GET SETTLED?
I HAVE A BIT MORE BUSINESS BUT I'LL COME GET YOU AS SOON AS I'M FINISHED.
DIDN'T YOU HEAR ME?
I'M HEADING INTO TO TOWN FOR--
ENOUGH OF THAT SILLINESS NOW, ABBY.
SILLINESS?
RAINBOW RIDGE MAY SOUND LIKE A CANDY CANE VILLAGE FROM ONE OF YOUR STORYBOOKS...
STORY-BOOKS?
...BUT IT'S NO PLACE AT ALL FOR A YOUNG WOMAN. YOU'LL STAY RIGHT HERE.
I'M NOT A LITTLE GIRL ANYMORE, FATHER.
"FATHER," NOW, IS IT?
I'M MORE THAN CAPABLE.
DON'T CONFUSE THIS FOR A DEBATE, ABIGAIL.
IF I HAD MY DRUTHERS, YOU'D HAVE NEVER COME WITHIN 1,000 MILES OF THIS FILTHY VIPER'S DEN.
BUT WITH YOUR MOTHER...
JUST...GIVE ME A FEW WEEKS TO FIND YOU A PROPER BOARDING SCHOOL. UNTIL THEN YOU'LL BE PERFECTLY FINE HERE IN THE HOUSE.
SAFE AND SOUND.
BUT...
...I...
TRUST THE OLD MAN, ABBY. THERE'S NOTHING WORTH SEEING DOWN THERE. I'VE ENOUGH TO WORRY ABOUT WITHOUT PUTTING YOU IN DANGER, TOO.
YES, DADDY.

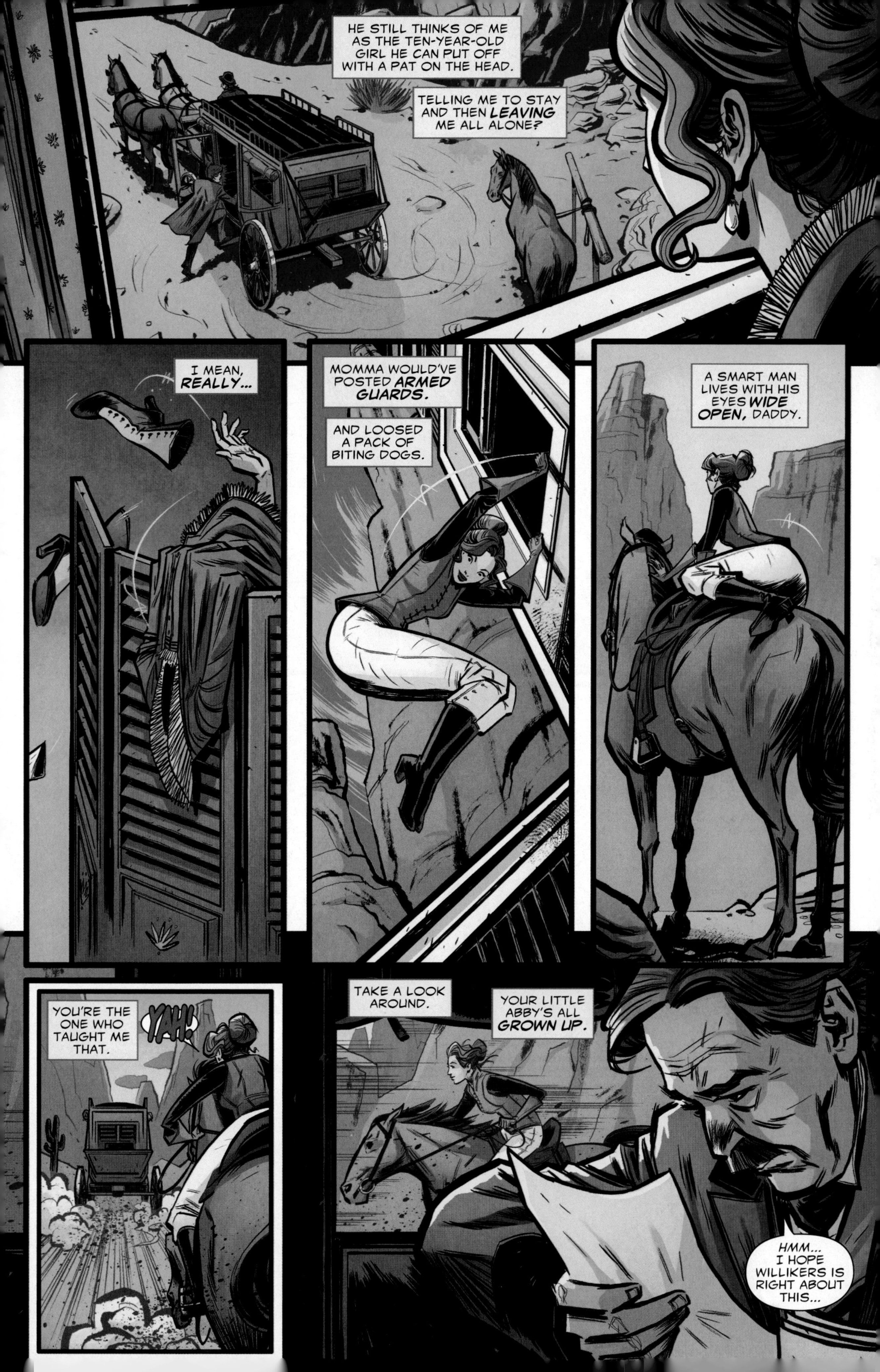
HE STILL THINKS OF ME AS THE TEN-YEAR-OLD GIRL HE CAN PUT OFF WITH A PAT ON THE HEAD.
TELLING ME TO STAY AND THEN LEAVING ME ALL ALONE?
I MEAN, REALLY...
MOMMA WOULD'VE POSTED ARMED GUARDS.
AND LOOSED A PACK OF BITING DOGS.
A SMART MAN LIVES WITH HIS EYES WIDE OPEN, DADDY.
YOU'RE THE ONE WHO TAUGHT ME THAT.
YAH!
TAKE A LOOK AROUND.
YOUR LITTLE ABBY'S ALL GROWN UP.
HMM... I HOPE WILLIKERS IS RIGHT ABOUT THIS...

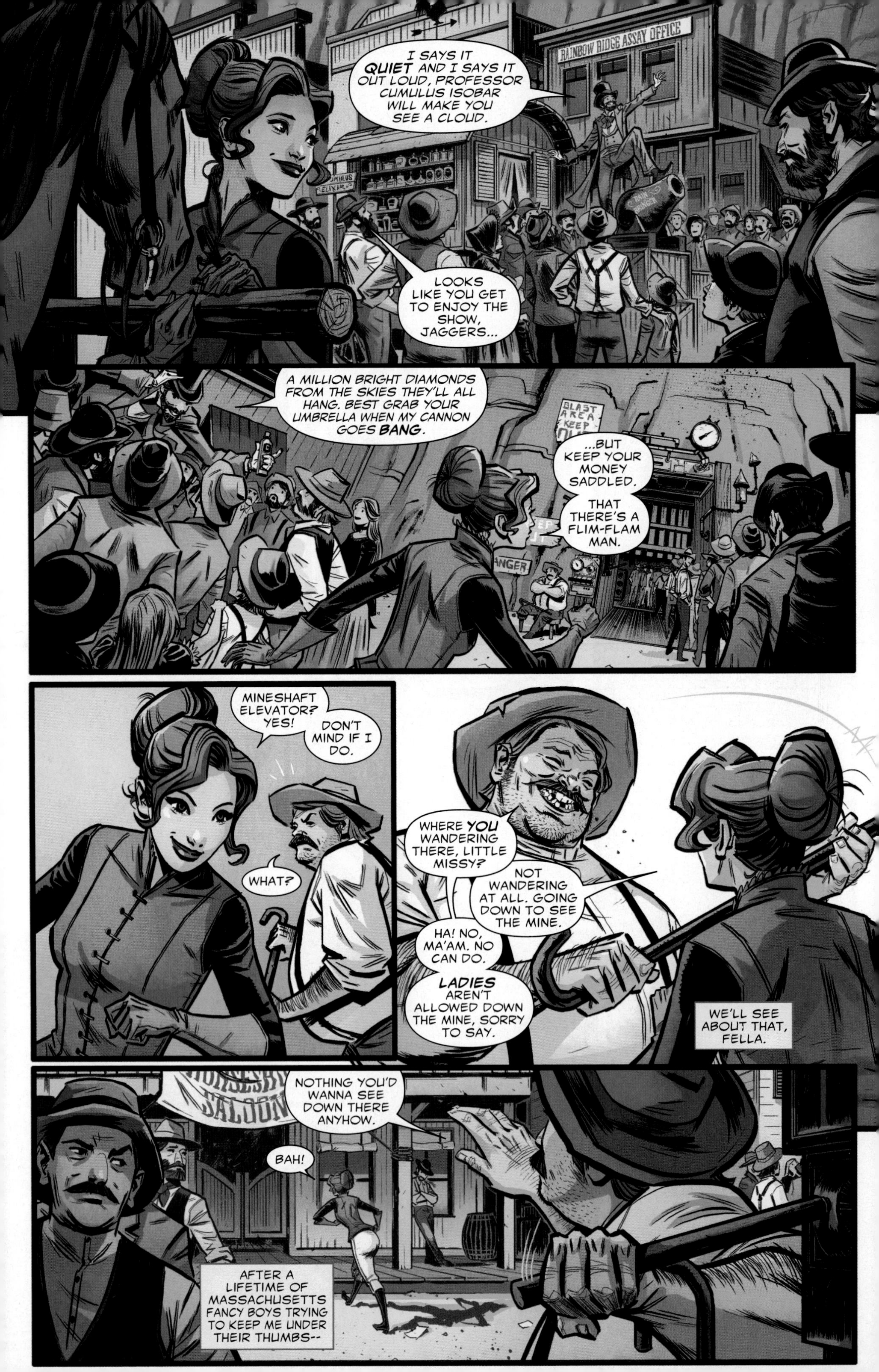
RAINBOW RIDGE ASSAY OFFICE
I SAYS IT QUIET AND I SAYS IT OUT LOUD, PROFESSOR CUMULUS ISOBAR WILL MAKE YOU SEE A CLOUD.
CUMULUS ELIXIR
RAIN BRINGER
LOOKS LIKE YOU GET TO ENJOY THE SHOW, JAGGERS...
A MILLION BRIGHT DIAMONDS FROM THE SKIES THEY'LL ALL HANG. BEST GRAB YOUR UMBRELLA WHEN MY CANNON GOES BANG.
BLAST AREA KEEP
...BUT KEEP YOUR MONEY SADDLED.
THAT THERE'S A FLIM-FLAM MAN.
ANGER
MINESHAFT ELEVATOR? YES!
DON'T MIND IF I DO.
WHAT?
WHERE YOU WANDERING THERE, LITTLE MISSY?
NOT WANDERING AT ALL. GOING DOWN TO SEE THE MINE.
HA! NO, MA'AM. NO CAN DO.
LADIES AREN'T ALLOWED DOWN THE MINE, SORRY TO SAY.
WE'LL SEE ABOUT THAT, FELLA.
SALOON
NOTHING YOU'D WANNA SEE DOWN THERE ANYHOW.
BAH!
AFTER A LIFETIME OF MASSACHUSETTS FANCY BOYS TRYING TO KEEP ME UNDER THEIR THUMBS--

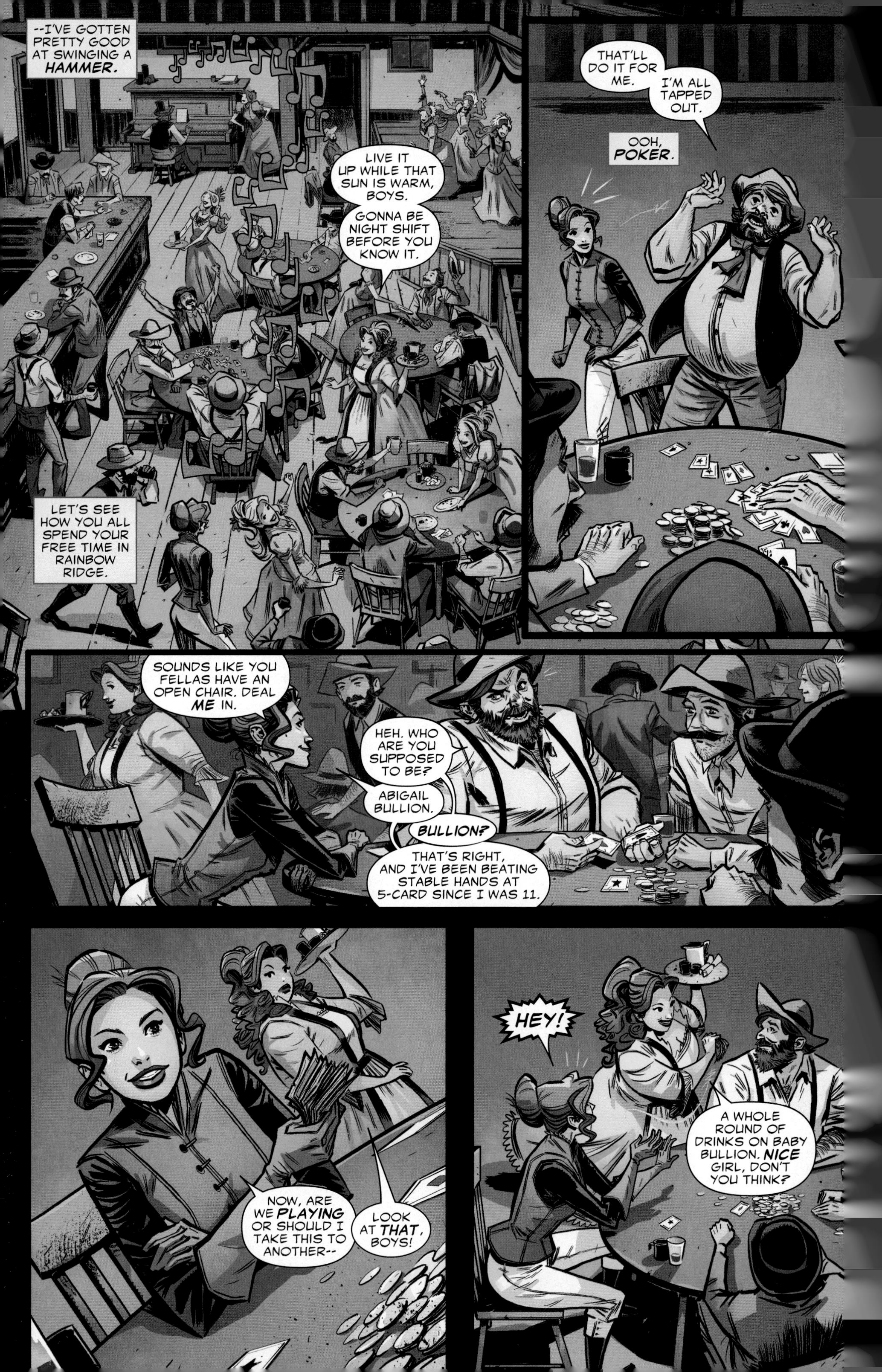
--I'VE GOTTEN PRETTY GOOD AT SWINGING A HAMMER.
LIVE IT UP WHILE THAT SUN IS WARM, BOYS.
GONNA BE NIGHT SHIFT BEFORE YOU KNOW IT.
LET'S SEE HOW YOU ALL SPEND YOUR FREE TIME IN RAINBOW RIDGE.
THAT'LL DO IT FOR ME.
I'M ALL TAPPED OUT.
OOH, POKER.
SOUNDS LIKE YOU FELLAS HAVE AN OPEN CHAIR. DEAL ME IN.
HEH. WHO ARE YOU SUPPOSED TO BE?
ABIGAIL BULLION.
BULLION?
THAT'S RIGHT, AND I'VE BEEN BEATING STABLE HANDS AT 5-CARD SINCE I WAS 11.
NOW, ARE WE PLAYING OR SHOULD I TAKE THIS TO ANOTHER--
LOOK AT THAT, BOYS!
HEY!
A WHOLE ROUND OF DRINKS ON BABY BULLION. NICE GIRL, DON'T YOU THINK?

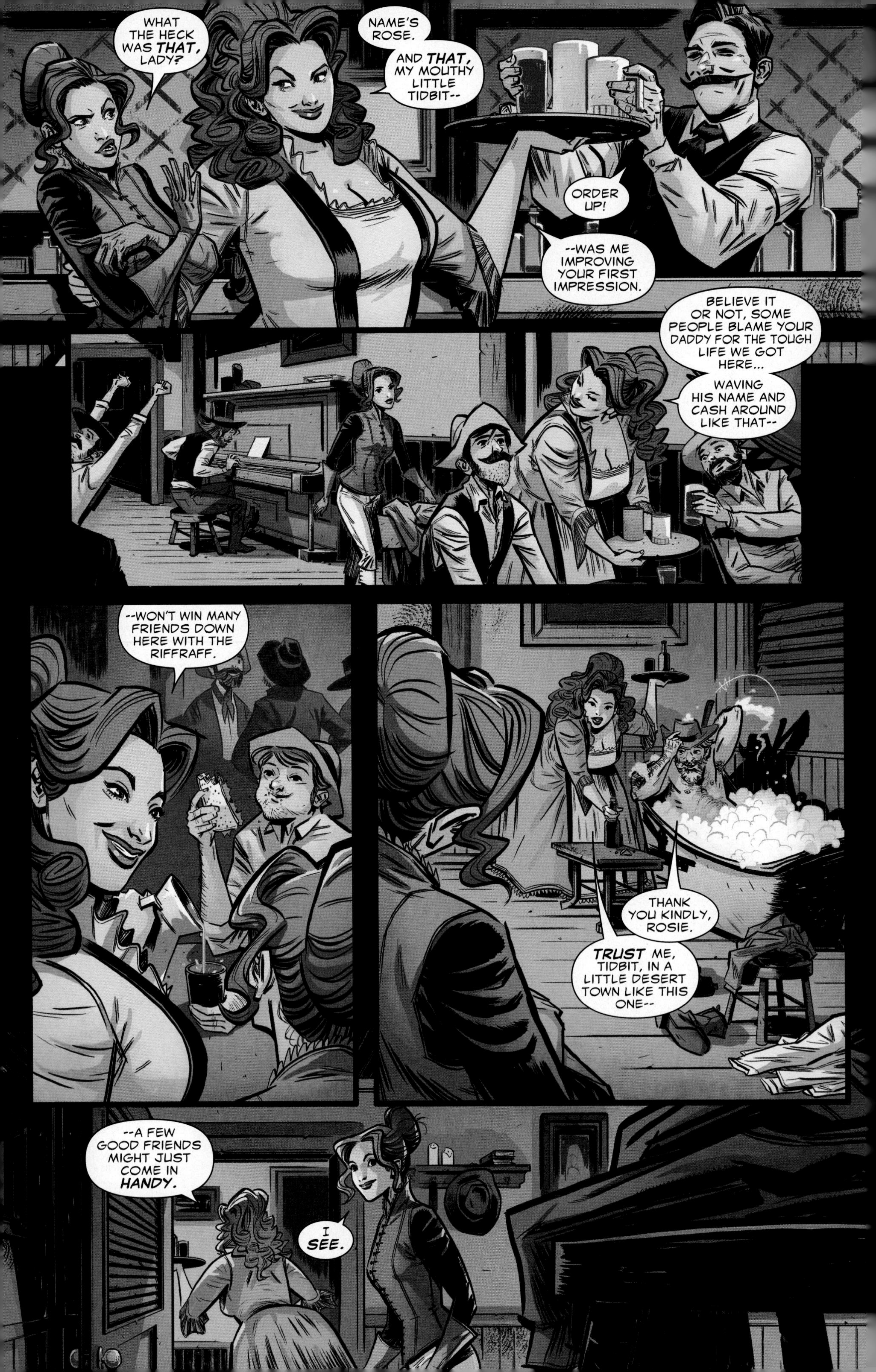
WHAT THE HECK WAS THAT, LADY?
NAME'S ROSE.
AND THAT, MY MOUTHY LITTLE TIDBIT--
ORDER UP!
--WAS ME IMPROVING YOUR FIRST IMPRESSION.
BELIEVE IT OR NOT, SOME PEOPLE BLAME YOUR DADDY FOR THE TOUGH LIFE WE GOT HERE...
WAVING HIS NAME AND CASH AROUND LIKE THAT--
--WON'T WIN MANY FRIENDS DOWN HERE WITH THE RIFFRAFF.
THANK YOU KINDLY, ROSIE.
TRUST ME, TIDBIT, IN A LITTLE DESERT TOWN LIKE THIS ONE--
--A FEW GOOD FRIENDS MIGHT JUST COME IN HANDY.
I SEE.

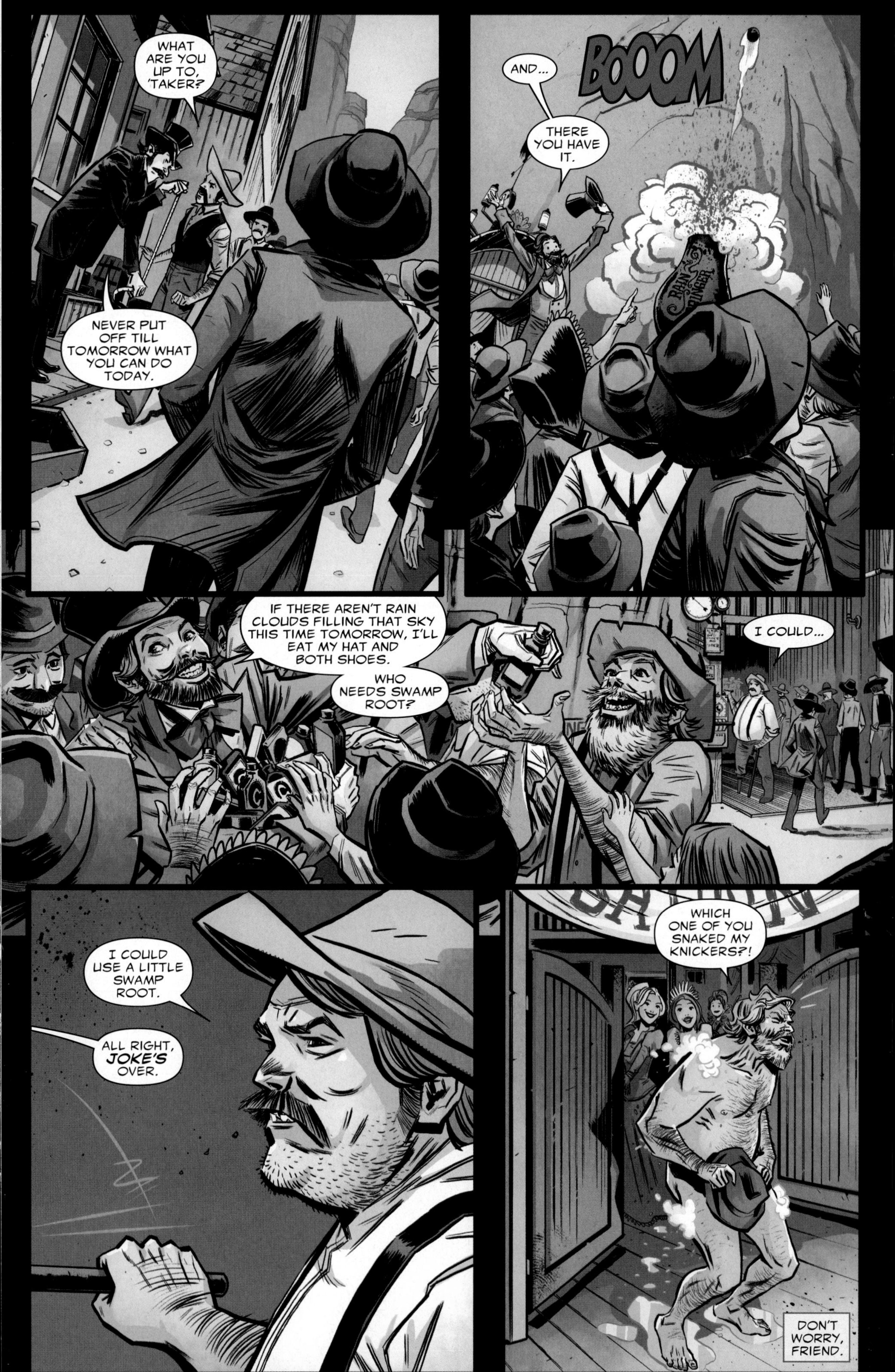

WHAT ARE YOU UP TO, 'TAKER?
NEVER PUT OFF TILL TOMORROW WHAT YOU CAN DO TODAY.
AND...
BOOOM
THERE YOU HAVE IT.
IF THERE AREN'T RAIN CLOUDS FILLING THAT SKY THIS TIME TOMORROW, I'LL EAT MY HAT AND BOTH SHOES.
WHO NEEDS SWAMP ROOT?
I COULD...
I COULD USE A LITTLE SWAMP ROOT.
ALL RIGHT, JOKE'S OVER.
WHICH ONE OF YOU SNAKED MY KNICKERS?!
DON'T WORRY, FRIEND.

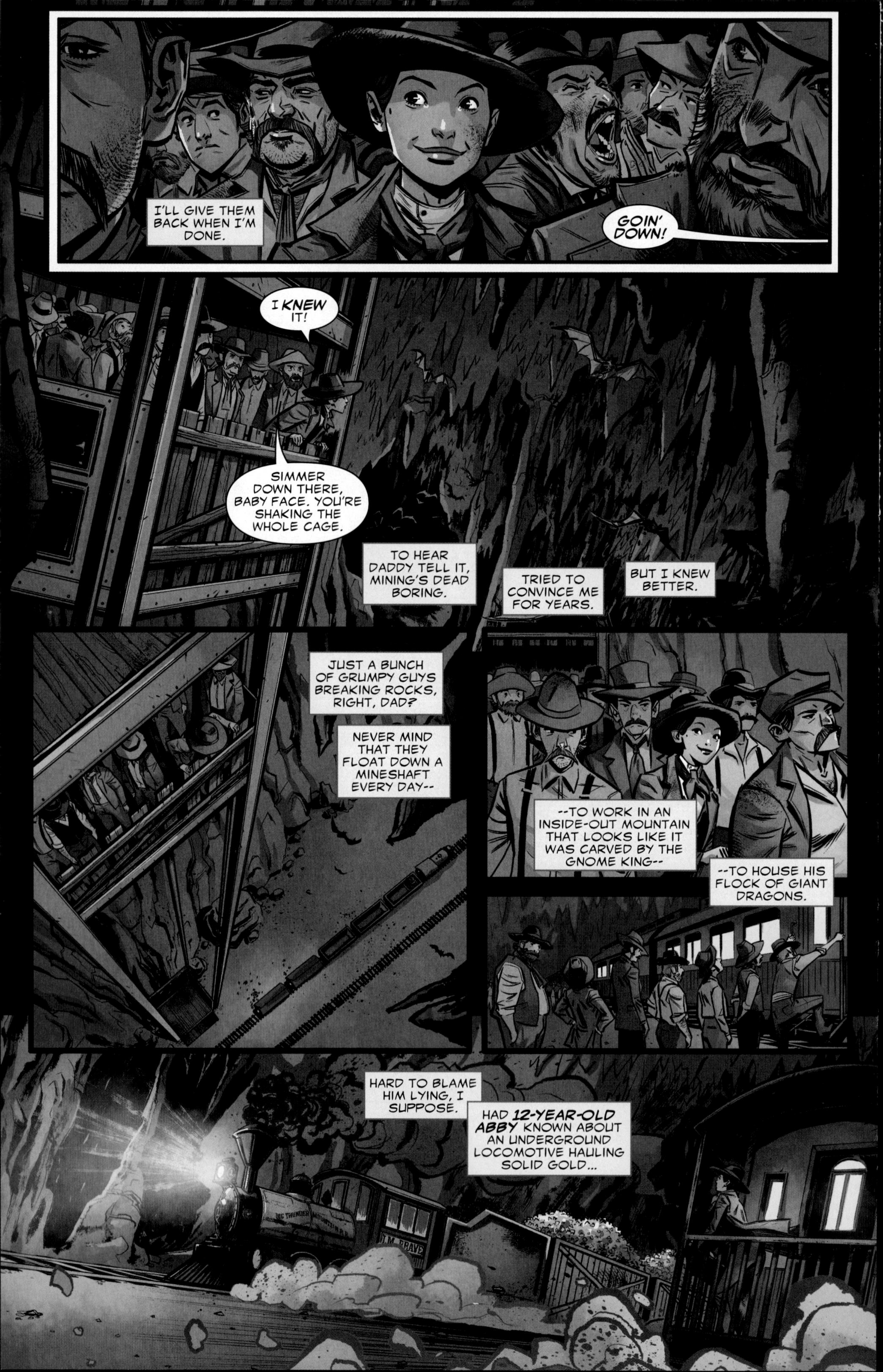
I'LL GIVE THEM BACK WHEN I'M DONE.
GOIN' DOWN!
I KNEW IT!
SIMMER DOWN THERE, BABY FACE. YOU'RE SHAKING THE WHOLE CAGE.
TO HEAR DADDY TELL IT, MINING'S DEAD BORING.
TRIED TO CONVINCE ME FOR YEARS.
BUT I KNEW BETTER.
JUST A BUNCH OF GRUMPY GUYS BREAKING ROCKS, RIGHT, DAD?
NEVER MIND THAT THEY FLOAT DOWN A MINESHAFT EVERY DAY--
--TO WORK IN AN INSIDE-OUT MOUNTAIN THAT LOOKS LIKE IT WAS CARVED BY THE GNOME KING--
--TO HOUSE HIS FLOCK OF GIANT DRAGONS.
HARD TO BLAME HIM LYING, I SUPPOSE.
HAD 12-YEAR-OLD ABBY KNOWN ABOUT AN UNDERGROUND LOCOMOTIVE HAULING SOLID GOLD...
BIG THUNDER MOUNTAIN R.R.
I.M. BRAVE

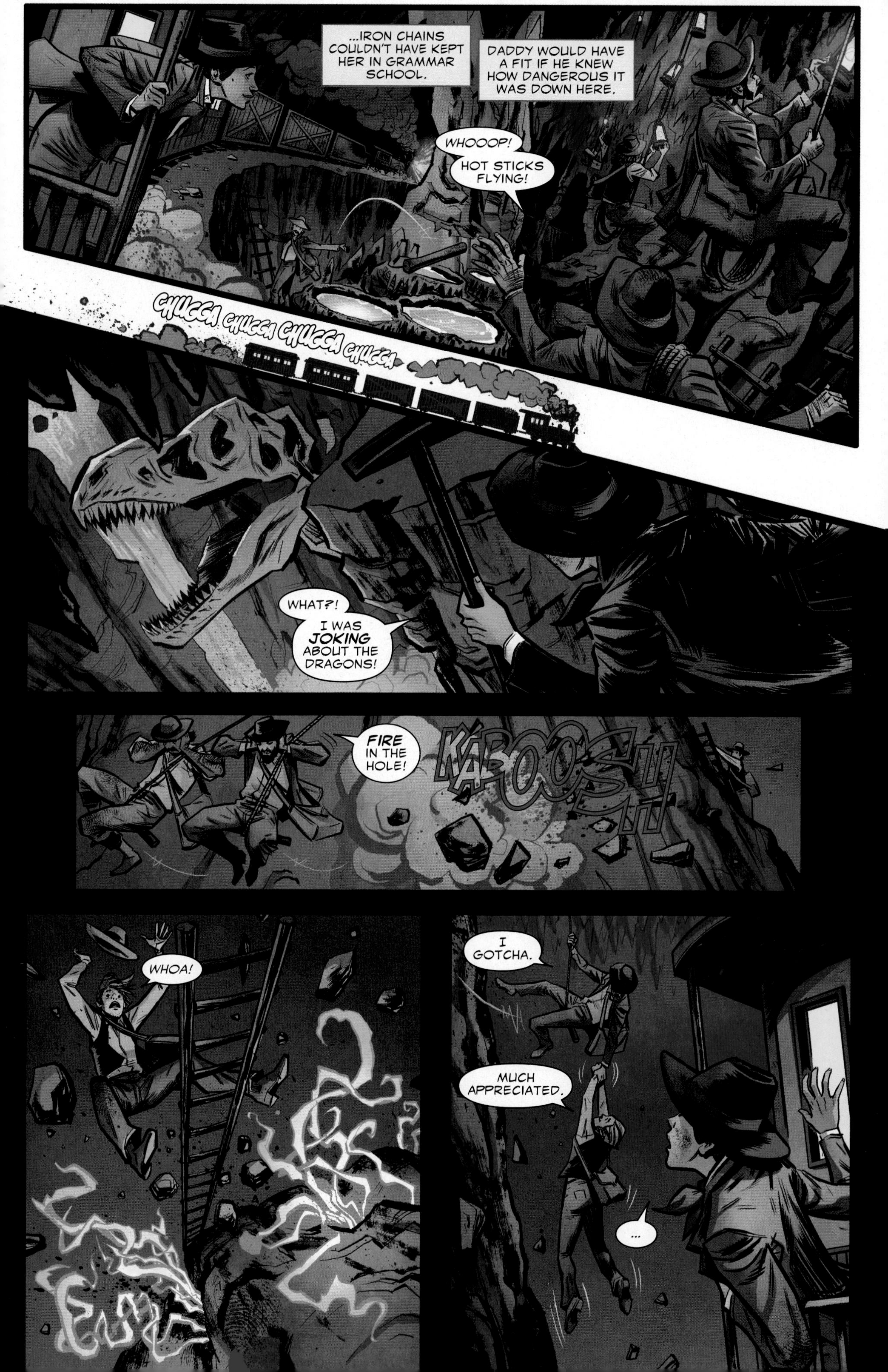
...IRON CHAINS COULDN'T HAVE KEPT HER IN GRAMMAR SCHOOL.
DADDY WOULD HAVE A FIT IF HE KNEW HOW DANGEROUS IT WAS DOWN HERE.
WHOOOP!
HOT STICKS FLYING!
CHUGGA CHUGGA CHUGGA CHUGGA
WHAT?!
I WAS JOKING ABOUT THE DRAGONS!
FIRE IN THE HOLE!
KABOOSH!!
WHOA!
I GOTCHA.
MUCH APPRECIATED.
...

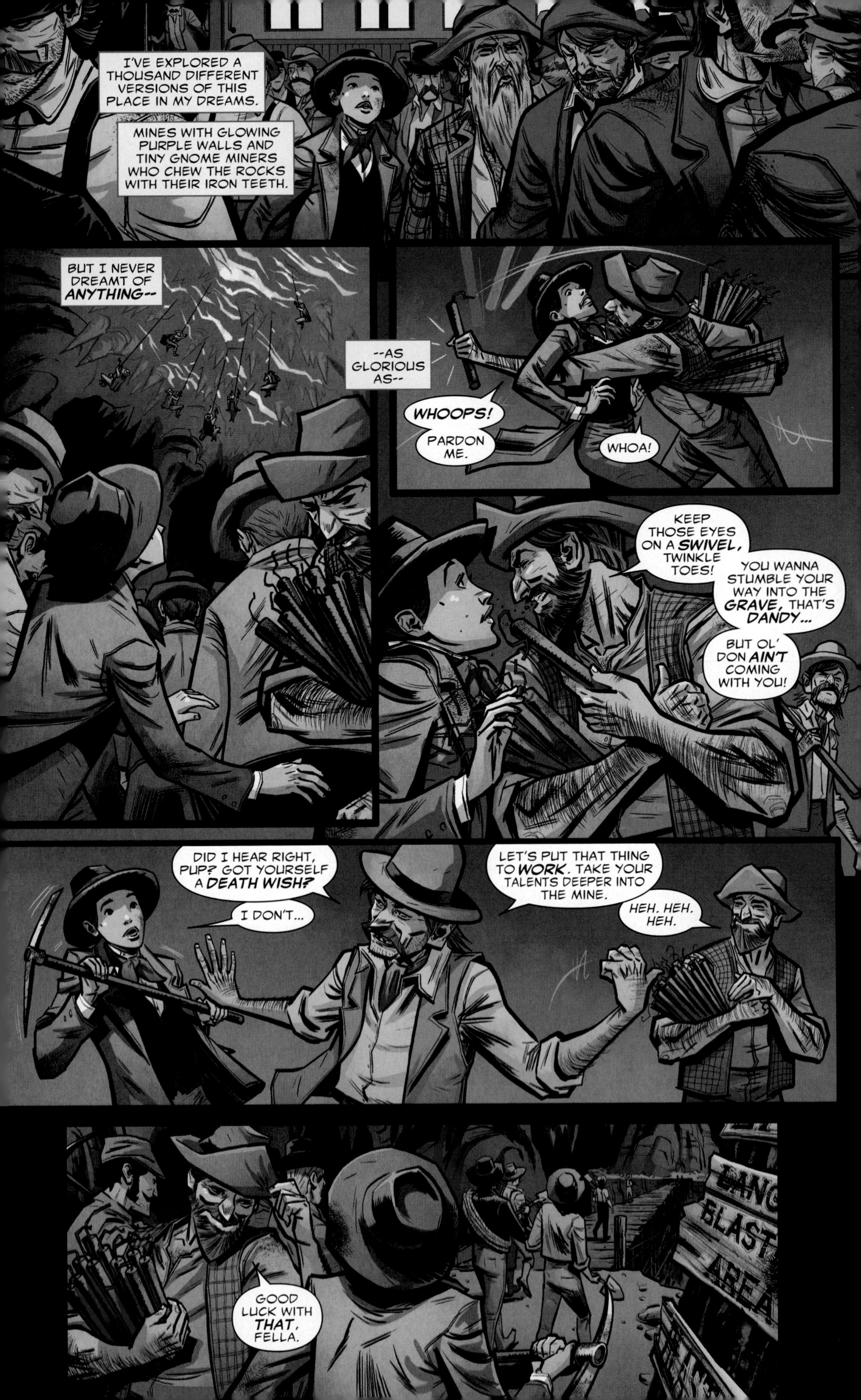
I'VE EXPLORED A THOUSAND DIFFERENT VERSIONS OF THIS PLACE IN MY DREAMS.
MINES WITH GLOWING PURPLE WALLS AND TINY GNOME MINERS WHO CHEW THE ROCKS WITH THEIR IRON TEETH.
BUT I NEVER DREAMT OF ANYTHING--
--AS GLORIOUS AS--
WHOOPS! PARDON ME.
WHOA!
KEEP THOSE EYES ON A SWIVEL, TWINKLE TOES!
YOU WANNA STUMBLE YOUR WAY INTO THE GRAVE, THAT'S DANDY...
BUT OL' DON AIN'T COMING WITH YOU!
DID I HEAR RIGHT, PUP? GOT YOURSELF A DEATH WISH?
I DON'T...
LET'S PUT THAT THING TO WORK. TAKE YOUR TALENTS DEEPER INTO THE MINE.
HEH. HEH. HEH.
GOOD LUCK WITH THAT, FELLA.

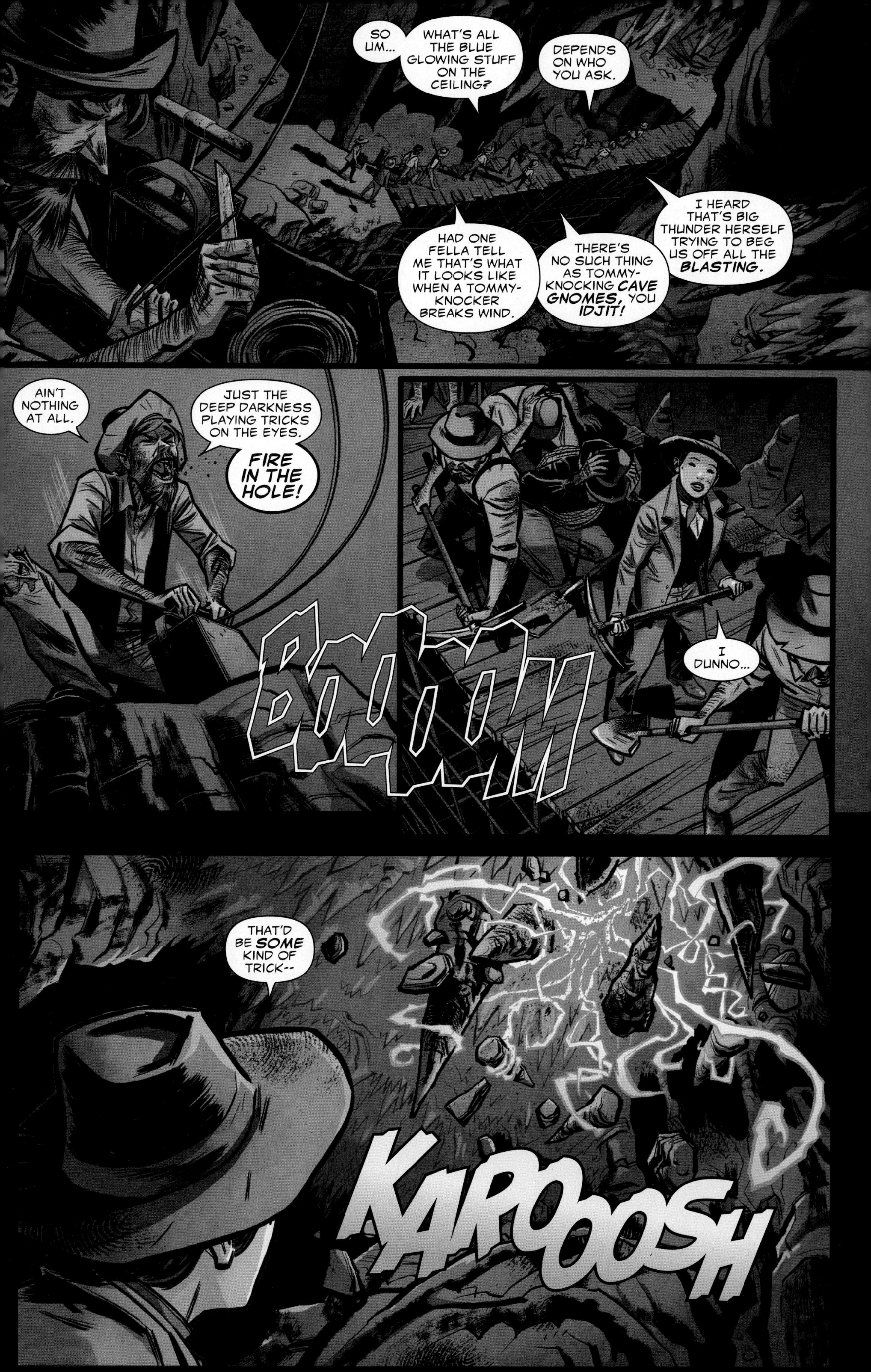
SO UM...
WHAT'S ALL THE BLUE GLOWING STUFF ON THE CEILING?
DEPENDS ON WHO YOU ASK.
HAD ONE FELLA TELL ME THAT'S WHAT IT LOOKS LIKE WHEN A TOMMY-KNOCKER BREAKS WIND.
THERE'S NO SUCH THING AS TOMMY-KNOCKING CAVE GNOMES, YOU IDJIT!
I HEARD THAT'S BIG THUNDER HERSELF TRYING TO BEG US OFF ALL THE BLASTING.
AIN'T NOTHING AT ALL.
JUST THE DEEP DARKNESS PLAYING TRICKS ON THE EYES.
FIRE IN THE HOLE!
BOOOOM
I DUNNO...
THAT'D BE SOME KIND OF TRICK--
KAPOOOSH

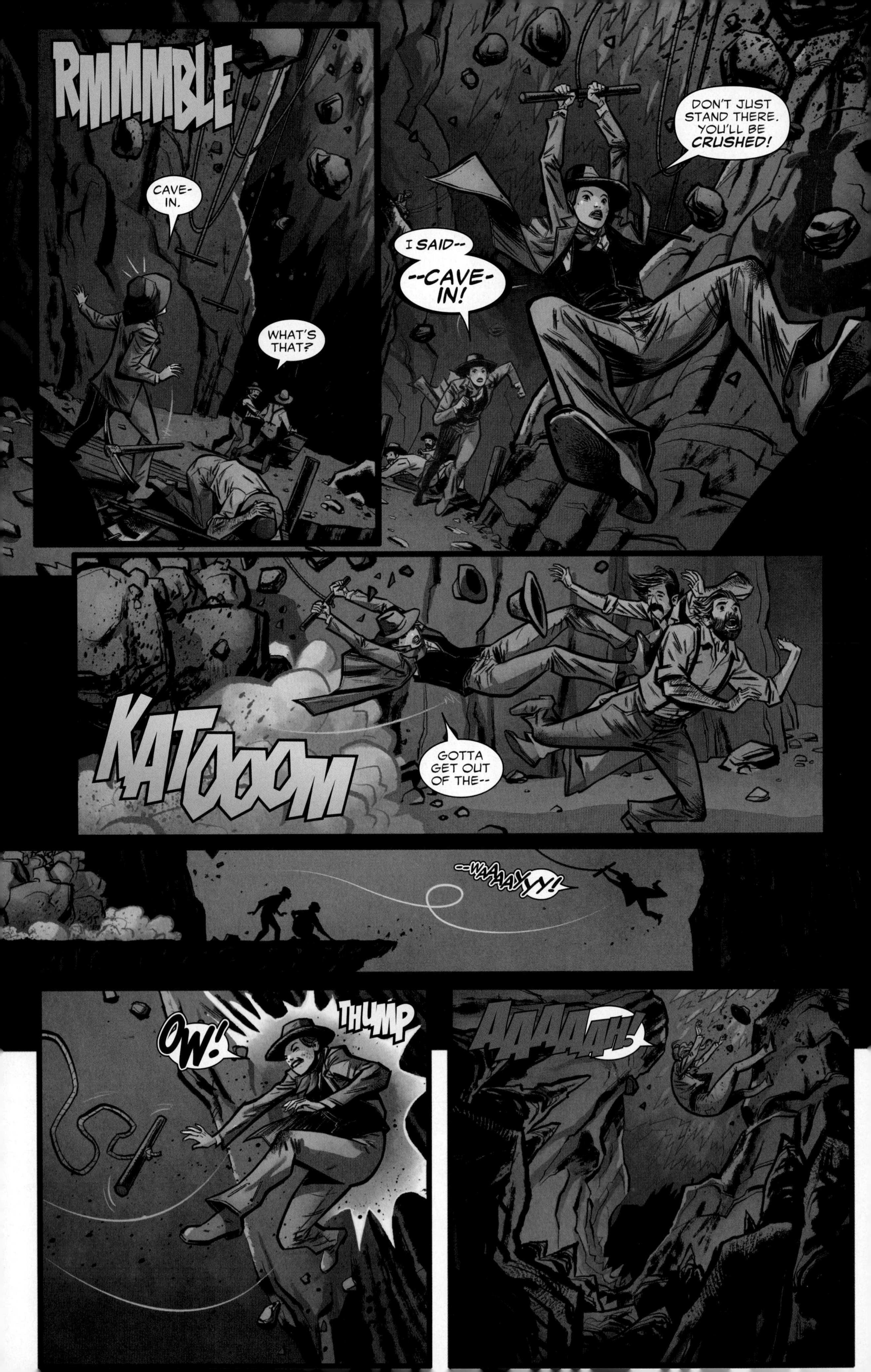
RMMMBLE
CAVE-IN.
WHAT'S THAT?
DON'T JUST STAND THERE. YOU'LL BE CRUSHED!
I SAID--
--CAVE-IN!
KATOOOM
GOTTA GET OUT OF THE--
--WAAAAYYY!
OW!
THUMP
AAAAAH!

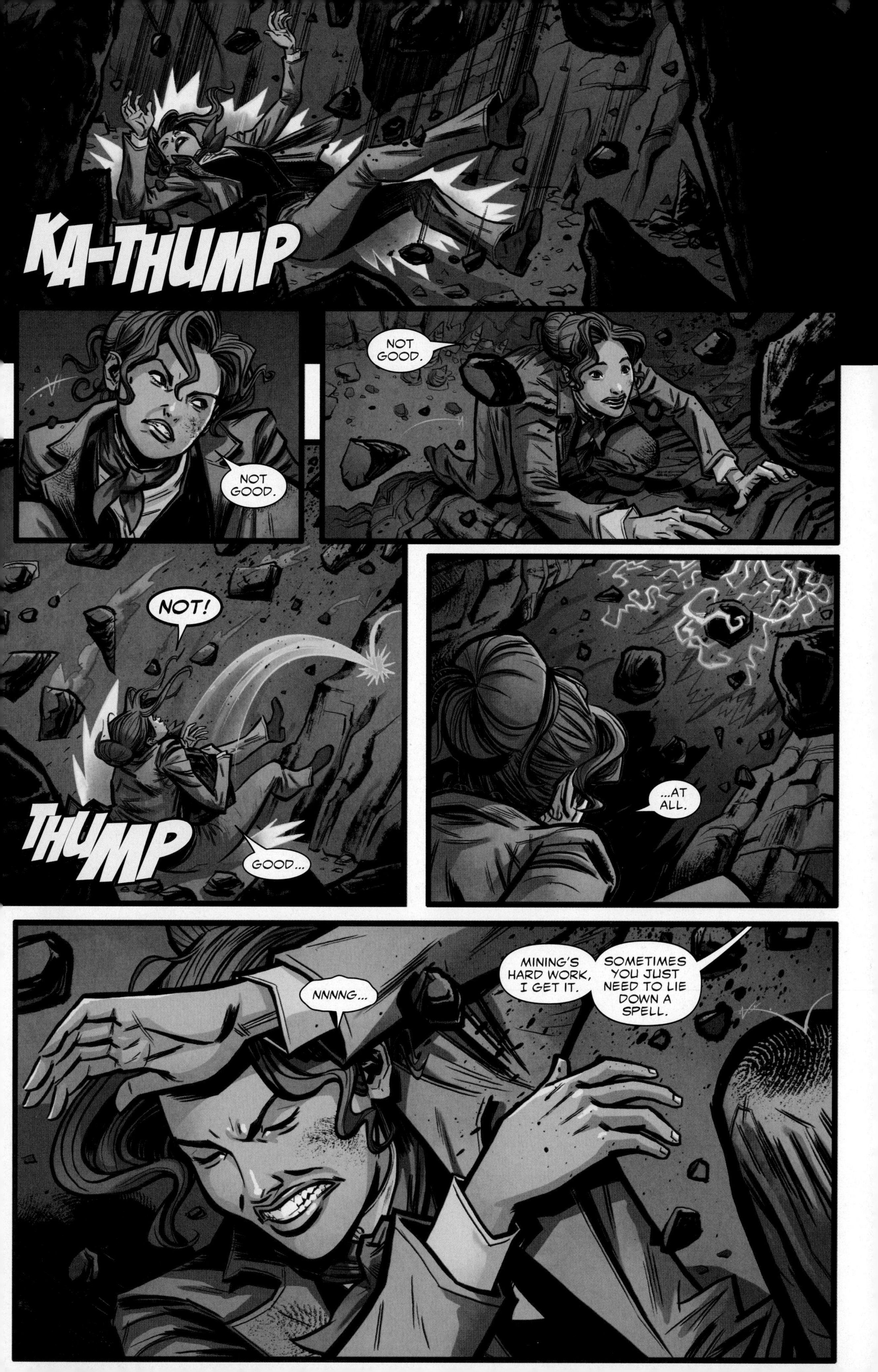
KA-THUMP
NOT GOOD.
NOT GOOD.
NOT!
THUMP
GOOD...
...AT ALL.
NNNNG...
MINING'S HARD WORK, I GET IT.
SOMETIMES YOU JUST NEED TO LIE DOWN A SPELL.

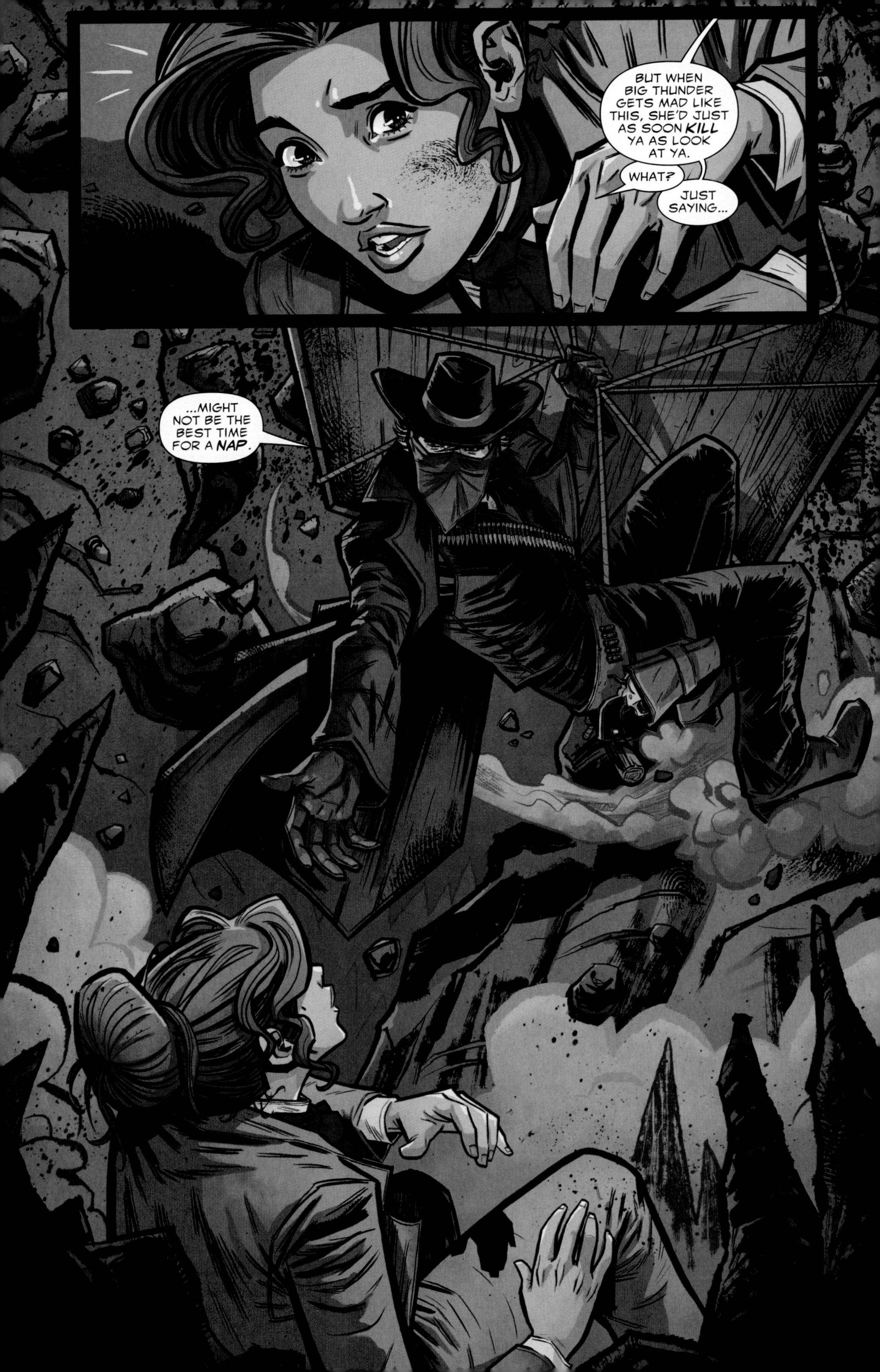
BUT WHEN BIG THUNDER GETS MAD LIKE THIS, SHE'D JUST AS SOON KILL YA AS LOOK AT YA.
WHAT?
JUST SAYING...
...MIGHT NOT BE THE BEST TIME FOR A NAP.

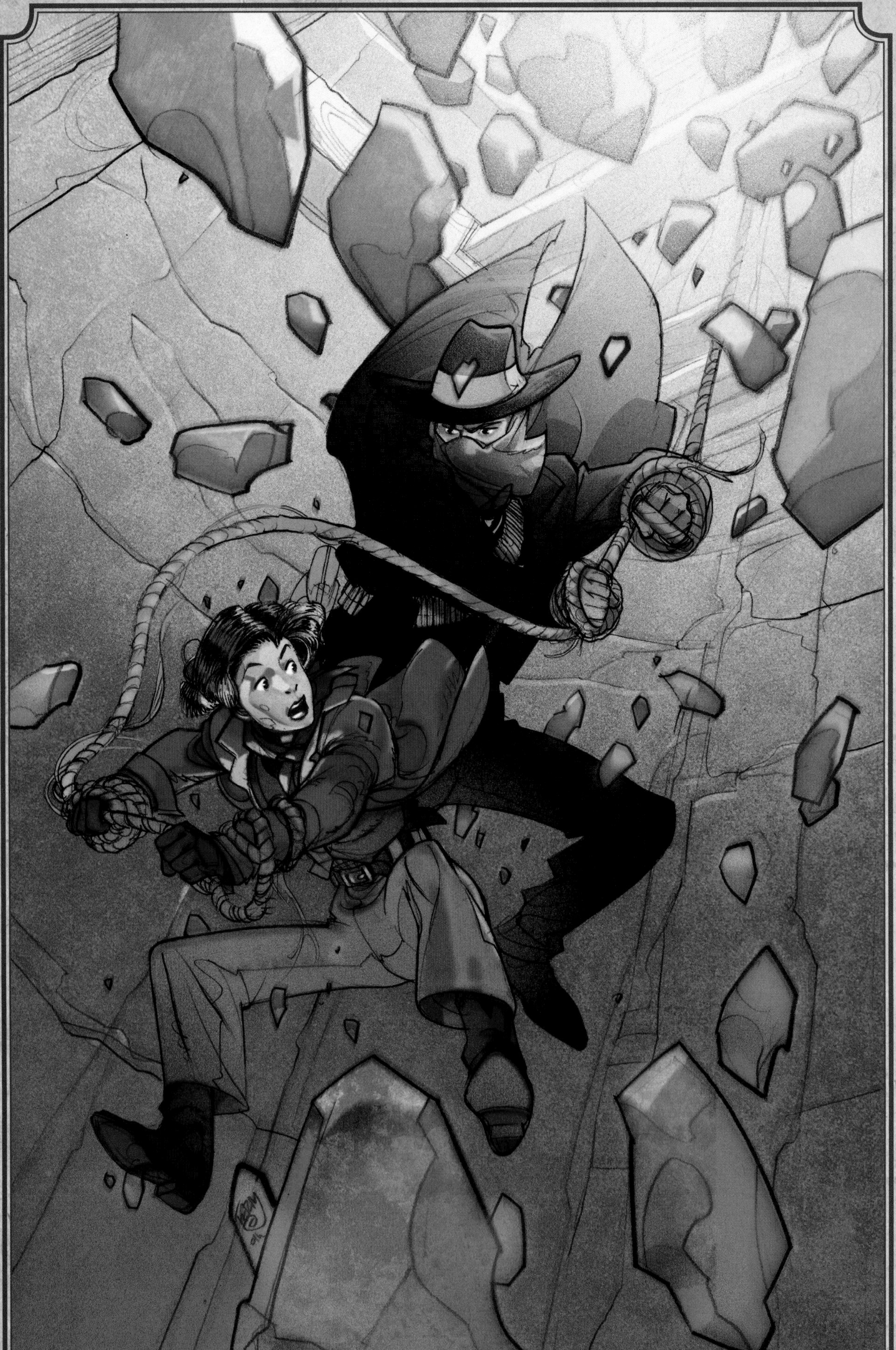

~ 2 ~

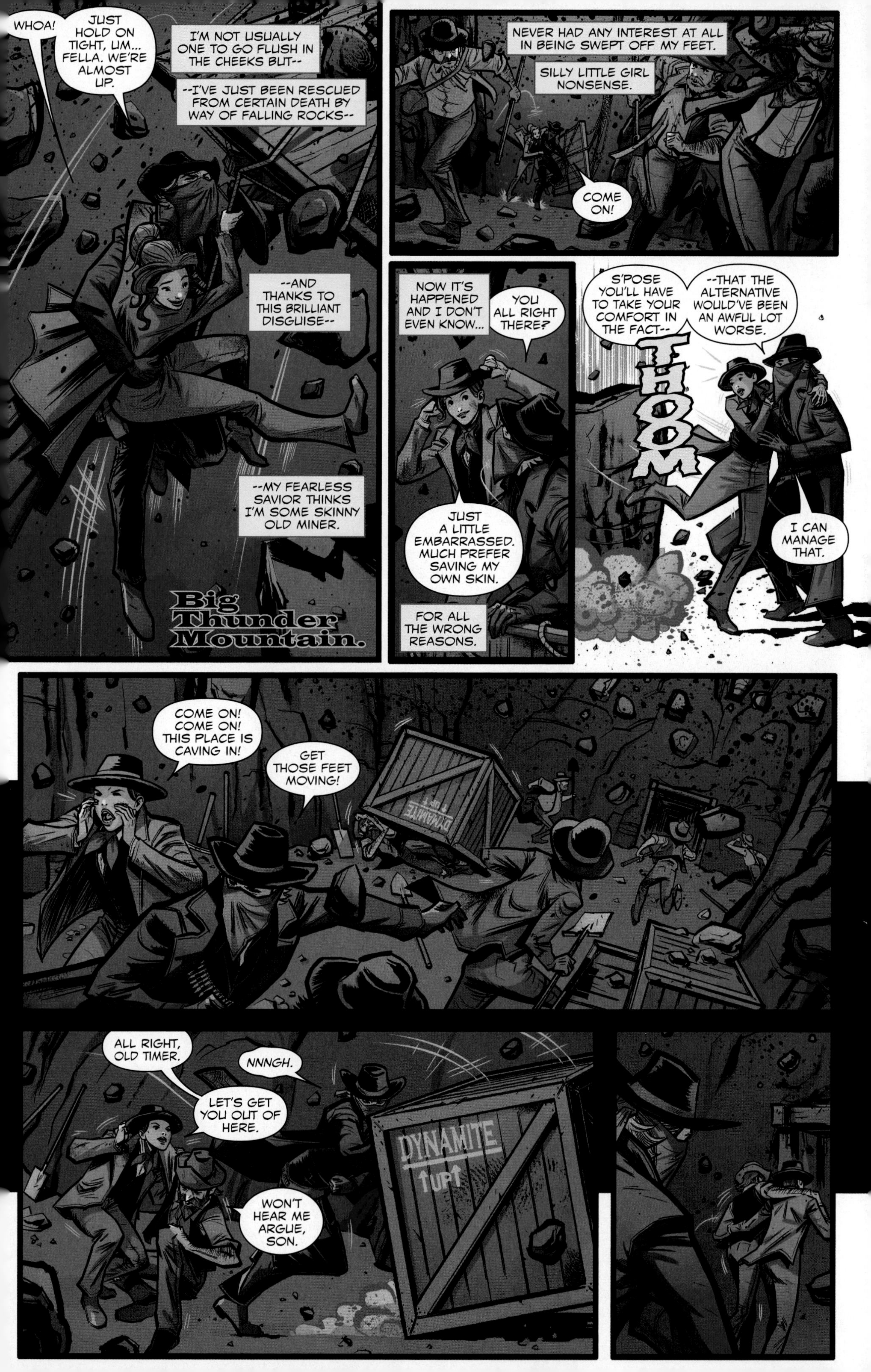

WHOA!
JUST HOLD ON TIGHT, UM... FELLA. WE'RE ALMOST UP.
I'M NOT USUALLY ONE TO GO FLUSH IN THE CHEEKS BUT--
--I'VE JUST BEEN RESCUED FROM CERTAIN DEATH BY WAY OF FALLING ROCKS--
--AND THANKS TO THIS BRILLIANT DISGUISE--
--MY FEARLESS SAVIOR THINKS I'M SOME SKINNY OLD MINER.
Big Thunder Mountain.
NEVER HAD ANY INTEREST AT ALL IN BEING SWEPT OFF MY FEET.
SILLY LITTLE GIRL NONSENSE.
COME ON!
NOW IT'S HAPPENED AND I DON'T EVEN KNOW...
YOU ALL RIGHT THERE?
JUST A LITTLE EMBARRASSED. MUCH PREFER SAVING MY OWN SKIN.
FOR ALL THE WRONG REASONS.
S'POSE YOU'LL HAVE TO TAKE YOUR COMFORT IN THE FACT--
THOOM
--THAT THE ALTERNATIVE WOULD'VE BEEN AN AWFUL LOT WORSE.
I CAN MANAGE THAT.
COME ON! COME ON! THIS PLACE IS CAVING IN!
GET THOSE FEET MOVING!
DYNAMITE
↑UP↑
ALL RIGHT, OLD TIMER.
NNNGH.
LET'S GET YOU OUT OF HERE.
WON'T HEAR ME ARGUE, SON.
DYNAMITE
↑UP↑

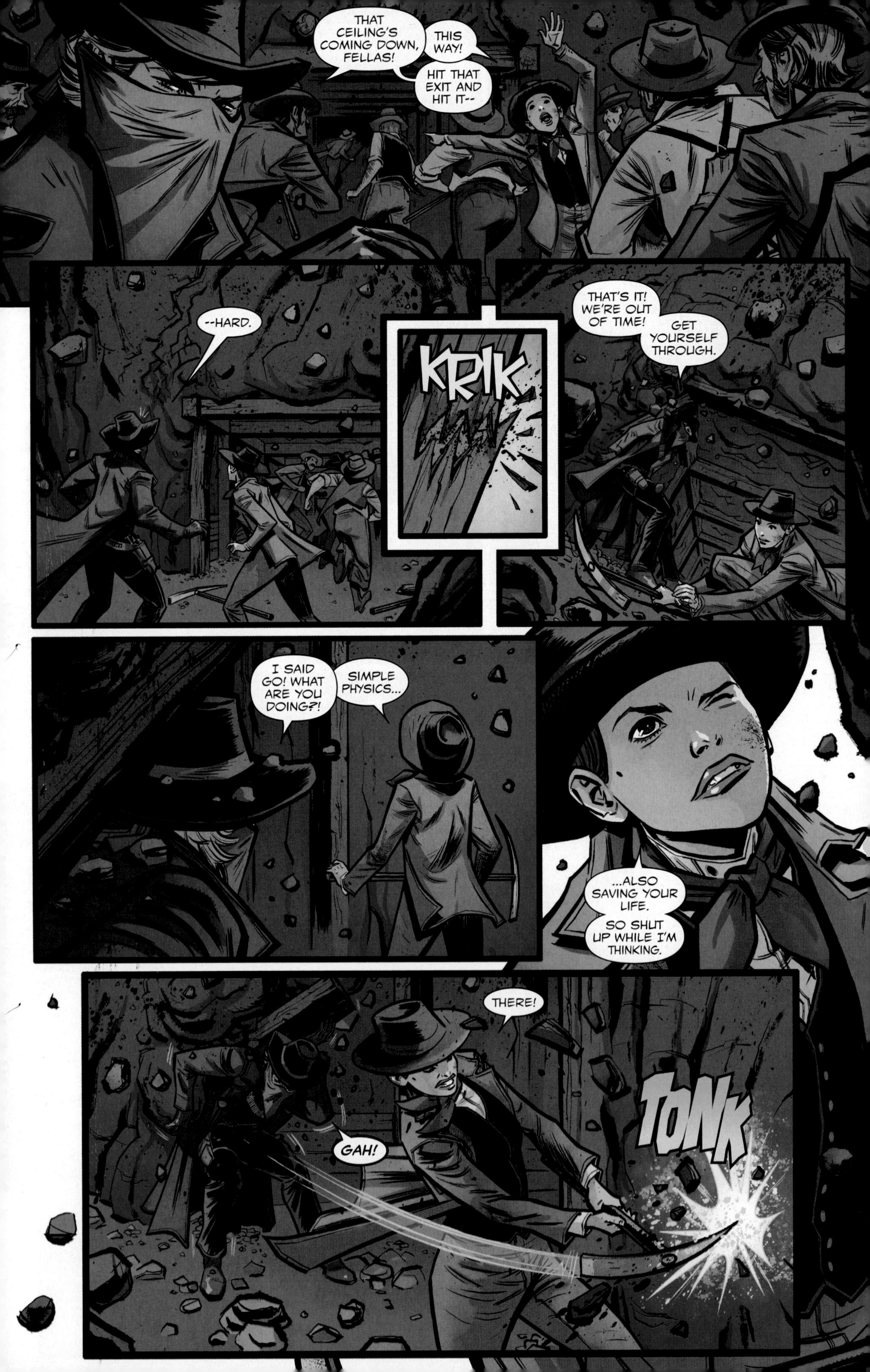
THAT CEILING'S COMING DOWN, FELLAS!
THIS WAY!
HIT THAT EXIT AND HIT IT--
--HARD.
KRIK
THAT'S IT! WE'RE OUT OF TIME!
GET YOURSELF THROUGH.
I SAID GO! WHAT ARE YOU DOING?!
SIMPLE PHYSICS...
...ALSO SAVING YOUR LIFE.
SO SHUT UP WHILE I'M THINKING.
THERE!
GAH!
TONK

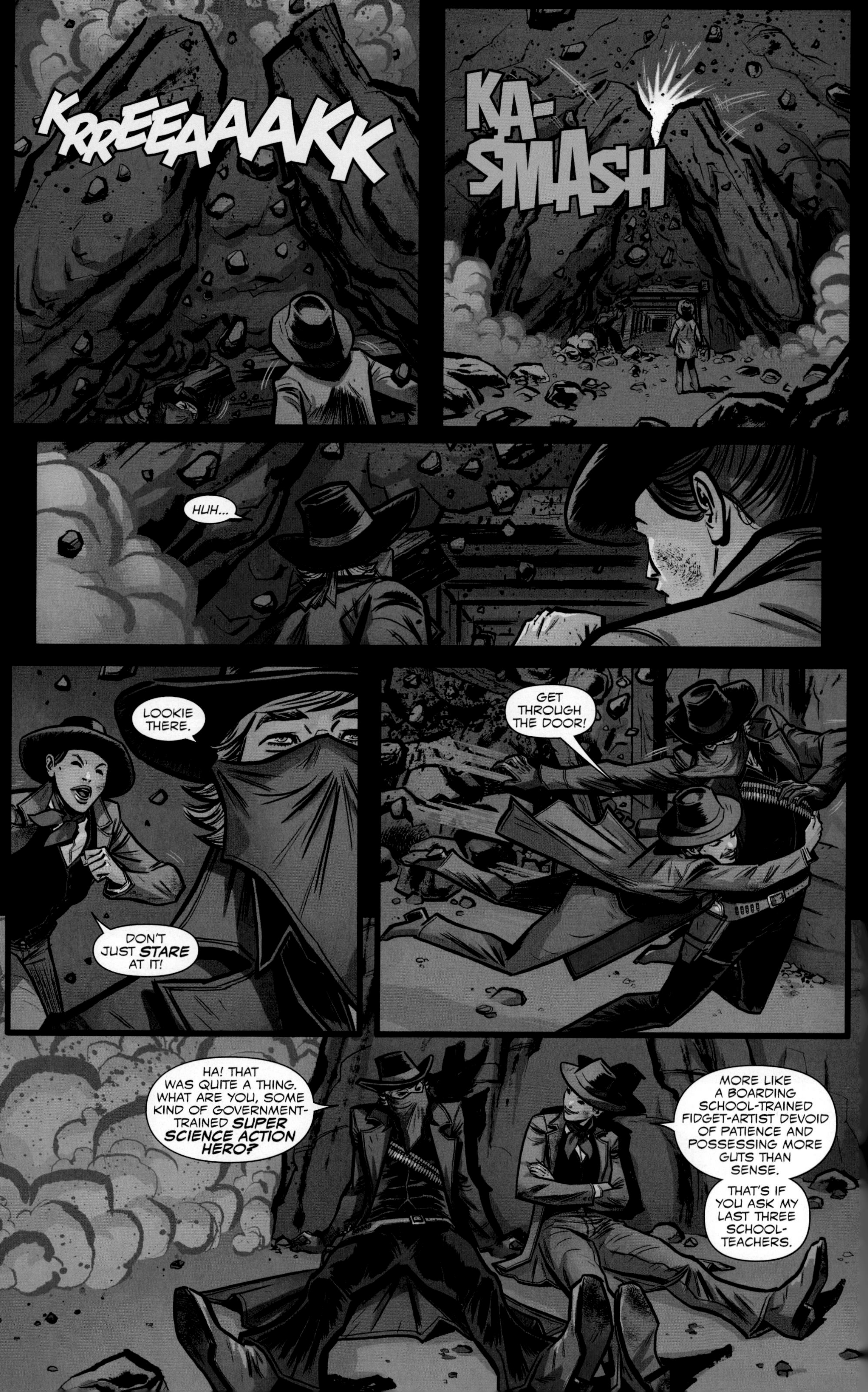
KRREEAAAKK
KA-SMASH
HUH...
LOOKIE THERE.
DON'T JUST STARE AT IT!
GET THROUGH THE DOOR!
HA! THAT WAS QUITE A THING. WHAT ARE YOU, SOME KIND OF GOVERNMENT-TRAINED SUPER SCIENCE ACTION HERO?
MORE LIKE A BOARDING SCHOOL-TRAINED FIDGET-ARTIST DEVOID OF PATIENCE AND POSSESSING MORE GUTS THAN SENSE.
THAT'S IF YOU ASK MY LAST THREE SCHOOL-TEACHERS.

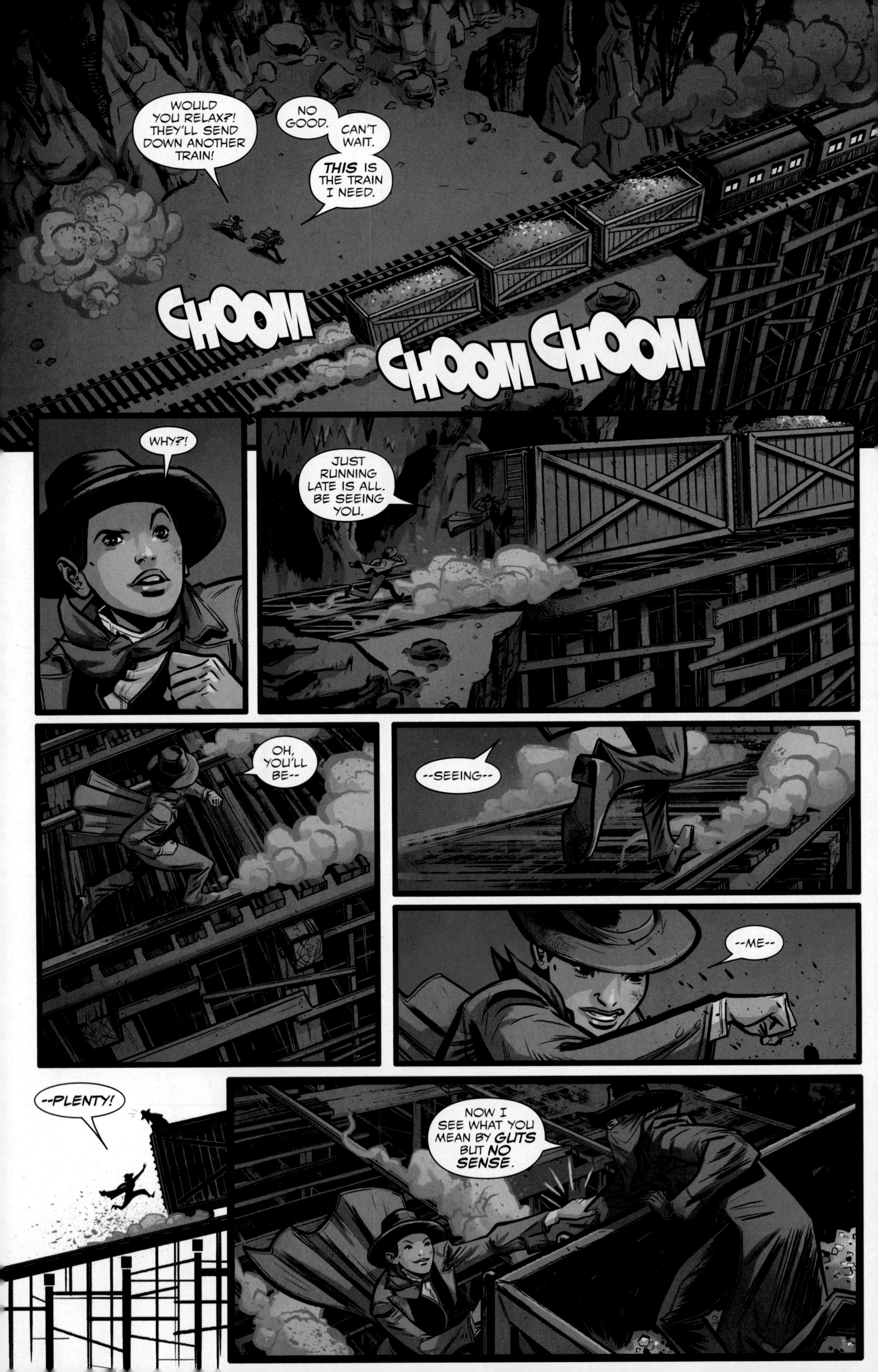
WOULD YOU RELAX?! THEY'LL SEND DOWN ANOTHER TRAIN!
NO GOOD.
CAN'T WAIT.
THIS IS THE TRAIN I NEED.
CHOOM
CHOOM CHOOM
WHY?!
JUST RUNNING LATE IS ALL. BE SEEING YOU.
OH, YOU'LL BE--
--SEEING--
--ME--
--PLENTY!
NOW I SEE WHAT YOU MEAN BY GUTS BUT NO SENSE.

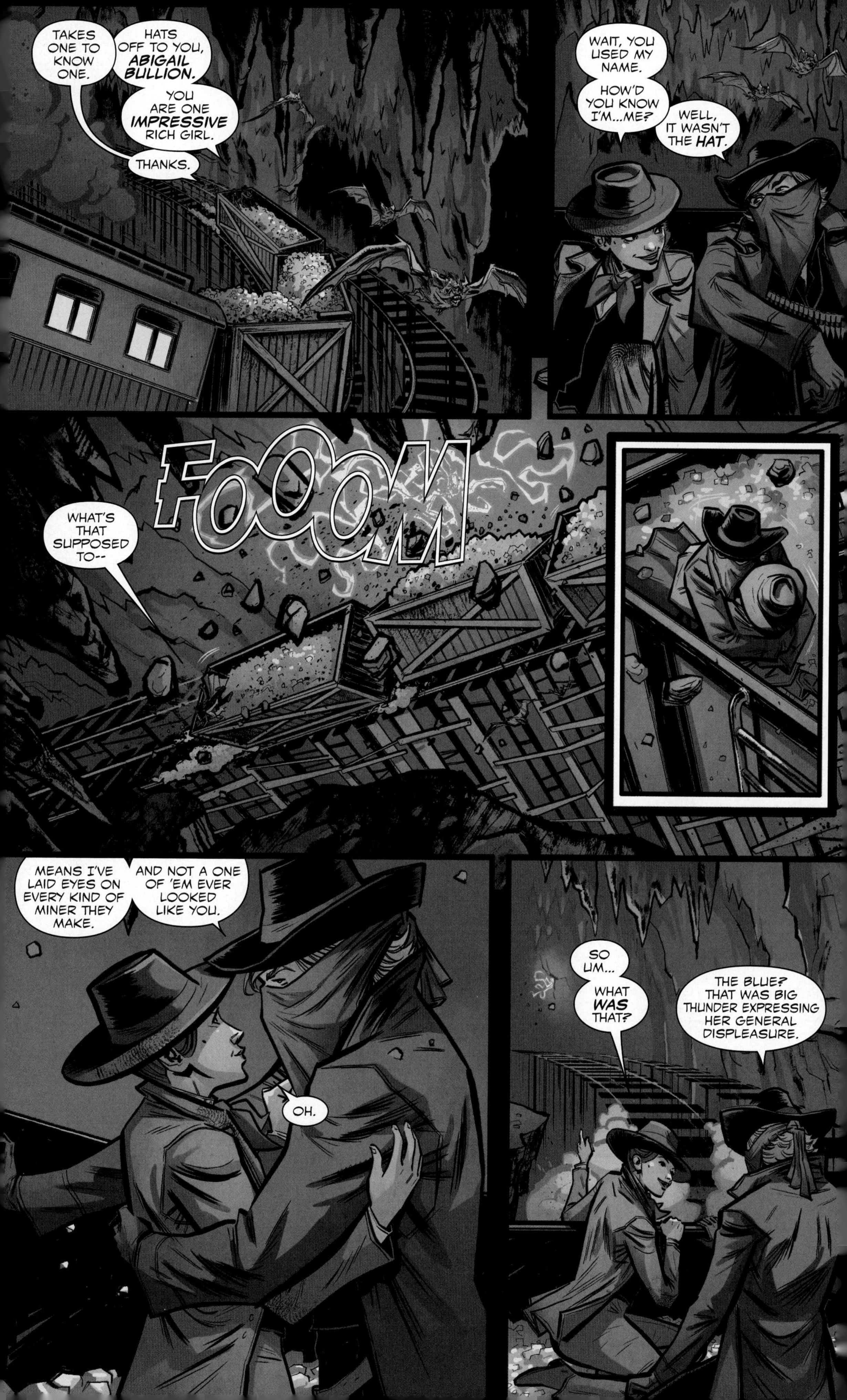
TAKES ONE TO KNOW ONE.
HATS OFF TO YOU, ABIGAIL BULLION.
YOU ARE ONE IMPRESSIVE RICH GIRL.
THANKS.
WAIT, YOU USED MY NAME.
HOW'D YOU KNOW I'M...ME?
WELL, IT WASN'T THE HAT.
FOOOM
WHAT'S THAT SUPPOSED TO--
MEANS I'VE LAID EYES ON EVERY KIND OF MINER THEY MAKE.
AND NOT A ONE OF 'EM EVER LOOKED LIKE YOU.
OH.
SO UM...
WHAT WAS THAT?
THE BLUE? THAT WAS BIG THUNDER EXPRESSING HER GENERAL DISPLEASURE.

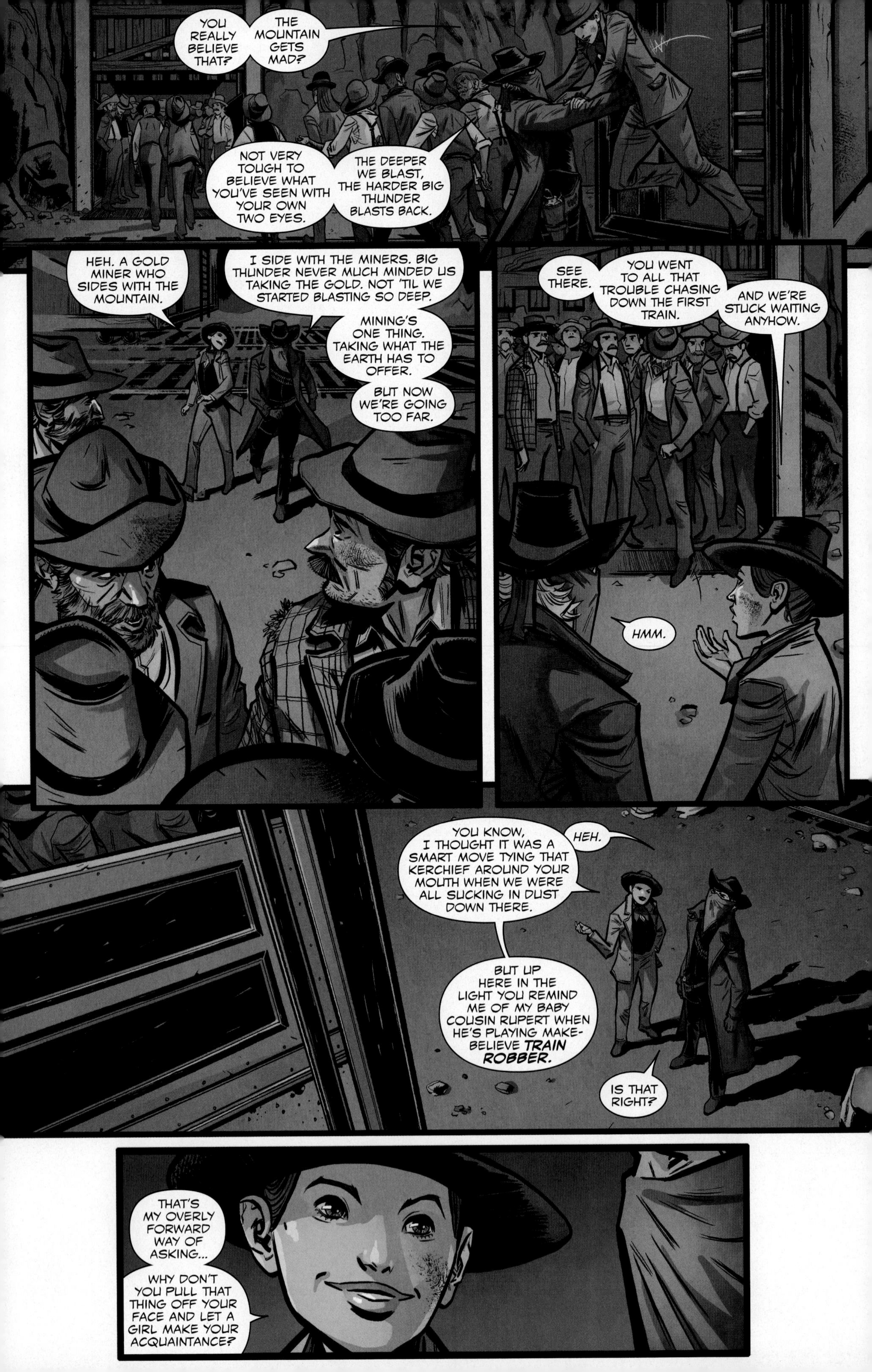
YOU REALLY BELIEVE THAT?
THE MOUNTAIN GETS MAD?
NOT VERY TOUGH TO BELIEVE WHAT YOU'VE SEEN WITH YOUR OWN TWO EYES.
THE DEEPER WE BLAST, THE HARDER BIG THUNDER BLASTS BACK.
HEH. A GOLD MINER WHO SIDES WITH THE MOUNTAIN.
I SIDE WITH THE MINERS. BIG THUNDER NEVER MUCH MINDED US TAKING THE GOLD. NOT 'TIL WE STARTED BLASTING SO DEEP.
MINING'S ONE THING. TAKING WHAT THE EARTH HAS TO OFFER.
BUT NOW WE'RE GOING TOO FAR.
SEE THERE.
YOU WENT TO ALL THAT TROUBLE CHASING DOWN THE FIRST TRAIN.
AND WE'RE STUCK WAITING ANYHOW.
HMM.
YOU KNOW, I THOUGHT IT WAS A SMART MOVE TYING THAT KERCHIEF AROUND YOUR MOUTH WHEN WE WERE ALL SUCKING IN DUST DOWN THERE.
HEH.
BUT UP HERE IN THE LIGHT YOU REMIND ME OF MY BABY COUSIN RUPERT WHEN HE'S PLAYING MAKE-BELIEVE ***TRAIN ROBBER.***
IS THAT RIGHT?
THAT'S MY OVERLY FORWARD WAY OF ASKING...
WHY DON'T YOU PULL THAT THING OFF YOUR FACE AND LET A GIRL MAKE YOUR ACQUAINTANCE?

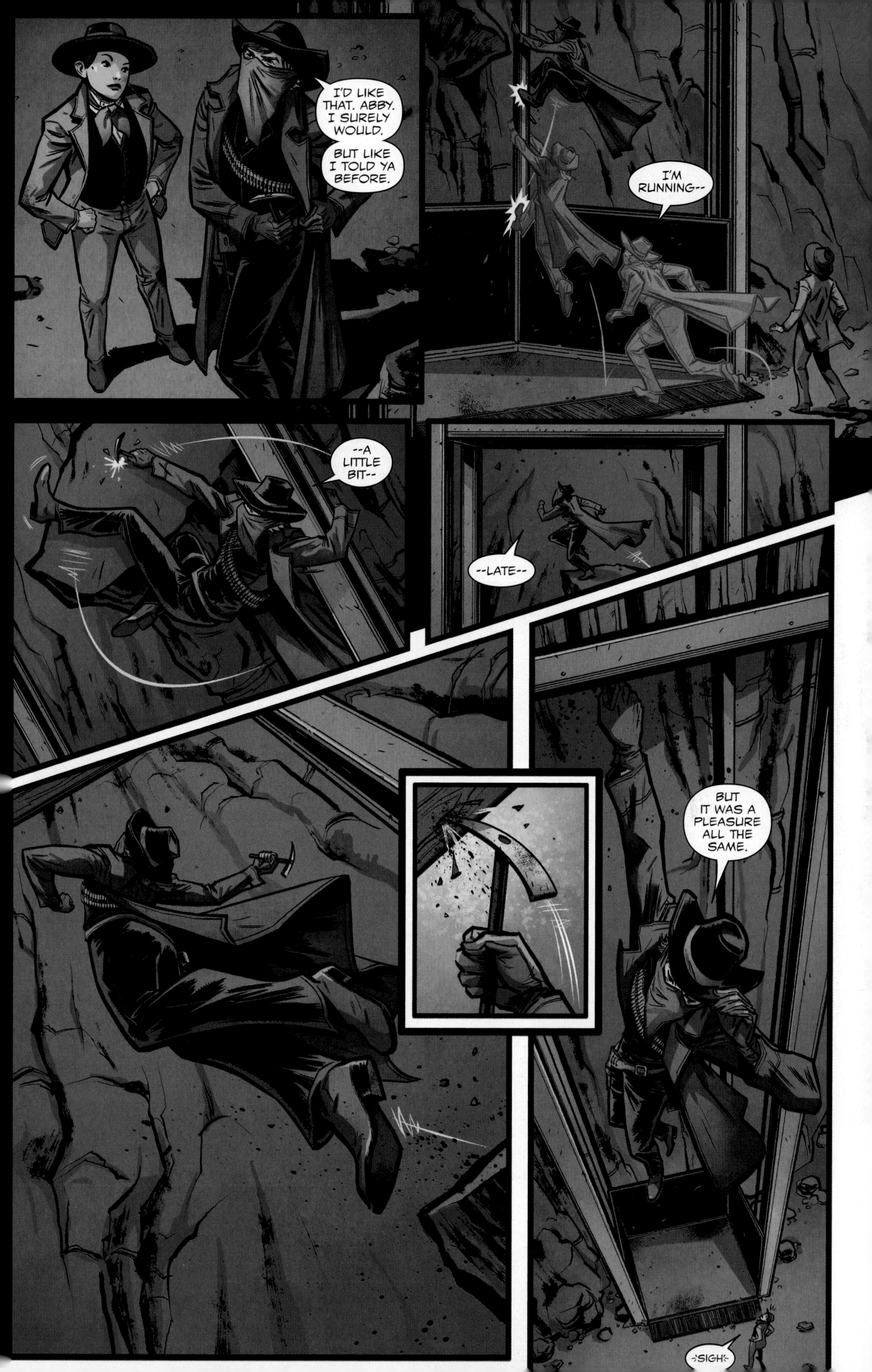
I'D LIKE THAT. ABBY. I SURELY WOULD.
BUT LIKE I TOLD YA BEFORE.
I'M RUNNING--
--A LITTLE BIT--
--LATE--
BUT IT WAS A PLEASURE ALL THE SAME.
SIGH

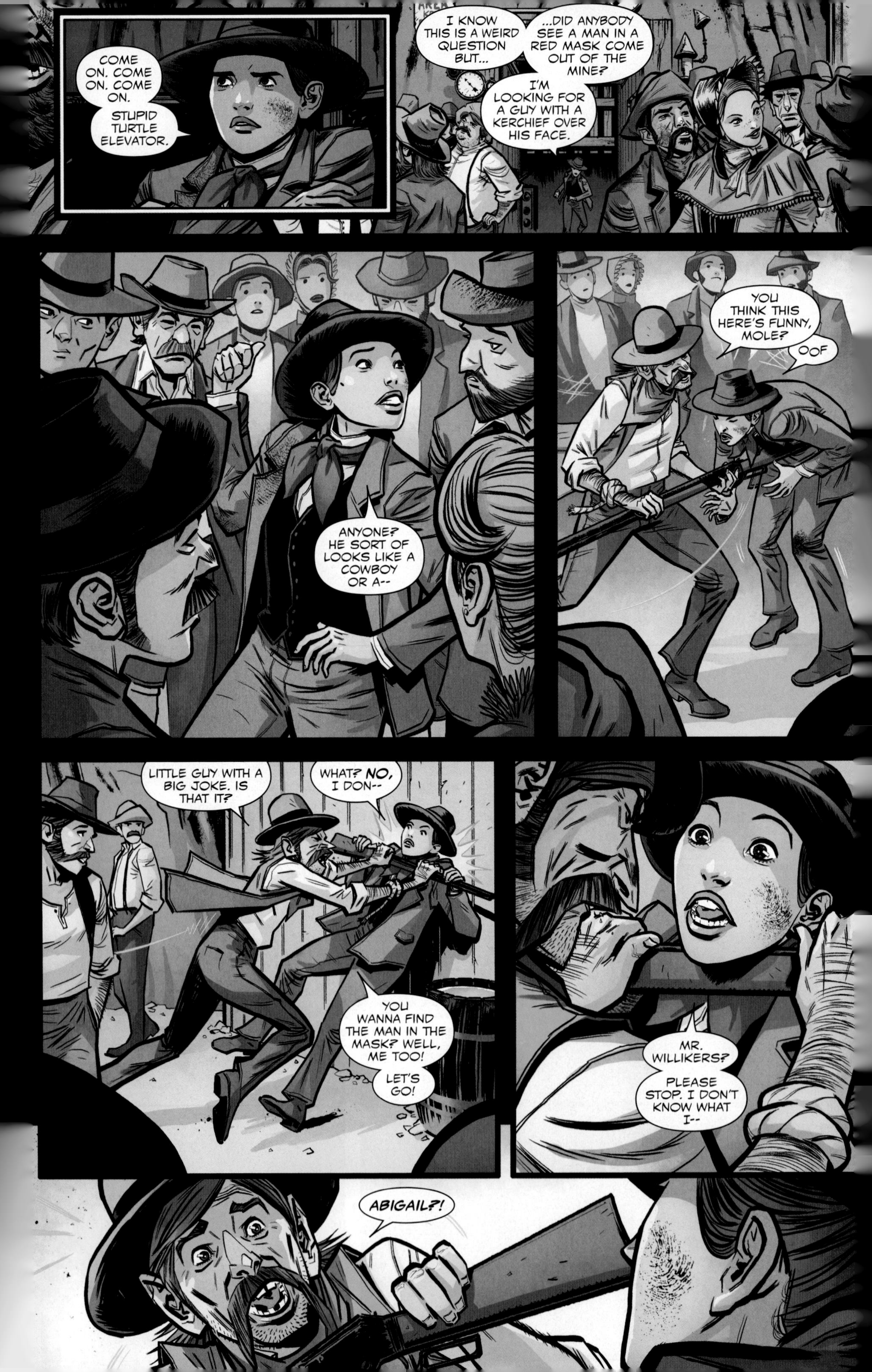

COME ON. COME ON. COME ON.
STUPID TURTLE ELEVATOR.
I KNOW THIS IS A WEIRD QUESTION BUT...
...DID ANYBODY SEE A MAN IN A RED MASK COME OUT OF THE MINE?
I'M LOOKING FOR A GUY WITH A KERCHIEF OVER HIS FACE.
ANYONE? HE SORT OF LOOKS LIKE A COWBOY OR A--
YOU THINK THIS HERE'S FUNNY, MOLE?
OOF
LITTLE GUY WITH A BIG JOKE. IS THAT IT?
WHAT? **NO,** I DON--
YOU WANNA FIND THE MAN IN THE MASK? WELL, ME TOO!
LET'S GO!
MR. WILLIKERS?
PLEASE STOP. I DON'T KNOW WHAT I--
ABIGAIL?!

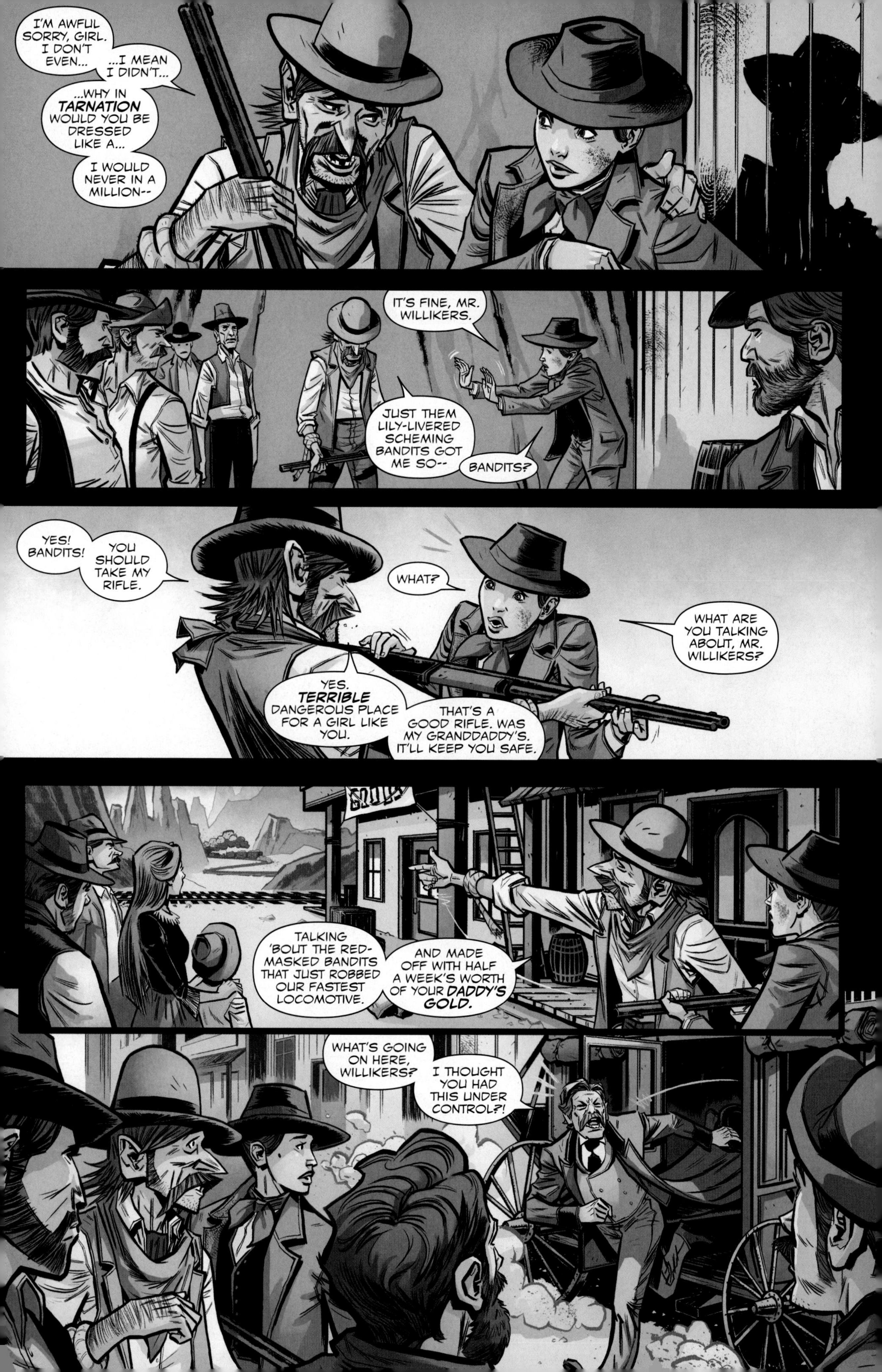
I'M AWFUL SORRY, GIRL. I DON'T EVEN...
...I MEAN I DIDN'T...
...WHY IN TARNATION WOULD YOU BE DRESSED LIKE A...
I WOULD NEVER IN A MILLION--
IT'S FINE, MR. WILLIKERS.
JUST THEM LILY-LIVERED SCHEMING BANDITS GOT ME SO--
BANDITS?
YES! BANDITS!
YOU SHOULD TAKE MY RIFLE.
WHAT?
WHAT ARE YOU TALKING ABOUT, MR. WILLIKERS?
YES. TERRIBLE DANGEROUS PLACE FOR A GIRL LIKE YOU.
THAT'S A GOOD RIFLE. WAS MY GRANDDADDY'S. IT'LL KEEP YOU SAFE.
TALKING 'BOUT THE RED-MASKED BANDITS THAT JUST ROBBED OUR FASTEST LOCOMOTIVE.
AND MADE OFF WITH HALF A WEEK'S WORTH OF YOUR DADDY'S GOLD.
WHAT'S GOING ON HERE, WILLIKERS?
I THOUGHT YOU HAD THIS UNDER CONTROL?!

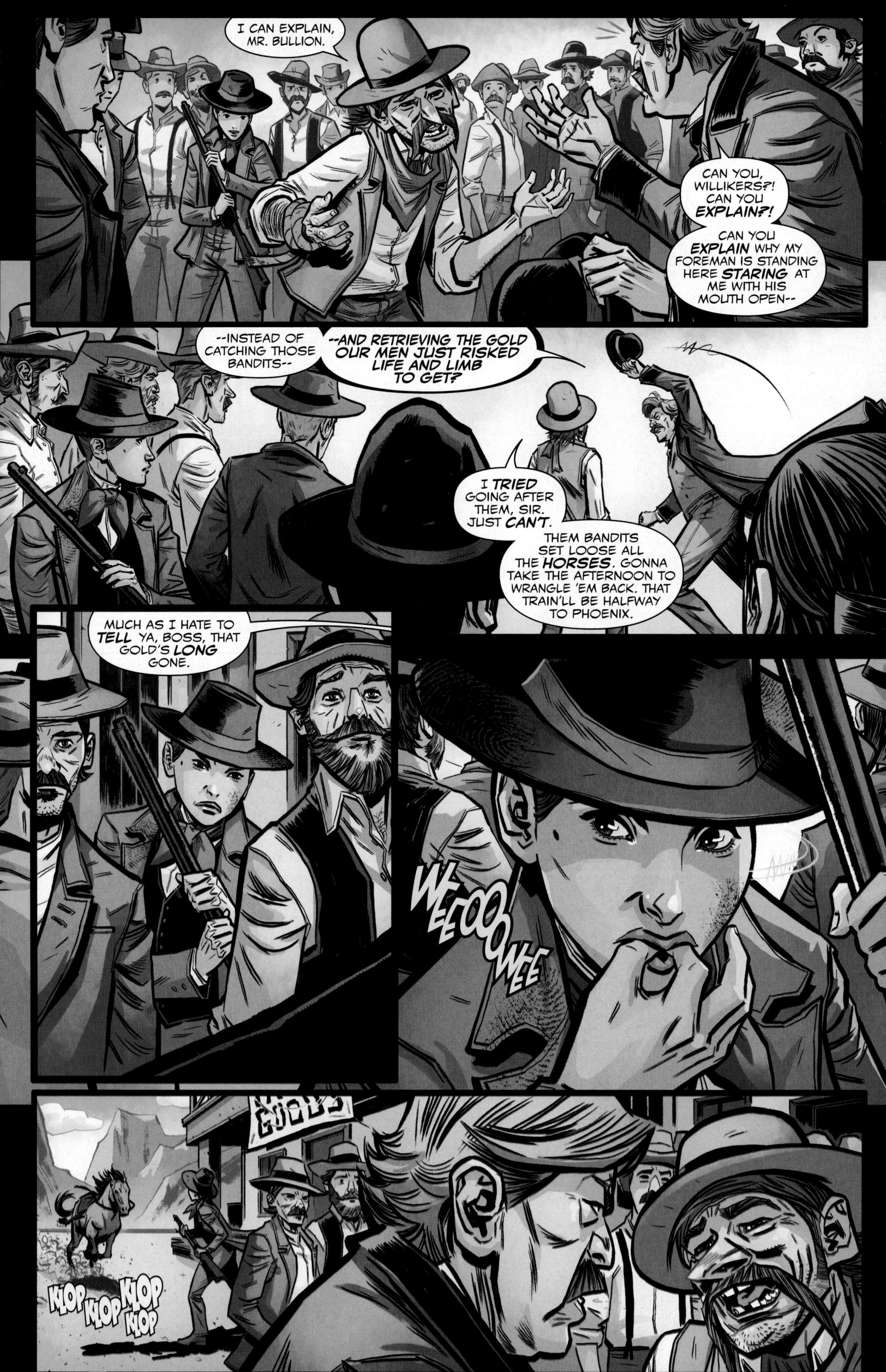
I CAN EXPLAIN, MR. BULLION.
CAN YOU, WILLIKERS?! CAN YOU EXPLAIN?!
CAN YOU EXPLAIN WHY MY FOREMAN IS STANDING HERE STARING AT ME WITH HIS MOUTH OPEN--
--INSTEAD OF CATCHING THOSE BANDITS--
--AND RETRIEVING THE GOLD OUR MEN JUST RISKED LIFE AND LIMB TO GET?
I TRIED GOING AFTER THEM, SIR. JUST CAN'T.
THEM BANDITS SET LOOSE ALL THE HORSES. GONNA TAKE THE AFTERNOON TO WRANGLE 'EM BACK. THAT TRAIN'LL BE HALFWAY TO PHOENIX.
MUCH AS I HATE TO TELL YA, BOSS, THAT GOLD'S LONG GONE.
WEEOOOWEE
KLOP KLOP KLOP KLOP

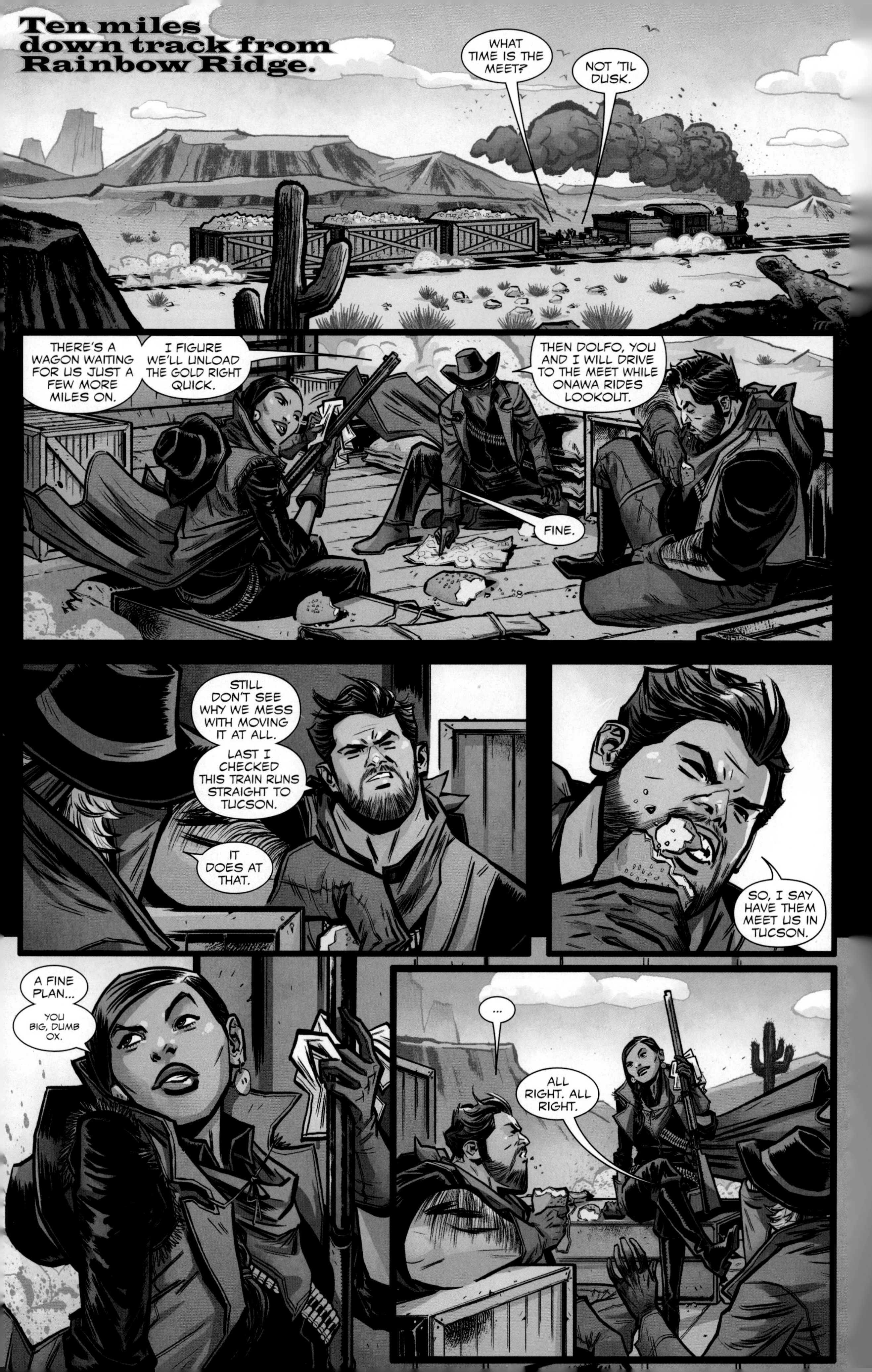

Ten miles down track from Rainbow Ridge.
WHAT TIME IS THE MEET?
NOT 'TIL DUSK.
THERE'S A WAGON WAITING FOR US JUST A FEW MORE MILES ON.
I FIGURE WE'LL UNLOAD THE GOLD RIGHT QUICK.
THEN DOLFO, YOU AND I WILL DRIVE TO THE MEET WHILE ONAWA RIDES LOOKOUT.
FINE.
STILL DON'T SEE WHY WE MESS WITH MOVING IT AT ALL.
LAST I CHECKED THIS TRAIN RUNS STRAIGHT TO TUCSON.
IT DOES AT THAT.
SO, I SAY HAVE THEM MEET US IN TUCSON.
A FINE PLAN...
YOU BIG, DUMB OX.
...
ALL RIGHT. ALL RIGHT.

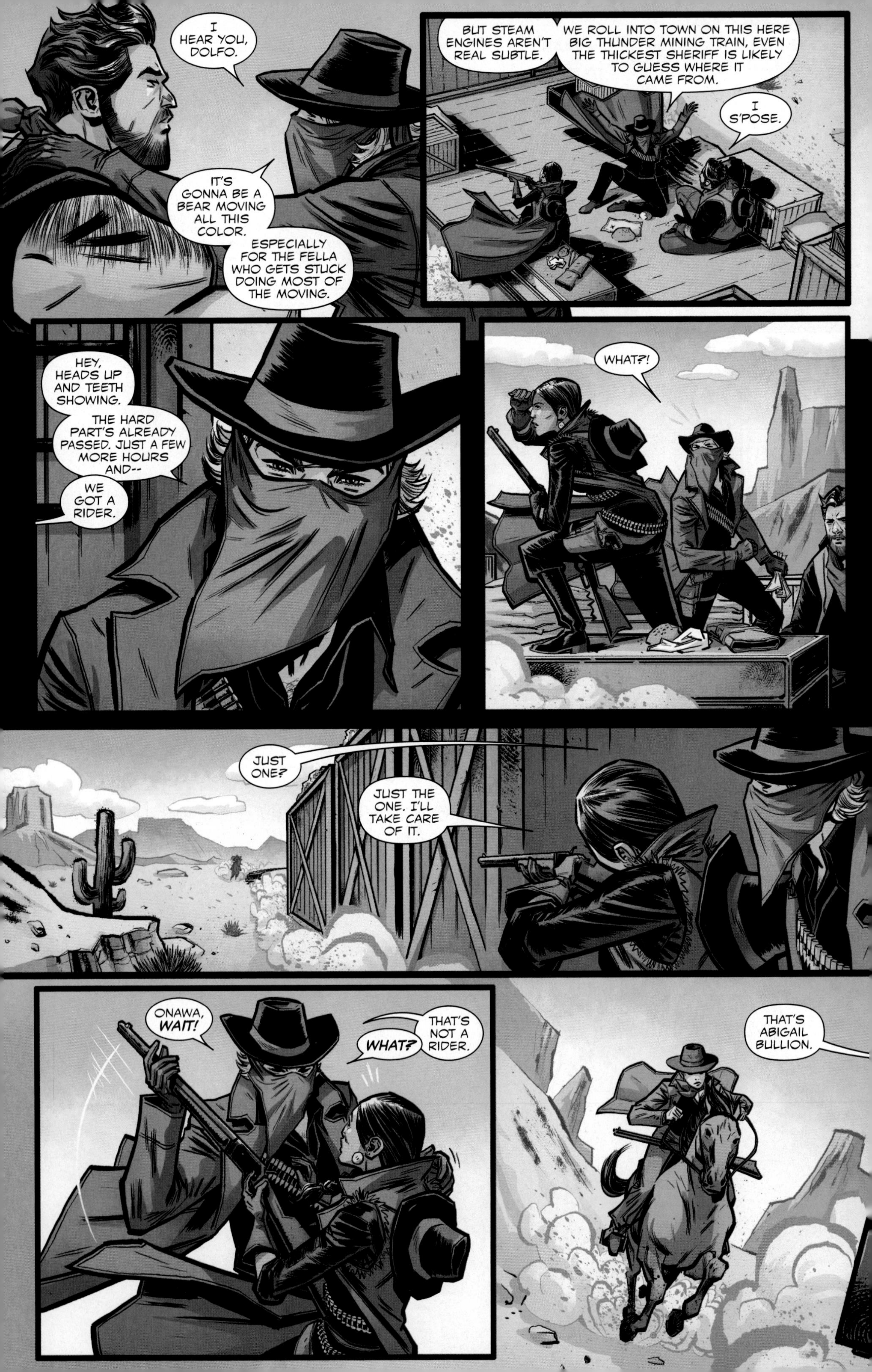
I HEAR YOU, DOLFO.
IT'S GONNA BE A BEAR MOVING ALL THIS COLOR.
ESPECIALLY FOR THE FELLA WHO GETS STUCK DOING MOST OF THE MOVING.
BUT STEAM ENGINES AREN'T REAL SUBTLE.
WE ROLL INTO TOWN ON THIS HERE BIG THUNDER MINING TRAIN, EVEN THE THICKEST SHERIFF IS LIKELY TO GUESS WHERE IT CAME FROM.
I S'POSE.
HEY, HEADS UP AND TEETH SHOWING.
THE HARD PART'S ALREADY PASSED. JUST A FEW MORE HOURS AND--
WE GOT A RIDER.
WHAT?!
JUST ONE?
JUST THE ONE. I'LL TAKE CARE OF IT.
ONAWA, WAIT!
WHAT?
THAT'S NOT A RIDER.
THAT'S ABIGAIL BULLION.

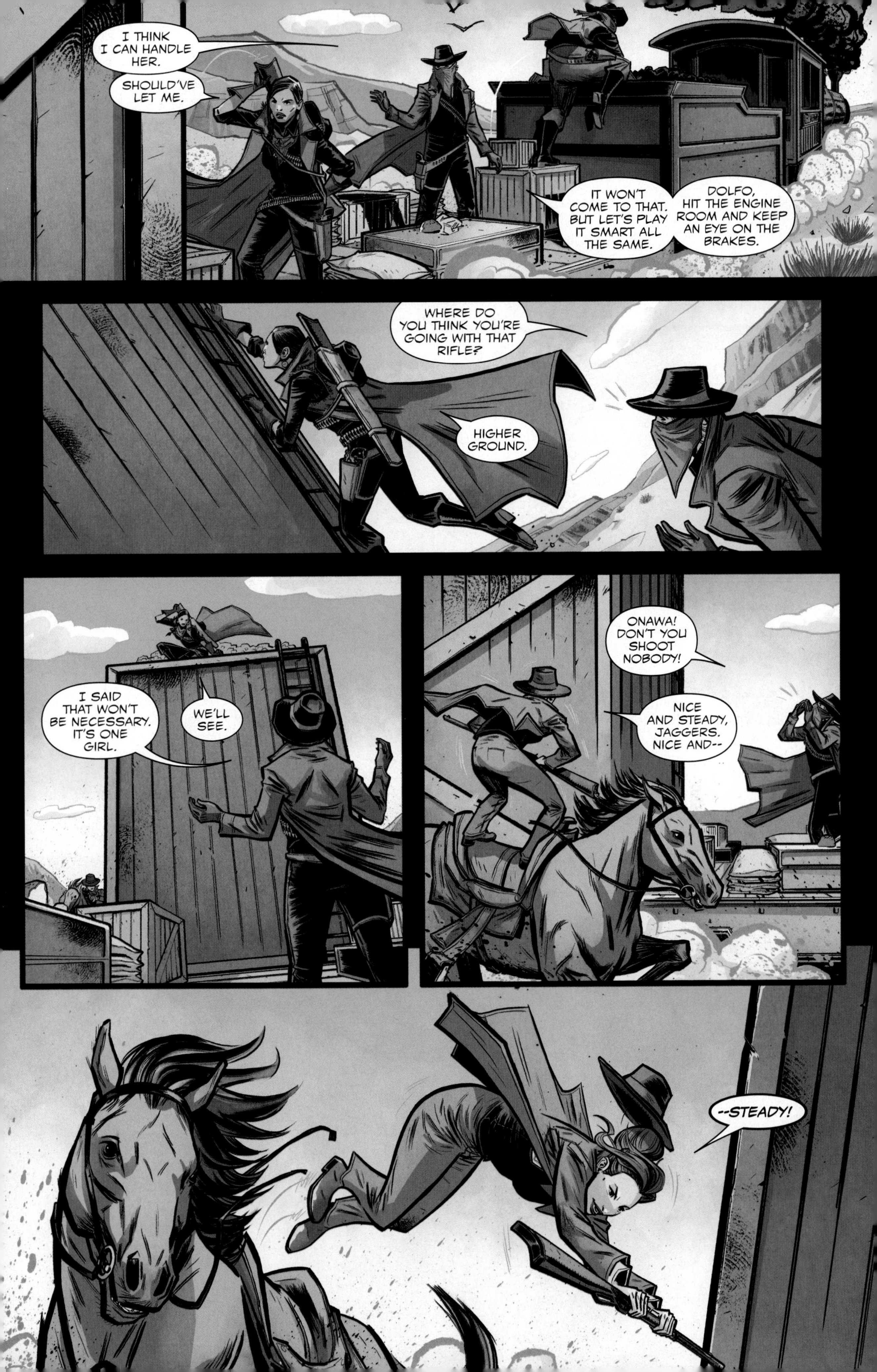
I THINK I CAN HANDLE HER.
SHOULD'VE LET ME.
IT WON'T COME TO THAT. BUT LET'S PLAY IT SMART ALL THE SAME.
DOLFO, HIT THE ENGINE ROOM AND KEEP AN EYE ON THE BRAKES.
WHERE DO YOU THINK YOU'RE GOING WITH THAT RIFLE?
HIGHER GROUND.
I SAID THAT WON'T BE NECESSARY. IT'S ONE GIRL.
WE'LL SEE.
ONAWA! DON'T YOU SHOOT NOBODY!
NICE AND STEADY, JAGGERS. NICE AND--
--STEADY!

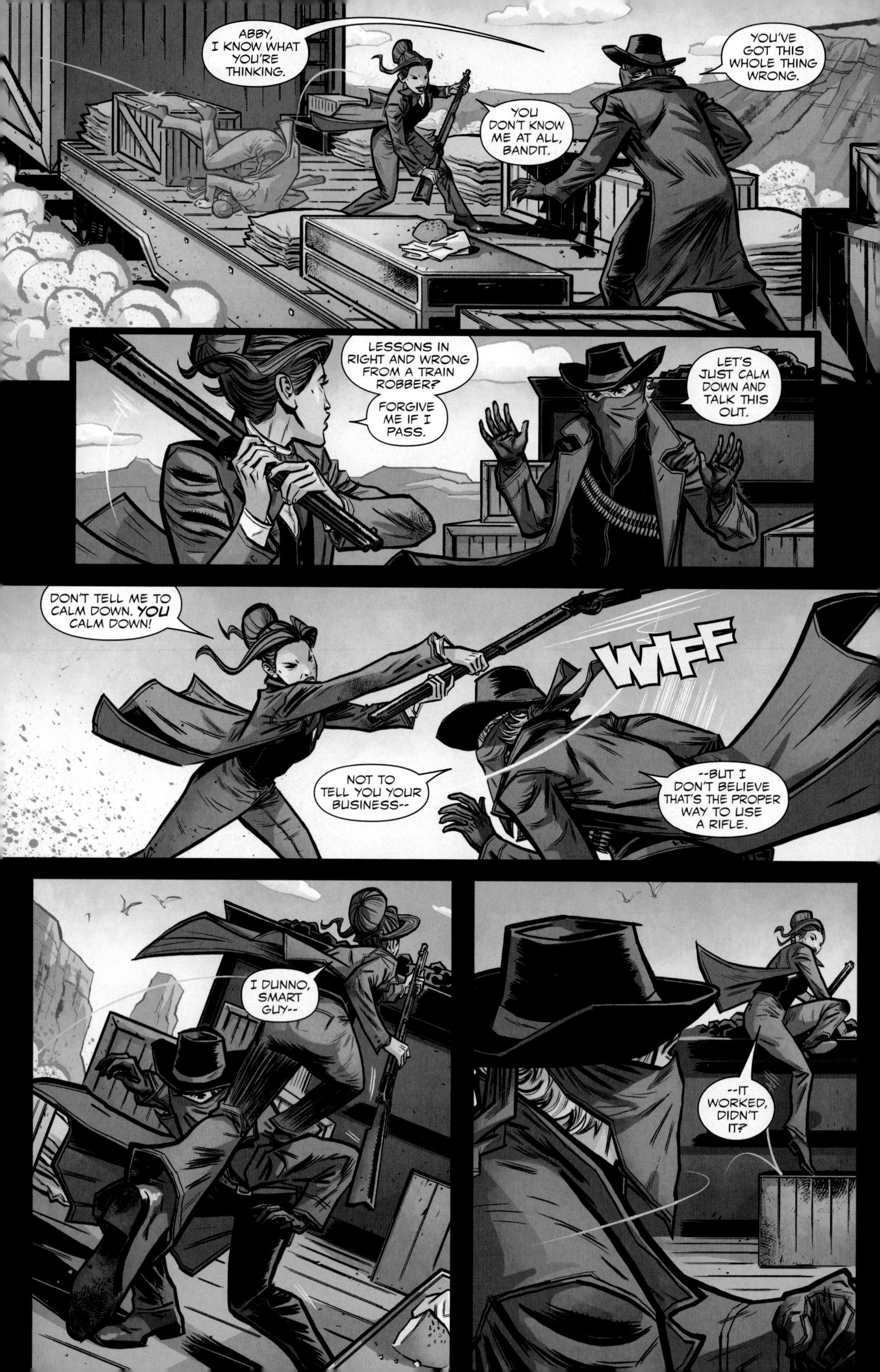
ABBY, I KNOW WHAT YOU'RE THINKING.
YOU'VE GOT THIS WHOLE THING WRONG.
YOU DON'T KNOW ME AT ALL, BANDIT.
LESSONS IN RIGHT AND WRONG FROM A TRAIN ROBBER?
FORGIVE ME IF I PASS.
LET'S JUST CALM DOWN AND TALK THIS OUT.
DON'T TELL ME TO CALM DOWN. YOU CALM DOWN!
WIFF
NOT TO TELL YOU YOUR BUSINESS--
--BUT I DON'T BELIEVE THAT'S THE PROPER WAY TO USE A RIFLE.
I DUNNO, SMART GUY--
--IT WORKED, DIDN'T IT?

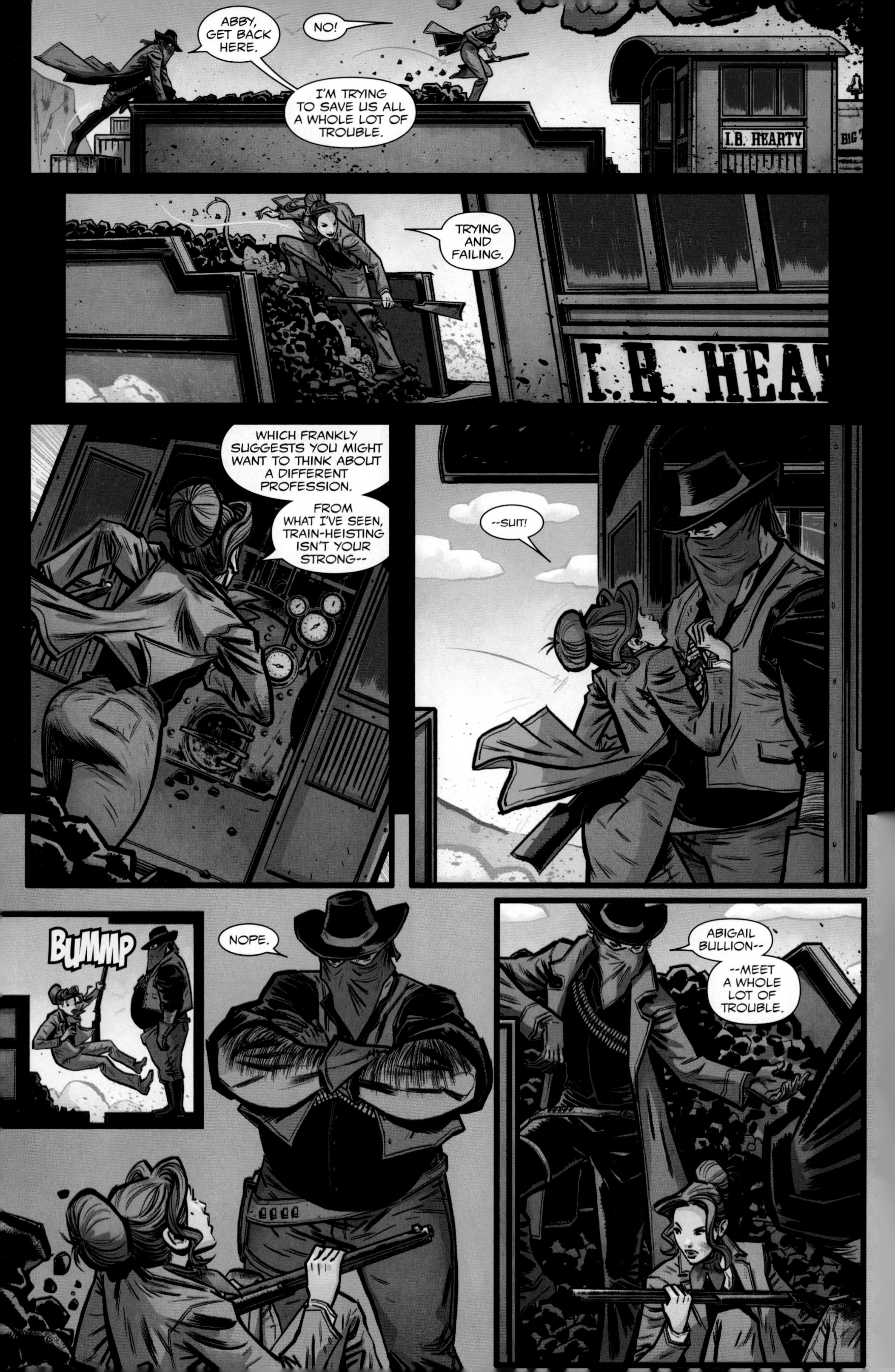
ABBY, GET BACK HERE.
NO!
I'M TRYING TO SAVE US ALL A WHOLE LOT OF TROUBLE.
I.B. HEARTY
TRYING AND FAILING.
I.B. HEA
WHICH FRANKLY SUGGESTS YOU MIGHT WANT TO THINK ABOUT A DIFFERENT PROFESSION.
FROM WHAT I'VE SEEN, TRAIN-HEISTING ISN'T YOUR STRONG--
--SUIT!
BUMMP
NOPE.
ABIGAIL BULLION--
--MEET A WHOLE LOT OF TROUBLE.

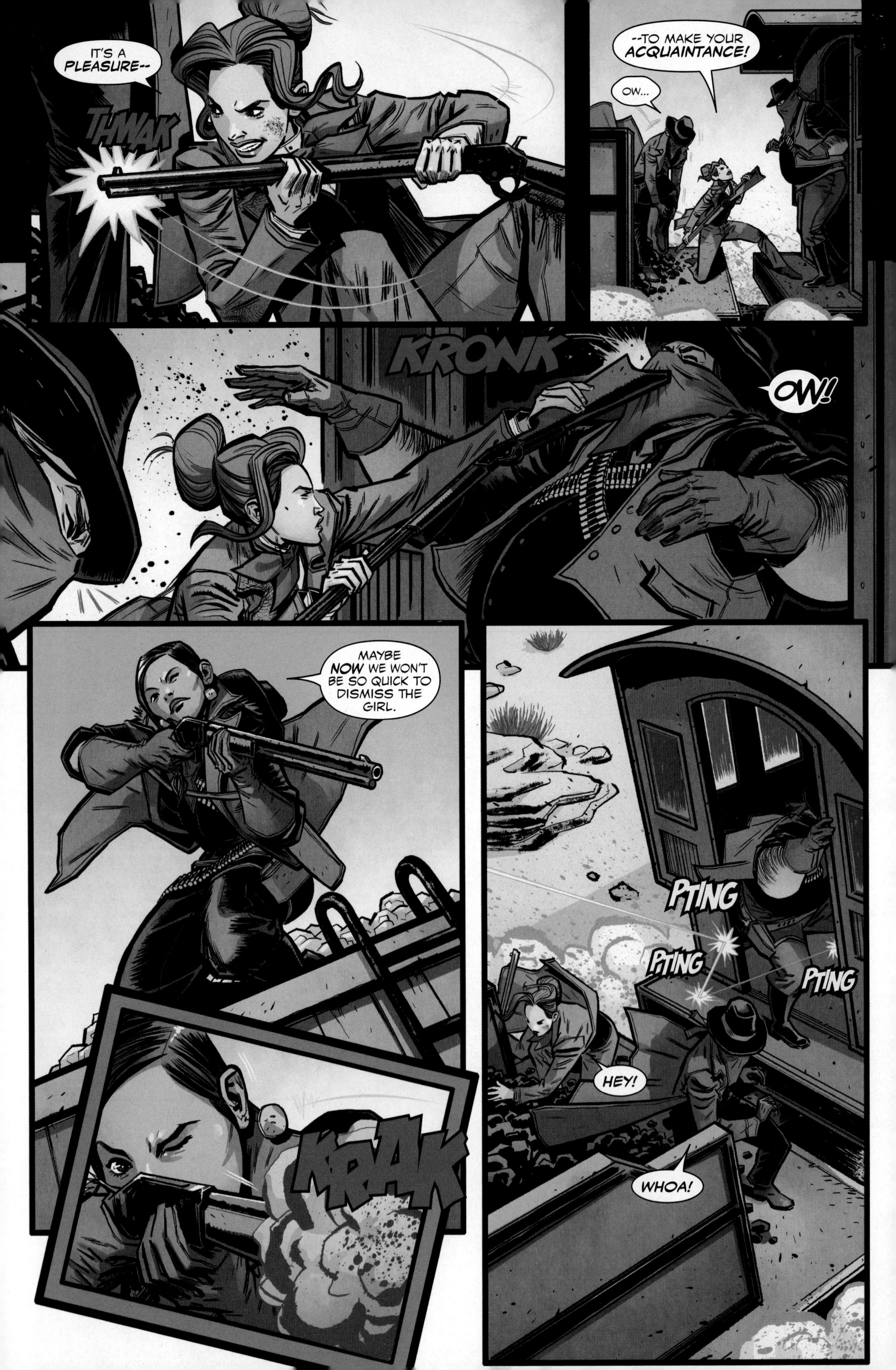
IT'S A PLEASURE--
THWAK
--TO MAKE YOUR ACQUAINTANCE!
OW...
KRONK
OW!
MAYBE NOW WE WON'T BE SO QUICK TO DISMISS THE GIRL.
KRAK
PTING
PTING
PTING
HEY!
WHOA!

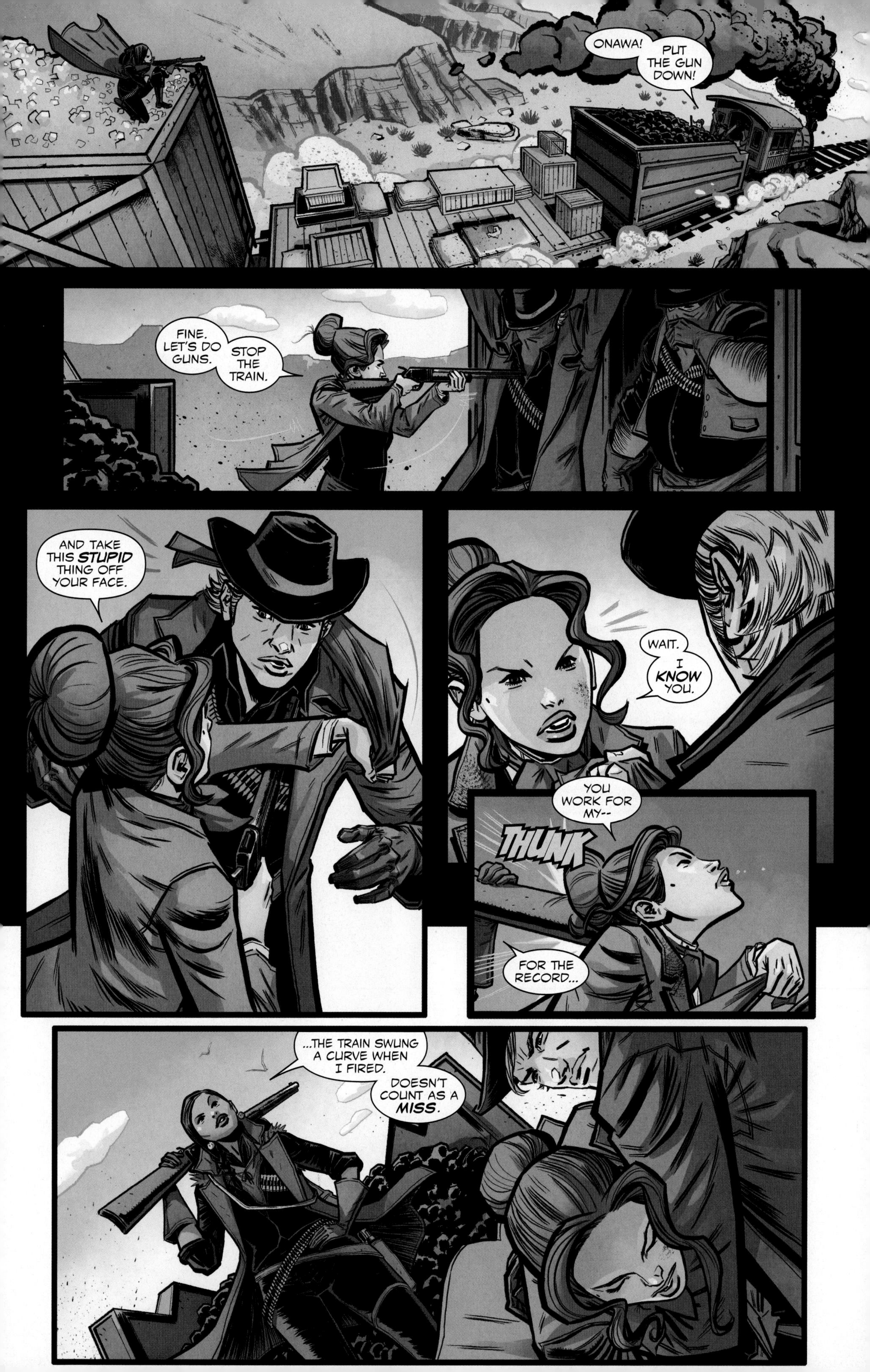
ONAWA!
PUT THE GUN DOWN!
FINE. LET'S DO GUNS.
STOP THE TRAIN.
AND TAKE THIS STUPID THING OFF YOUR FACE.
WAIT.
I KNOW YOU.
YOU WORK FOR MY--
THUNK
FOR THE RECORD...
...THE TRAIN SWUNG A CURVE WHEN I FIRED.
DOESN'T COUNT AS A MISS.

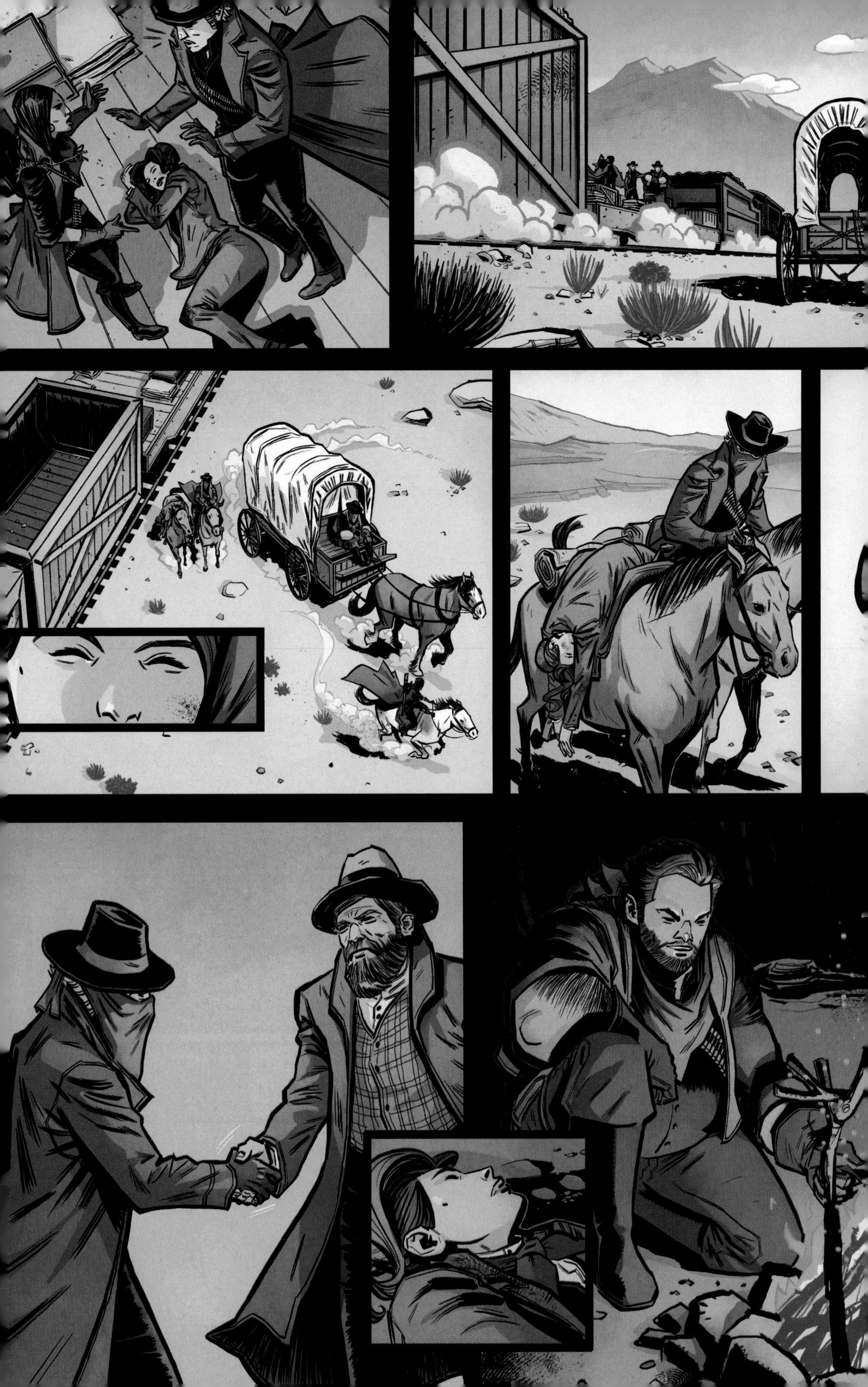

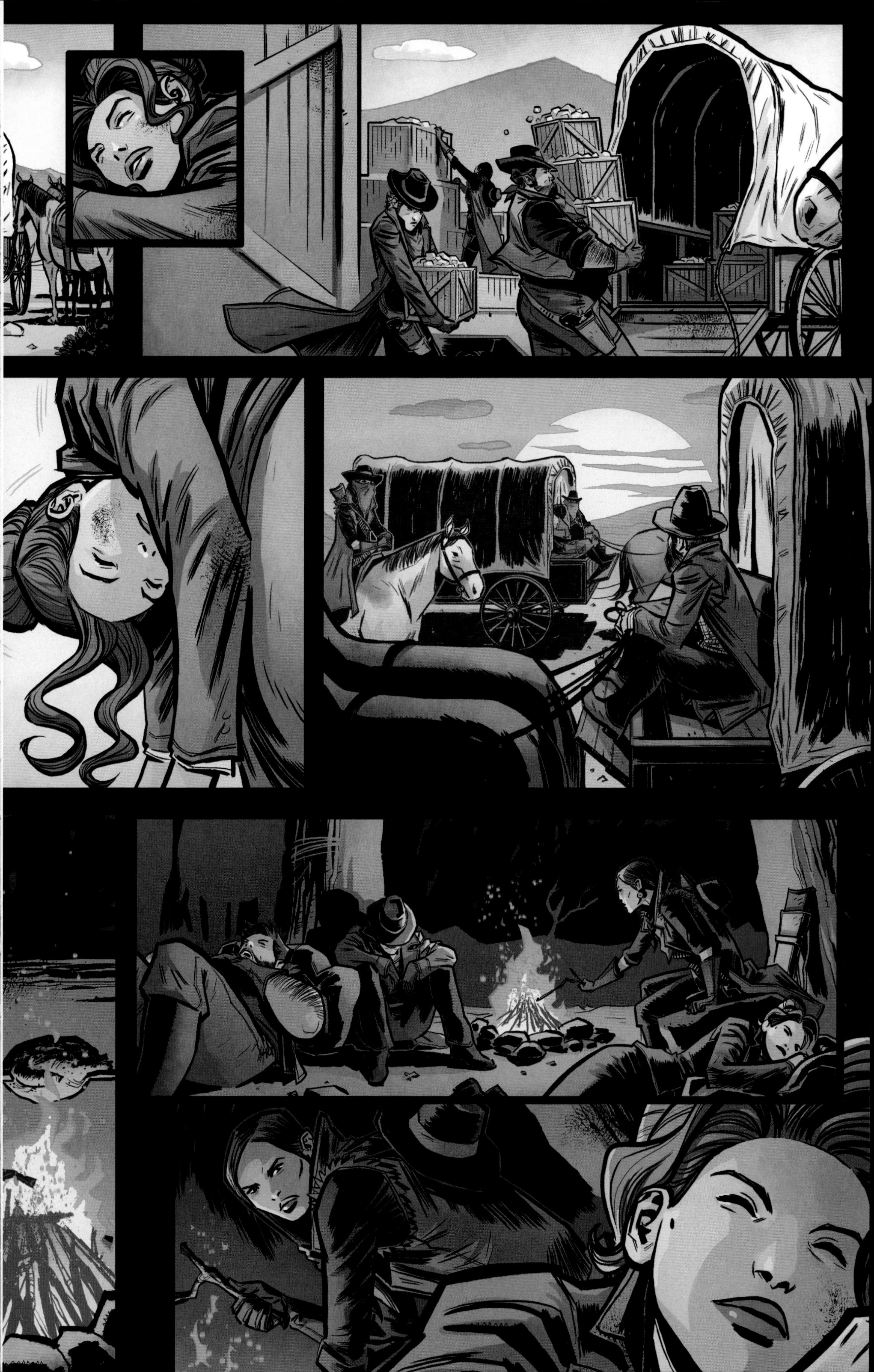

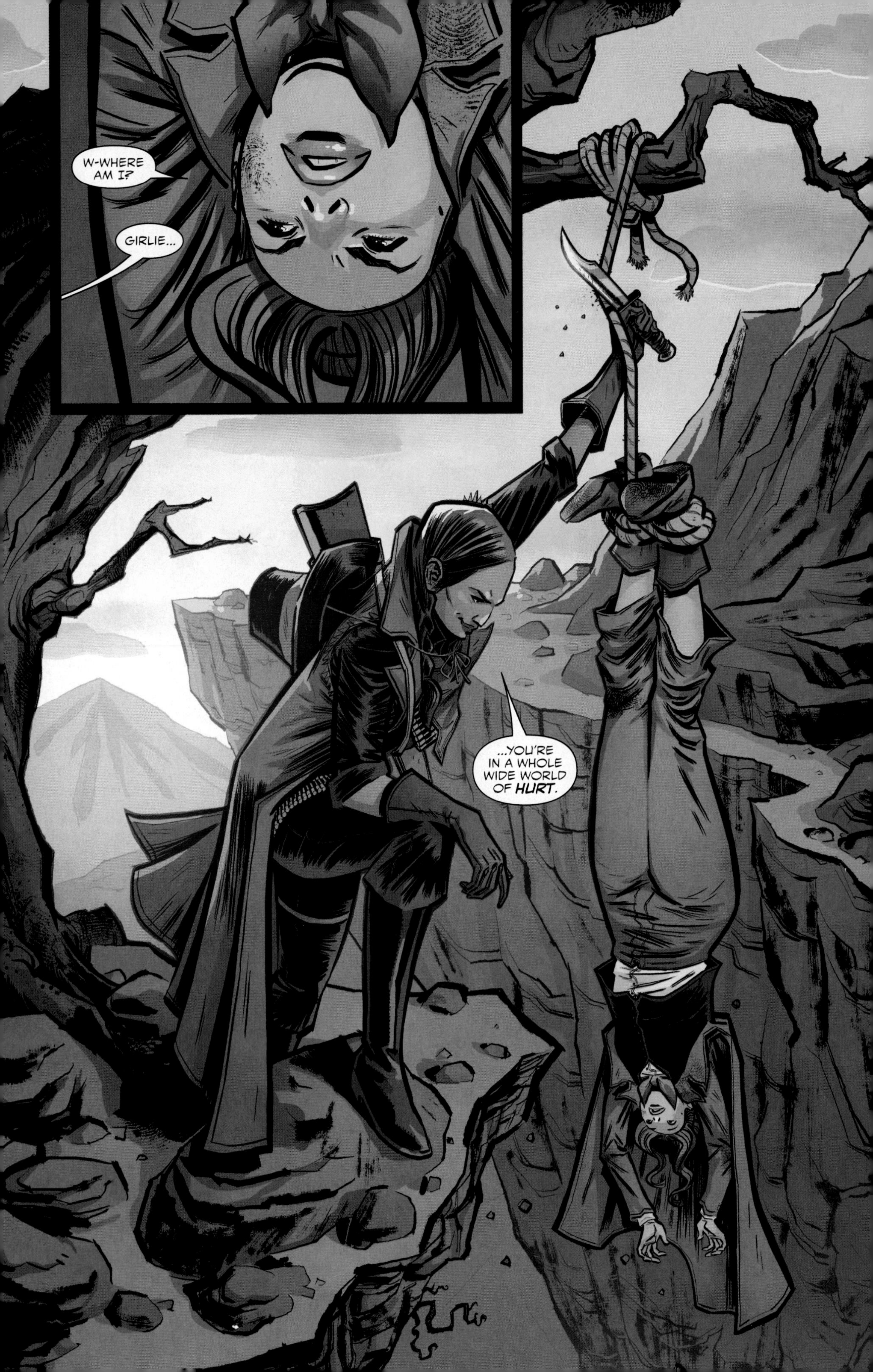
W-WHERE AM I?
GIRLIE...
...YOU'RE IN A WHOLE WIDE WORLD OF **HURT**.

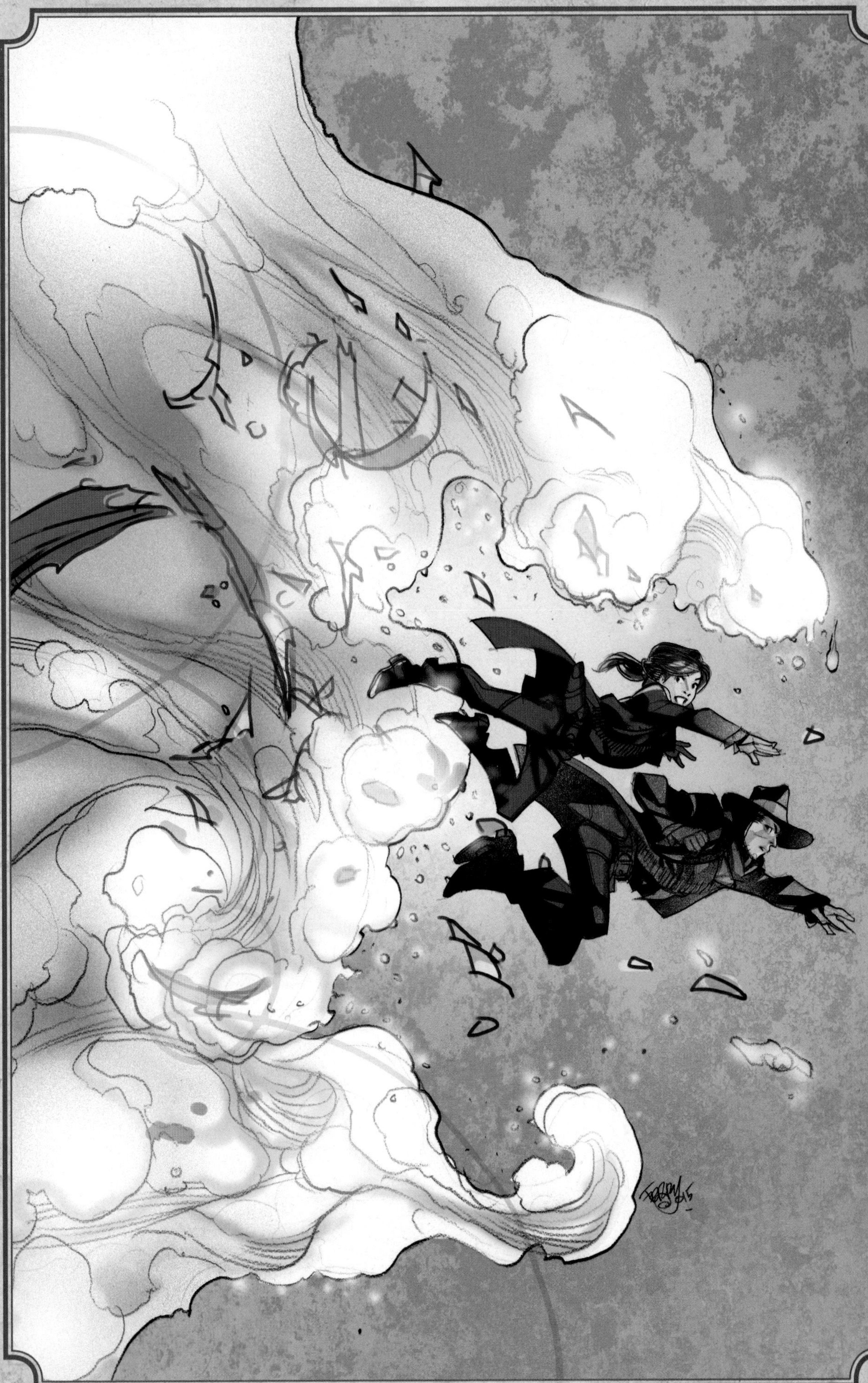

~ 3 ~

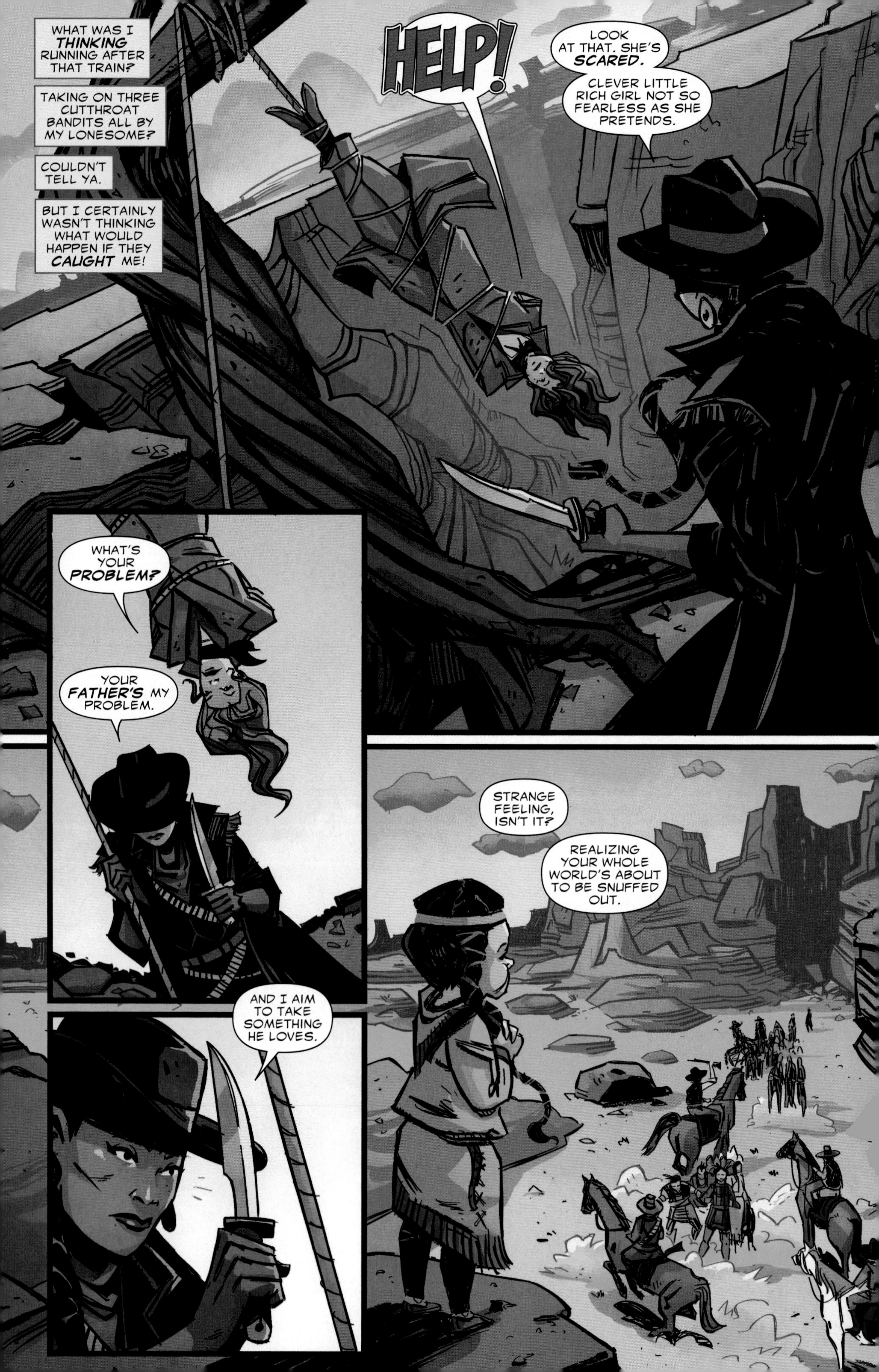
WHAT WAS I THINKING RUNNING AFTER THAT TRAIN?
TAKING ON THREE CUTTHROAT BANDITS ALL BY MY LONESOME?
COULDN'T TELL YA.
BUT I CERTAINLY WASN'T THINKING WHAT WOULD HAPPEN IF THEY CAUGHT ME!
HELP!
LOOK AT THAT. SHE'S SCARED.
CLEVER LITTLE RICH GIRL NOT SO FEARLESS AS SHE PRETENDS.
WHAT'S YOUR PROBLEM?
YOUR FATHER'S MY PROBLEM.
AND I AIM TO TAKE SOMETHING HE LOVES.
STRANGE FEELING, ISN'T IT?
REALIZING YOUR WHOLE WORLD'S ABOUT TO BE SNUFFED OUT.

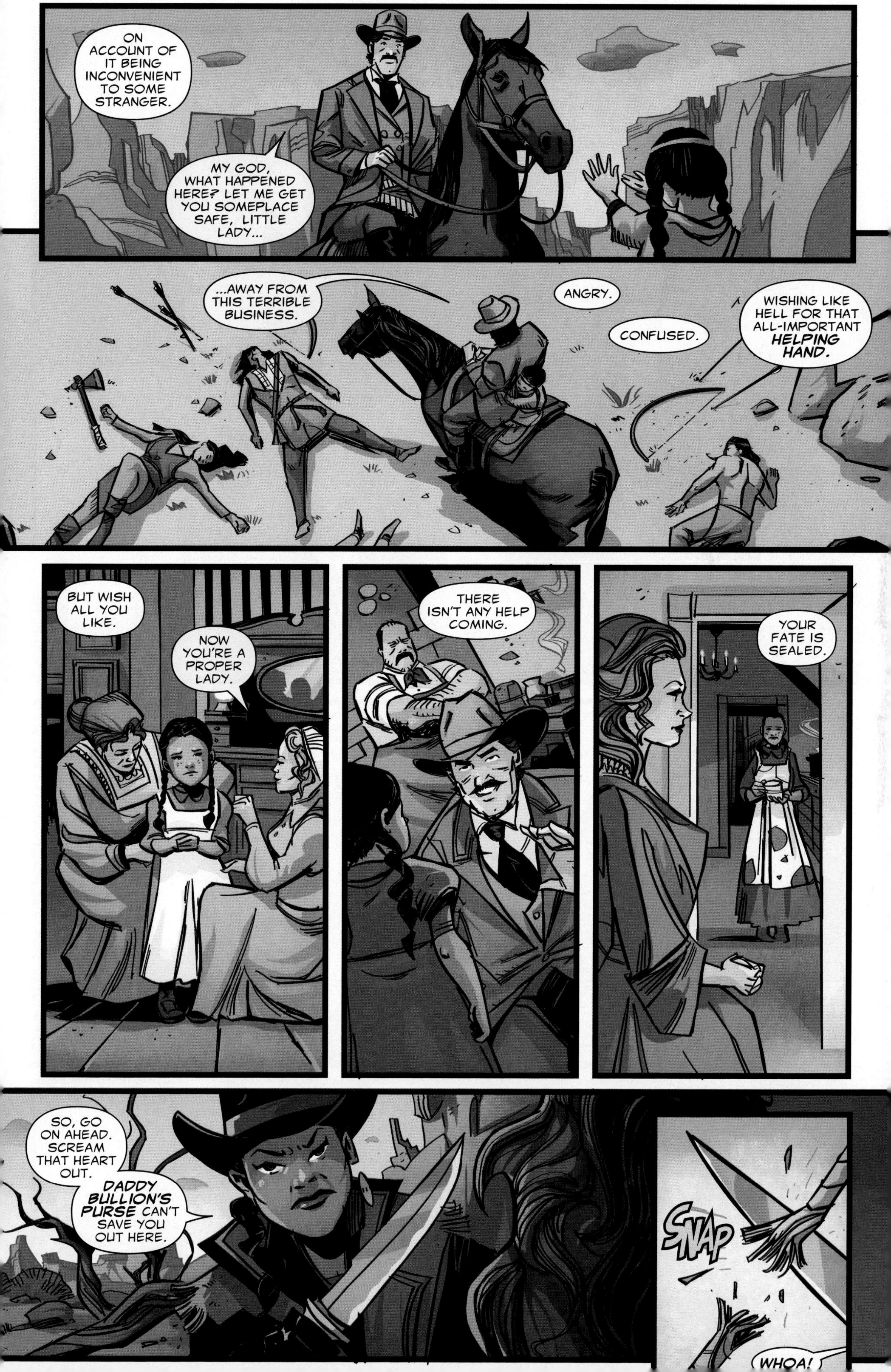
ON ACCOUNT OF IT BEING INCONVENIENT TO SOME STRANGER.
MY GOD, WHAT HAPPENED HERE? LET ME GET YOU SOMEPLACE SAFE, LITTLE LADY...
...AWAY FROM THIS TERRIBLE BUSINESS.
ANGRY.
CONFUSED.
WISHING LIKE HELL FOR THAT ALL-IMPORTANT HELPING HAND.
BUT WISH ALL YOU LIKE.
NOW YOU'RE A PROPER LADY.
THERE ISN'T ANY HELP COMING.
YOUR FATE IS SEALED.
SO, GO ON AHEAD. SCREAM THAT HEART OUT.
DADDY BULLION'S PURSE CAN'T SAVE YOU OUT HERE.
SNAP
WHOA!

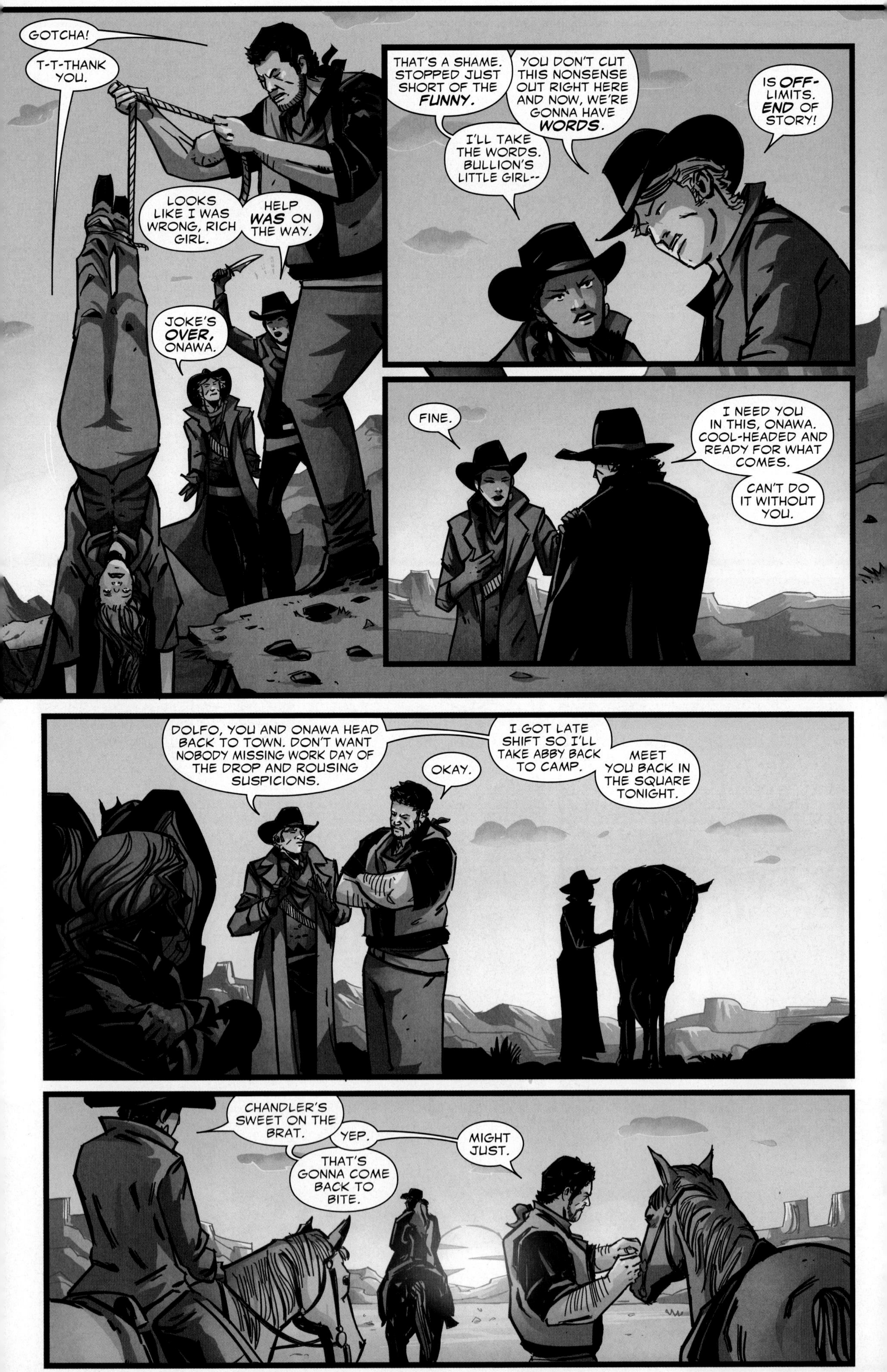
GOTCHA!
T-T-THANK YOU.
LOOKS LIKE I WAS WRONG, RICH GIRL.
HELP WAS ON THE WAY.
JOKE'S OVER, ONAWA.
THAT'S A SHAME. STOPPED JUST SHORT OF THE FUNNY.
YOU DON'T CUT THIS NONSENSE OUT RIGHT HERE AND NOW, WE'RE GONNA HAVE WORDS.
I'LL TAKE THE WORDS. BULLION'S LITTLE GIRL--
IS OFF-LIMITS. END OF STORY!
FINE.
I NEED YOU IN THIS, ONAWA. COOL-HEADED AND READY FOR WHAT COMES.
CAN'T DO IT WITHOUT YOU.
DOLFO, YOU AND ONAWA HEAD BACK TO TOWN. DON'T WANT NOBODY MISSING WORK DAY OF THE DROP AND ROUSING SUSPICIONS.
OKAY.
I GOT LATE SHIFT SO I'LL TAKE ABBY BACK TO CAMP.
MEET YOU BACK IN THE SQUARE TONIGHT.
CHANDLER'S SWEET ON THE BRAT.
YEP.
THAT'S GONNA COME BACK TO BITE.
MIGHT JUST.

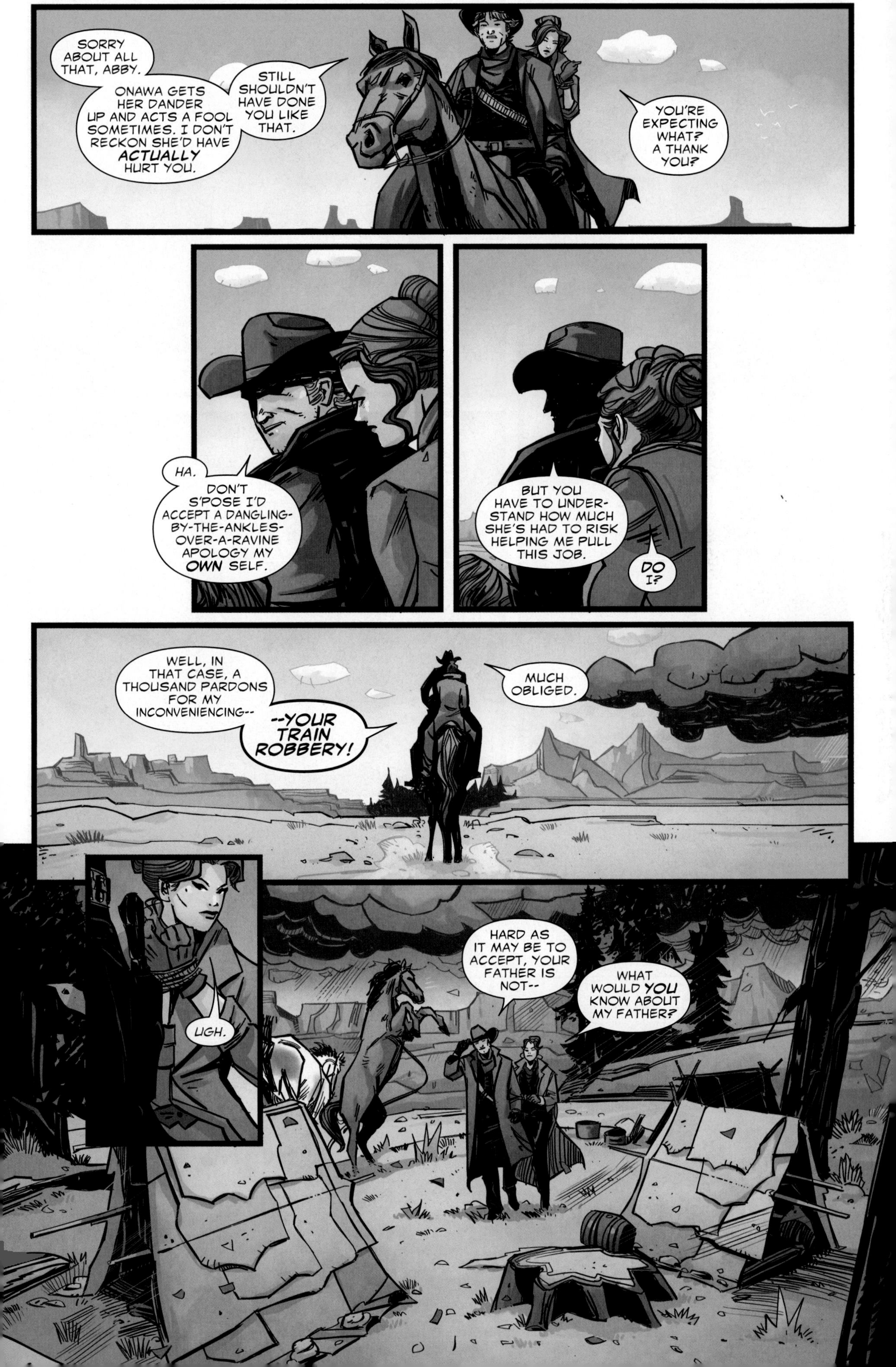
SORRY ABOUT ALL THAT, ABBY.
ONAWA GETS HER DANDER UP AND ACTS A FOOL SOMETIMES. I DON'T RECKON SHE'D HAVE ACTUALLY HURT YOU.
STILL SHOULDN'T HAVE DONE YOU LIKE THAT.
YOU'RE EXPECTING WHAT? A THANK YOU?
HA.
DON'T S'POSE I'D ACCEPT A DANGLING-BY-THE-ANKLES-OVER-A-RAVINE APOLOGY MY OWN SELF.
BUT YOU HAVE TO UNDERSTAND HOW MUCH SHE'S HAD TO RISK HELPING ME PULL THIS JOB.
DO I?
WELL, IN THAT CASE, A THOUSAND PARDONS FOR MY INCONVENIENCING--
--YOUR TRAIN ROBBERY!
MUCH OBLIGED.
UGH.
HARD AS IT MAY BE TO ACCEPT, YOUR FATHER IS NOT--
WHAT WOULD YOU KNOW ABOUT MY FATHER?

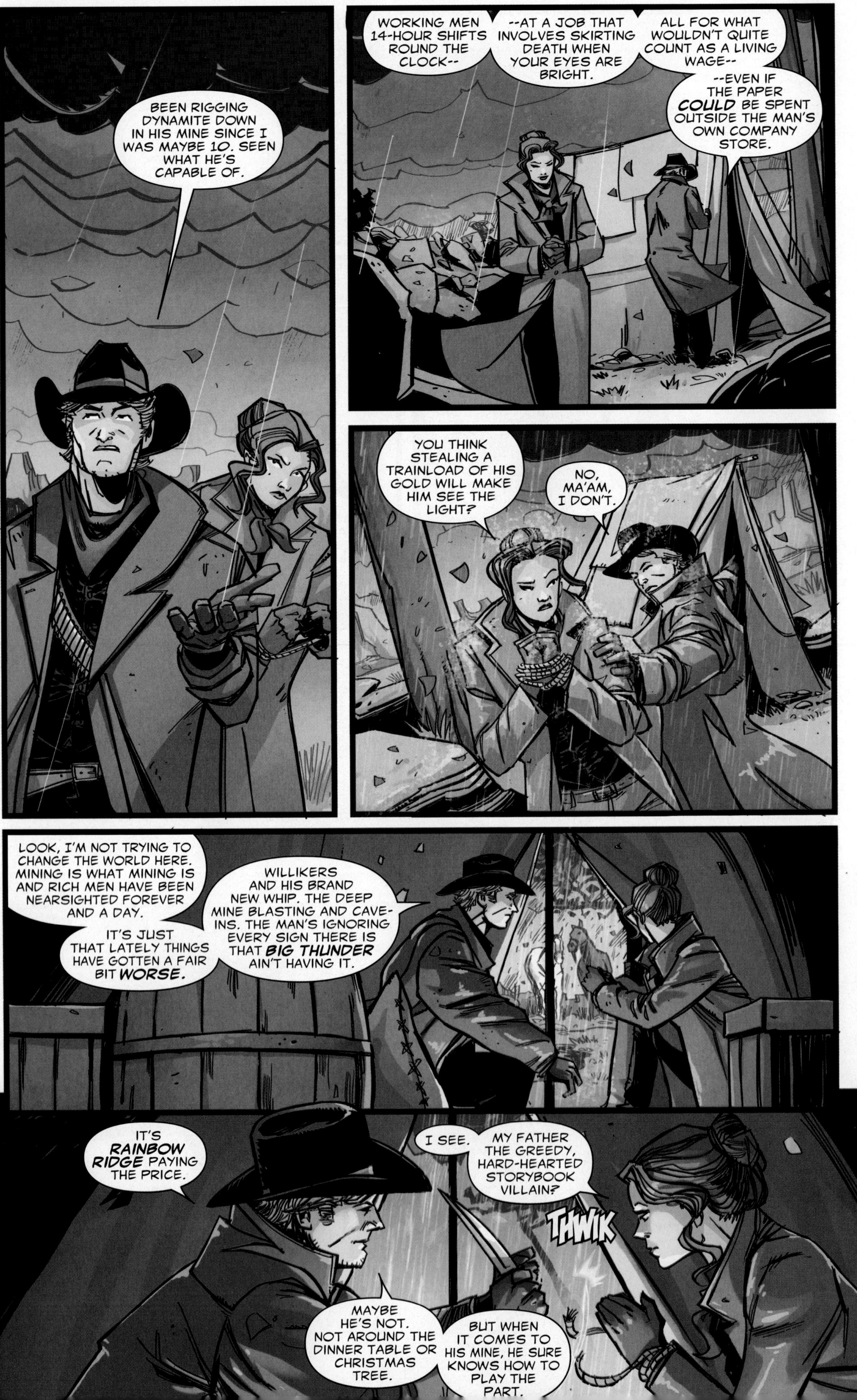
BEEN RIGGING DYNAMITE DOWN IN HIS MINE SINCE I WAS MAYBE 10. SEEN WHAT HE'S CAPABLE OF.
WORKING MEN 14-HOUR SHIFTS ROUND THE CLOCK--
--AT A JOB THAT INVOLVES SKIRTING DEATH WHEN YOUR EYES ARE BRIGHT.
ALL FOR WHAT WOULDN'T QUITE COUNT AS A LIVING WAGE--
--EVEN IF THE PAPER COULD BE SPENT OUTSIDE THE MAN'S OWN COMPANY STORE.
YOU THINK STEALING A TRAINLOAD OF HIS GOLD WILL MAKE HIM SEE THE LIGHT?
NO, MA'AM, I DON'T.
LOOK, I'M NOT TRYING TO CHANGE THE WORLD HERE. MINING IS WHAT MINING IS AND RICH MEN HAVE BEEN NEARSIGHTED FOREVER AND A DAY.
IT'S JUST THAT LATELY THINGS HAVE GOTTEN A FAIR BIT WORSE.
WILLIKERS AND HIS BRAND NEW WHIP. THE DEEP MINE BLASTING AND CAVE-INS. THE MAN'S IGNORING EVERY SIGN THERE IS THAT BIG THUNDER AIN'T HAVING IT.
IT'S RAINBOW RIDGE PAYING THE PRICE.
I SEE.
MY FATHER THE GREEDY, HARD-HEARTED STORYBOOK VILLAIN?
THWIK
MAYBE HE'S NOT. NOT AROUND THE DINNER TABLE OR CHRISTMAS TREE.
BUT WHEN IT COMES TO HIS MINE, HE SURE KNOWS HOW TO PLAY THE PART.

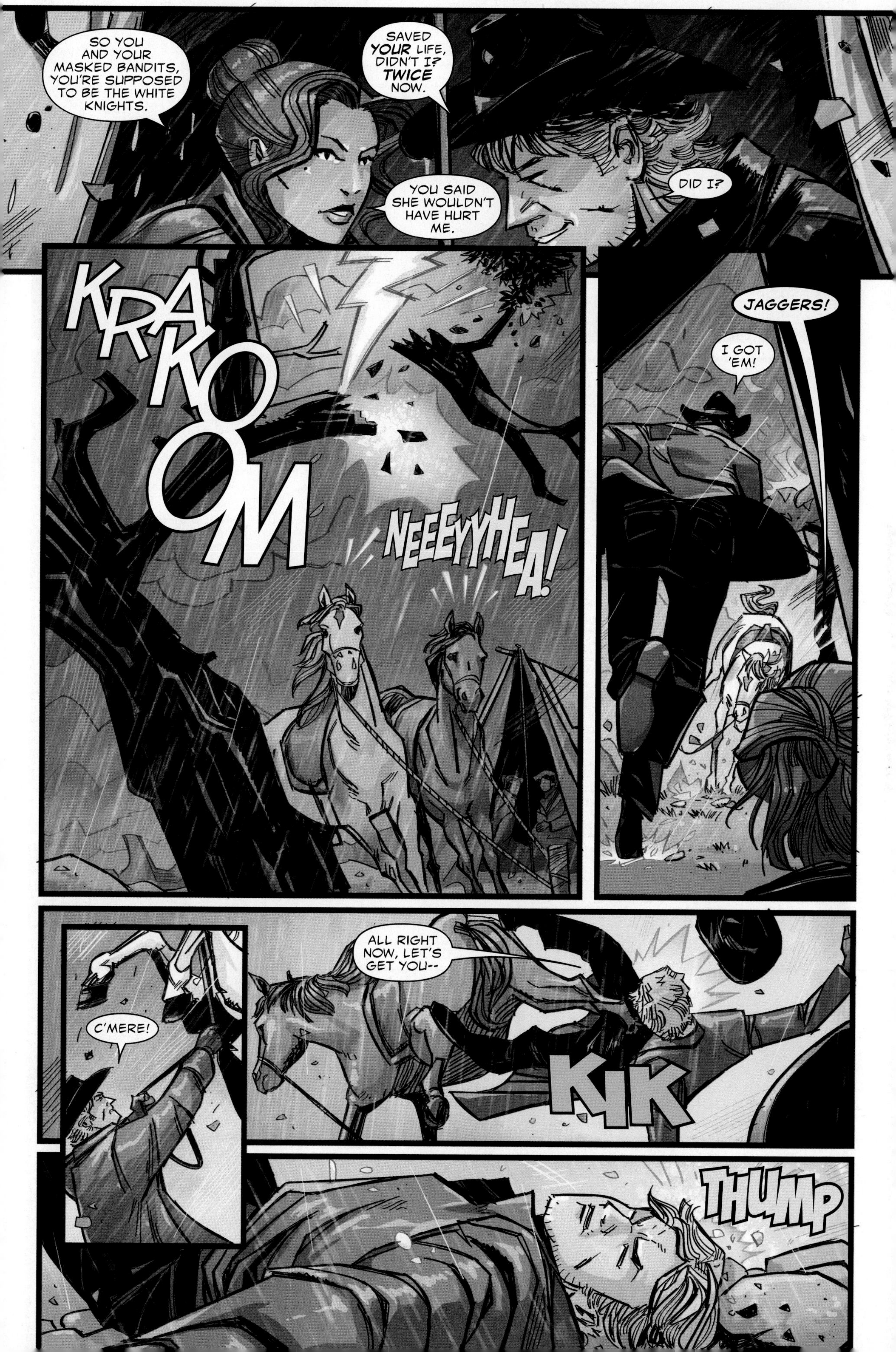

SO YOU AND YOUR MASKED BANDITS, YOU'RE SUPPOSED TO BE THE WHITE KNIGHTS.
SAVED YOUR LIFE, DIDN'T I? TWICE NOW.
YOU SAID SHE WOULDN'T HAVE HURT ME.
DID I?
KRAKOOM
NEEEYYHEA!
JAGGERS!
I GOT 'EM!
C'MERE!
ALL RIGHT NOW, LET'S GET YOU--
KLIK
THUMP

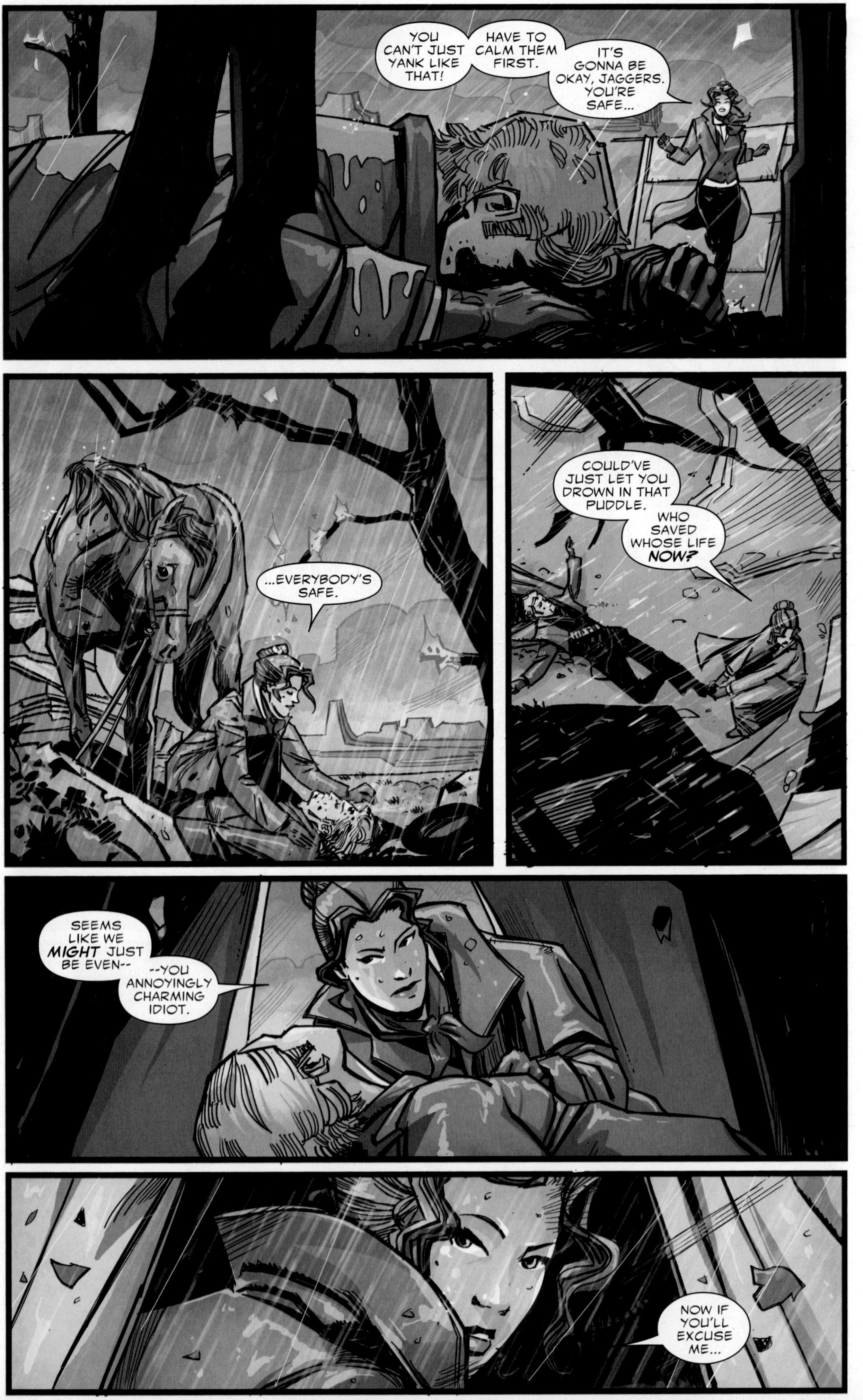

YOU CAN'T JUST YANK LIKE THAT!
HAVE TO CALM THEM FIRST.
IT'S GONNA BE OKAY, JAGGERS. YOU'RE SAFE...
...EVERYBODY'S SAFE.
COULD'VE JUST LET YOU DROWN IN THAT PUDDLE.
WHO SAVED WHOSE LIFE NOW?
SEEMS LIKE WE MIGHT JUST BE EVEN--
--YOU ANNOYINGLY CHARMING IDIOT.
NOW IF YOU'LL EXCUSE ME...

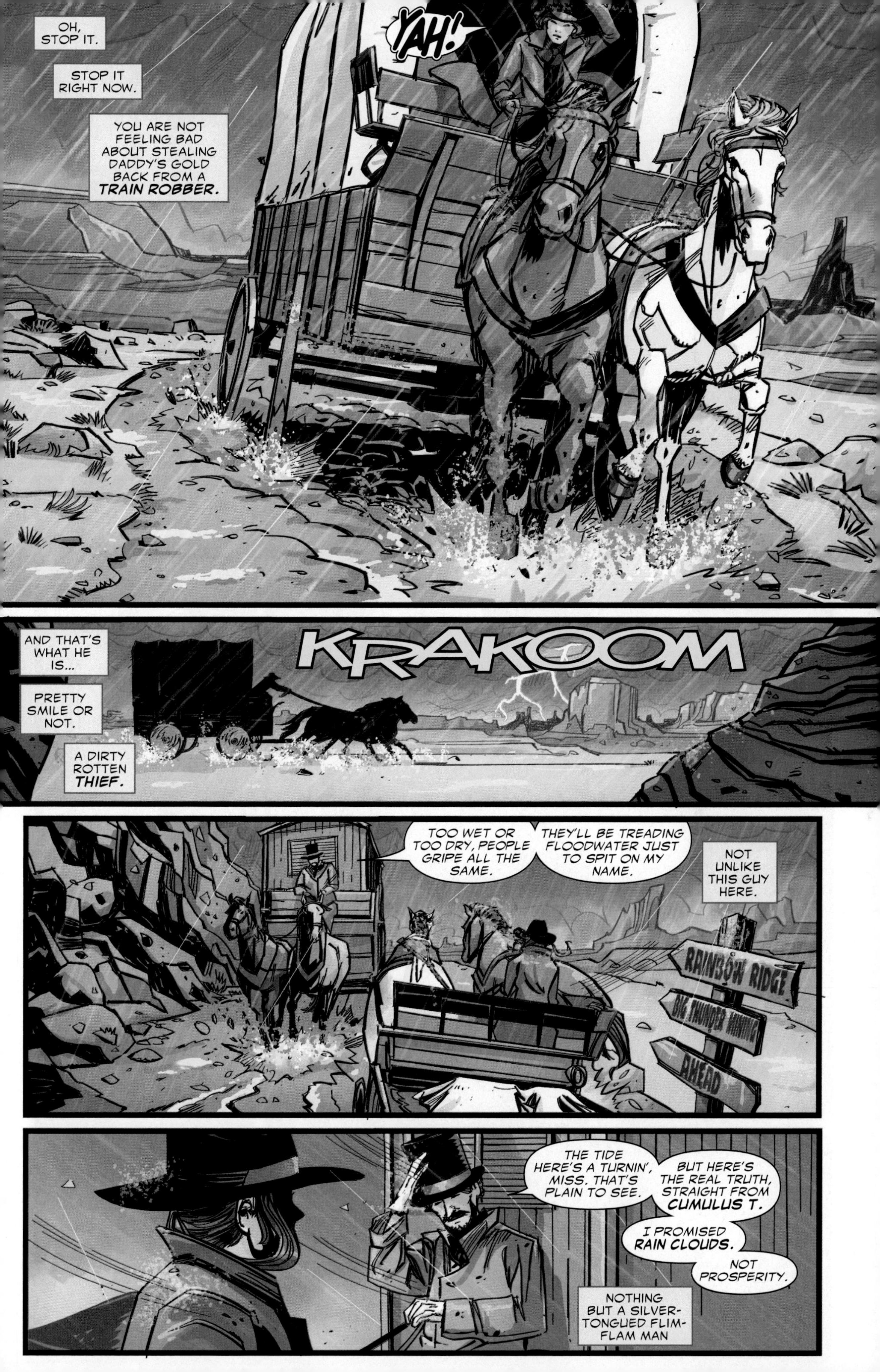
OH, STOP IT.
STOP IT RIGHT NOW.
YOU ARE NOT FEELING BAD ABOUT STEALING DADDY'S GOLD BACK FROM A TRAIN ROBBER.
YAH!
AND THAT'S WHAT HE IS...
PRETTY SMILE OR NOT.
A DIRTY ROTTEN THIEF.
KRAKOOM
TOO WET OR TOO DRY, PEOPLE GRIPE ALL THE SAME.
THEY'LL BE TREADING FLOODWATER JUST TO SPIT ON MY NAME.
NOT UNLIKE THIS GUY HERE.
RAINBOW RIDGE
BIG THUNDER MINING
AHEAD
THE TIDE HERE'S A TURNIN', MISS. THAT'S PLAIN TO SEE.
BUT HERE'S THE REAL TRUTH, STRAIGHT FROM CUMULUS T.
I PROMISED RAIN CLOUDS.
NOT PROSPERITY.
NOTHING BUT A SILVER-TONGUED FLIM-FLAM MAN

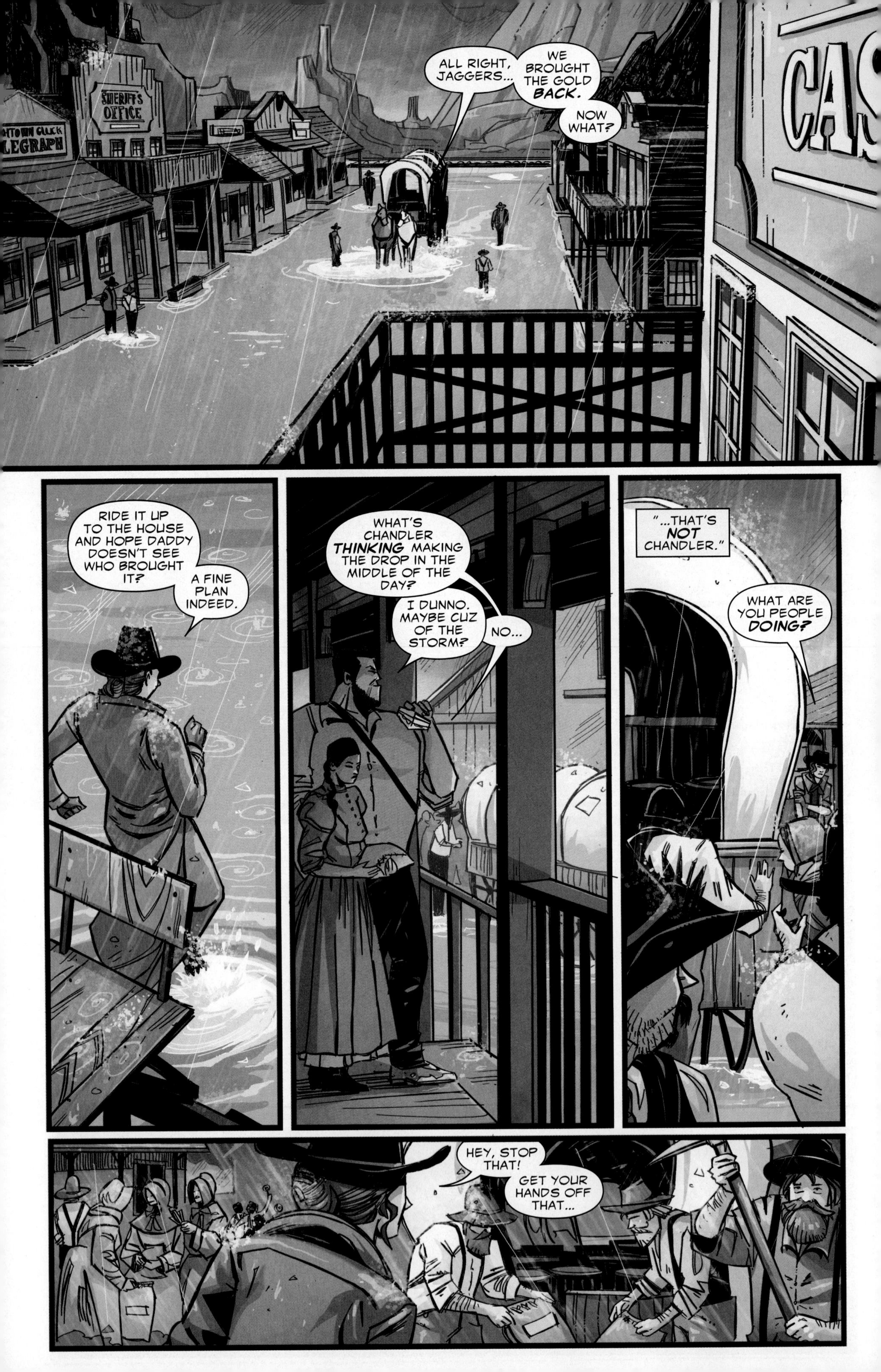
SHERIFF'S OFFICE
ALL RIGHT, JAGGERS...
WE BROUGHT THE GOLD BACK.
NOW WHAT?
RIDE IT UP TO THE HOUSE AND HOPE DADDY DOESN'T SEE WHO BROUGHT IT?
A FINE PLAN INDEED.
WHAT'S CHANDLER THINKING MAKING THE DROP IN THE MIDDLE OF THE DAY?
I DUNNO. MAYBE CUZ OF THE STORM?
NO...
"...THAT'S NOT CHANDLER."
WHAT ARE YOU PEOPLE DOING?
HEY, STOP THAT!
GET YOUR HANDS OFF THAT...

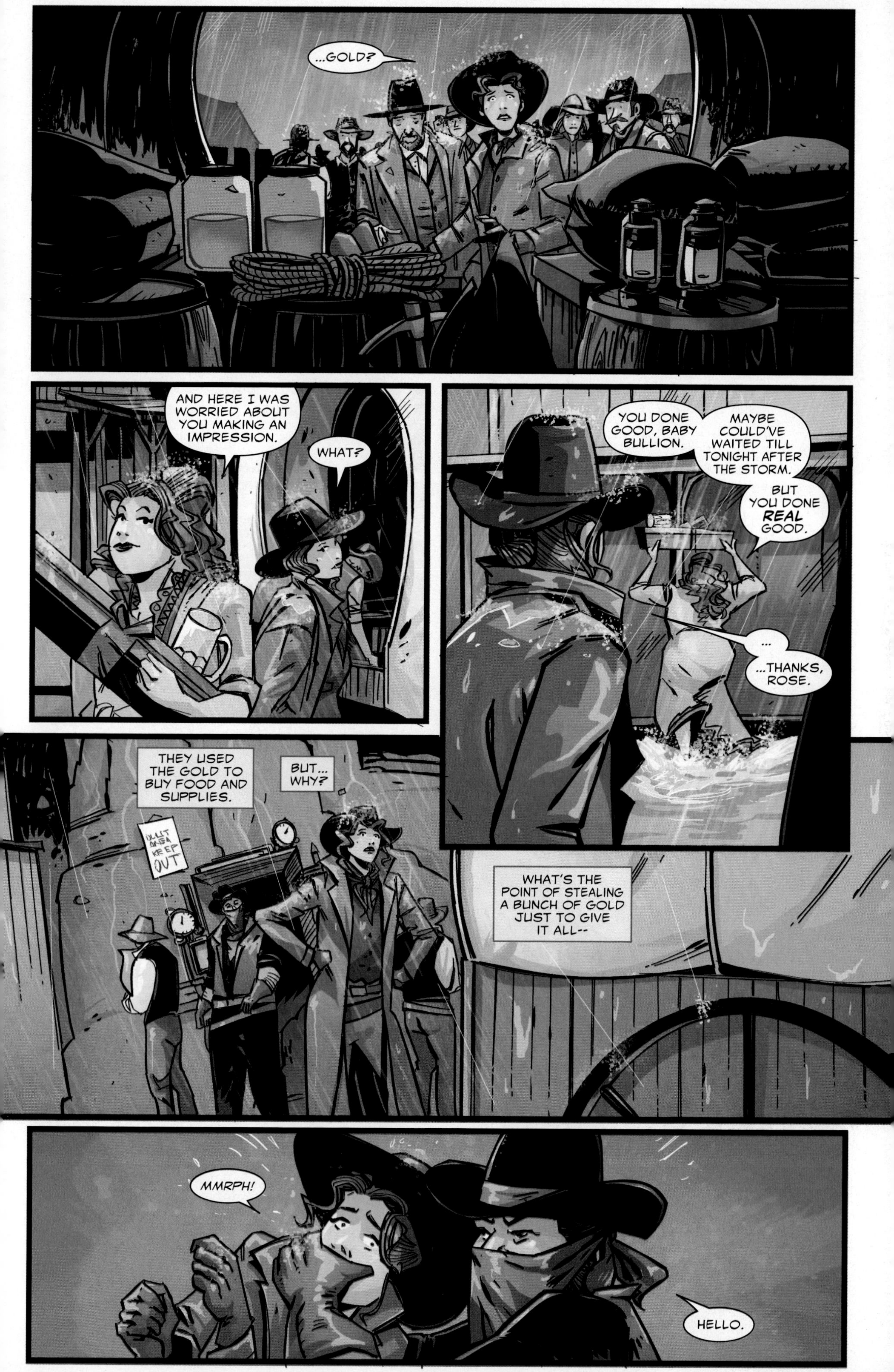
...GOLD?
AND HERE I WAS WORRIED ABOUT YOU MAKING AN IMPRESSION.
WHAT?
YOU DONE GOOD, BABY BULLION.
MAYBE COULD'VE WAITED TILL TONIGHT AFTER THE STORM.
BUT YOU DONE **REAL** GOOD.
...
...THANKS, ROSE.
THEY USED THE GOLD TO BUY FOOD AND SUPPLIES.
BUT... WHY?
KEEP OUT
WHAT'S THE POINT OF STEALING A BUNCH OF GOLD JUST TO GIVE IT ALL--
MMRPH!
HELLO.

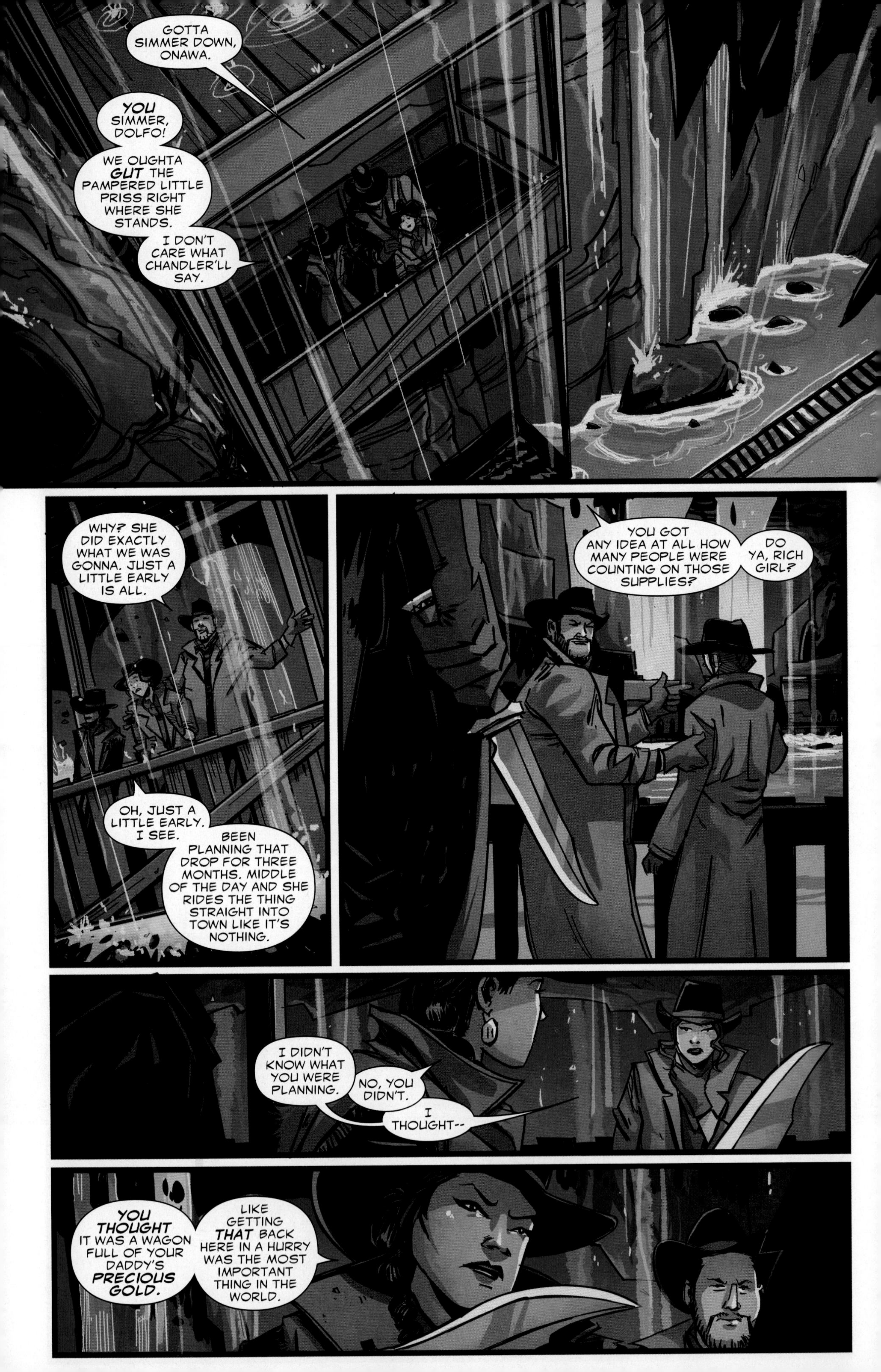
GOTTA SIMMER DOWN, ONAWA.
YOU SIMMER, DOLFO!
WE OUGHTA GUT THE PAMPERED LITTLE PRISS RIGHT WHERE SHE STANDS.
I DON'T CARE WHAT CHANDLER'LL SAY.
WHY? SHE DID EXACTLY WHAT WE WAS GONNA. JUST A LITTLE EARLY IS ALL.
OH, JUST A LITTLE EARLY. I SEE.
BEEN PLANNING THAT DROP FOR THREE MONTHS. MIDDLE OF THE DAY AND SHE RIDES THE THING STRAIGHT INTO TOWN LIKE IT'S NOTHING.
YOU GOT ANY IDEA AT ALL HOW MANY PEOPLE WERE COUNTING ON THOSE SUPPLIES?
DO YA, RICH GIRL?
I DIDN'T KNOW WHAT YOU WERE PLANNING.
NO, YOU DIDN'T.
I THOUGHT--
YOU THOUGHT IT WAS A WAGON FULL OF YOUR DADDY'S PRECIOUS GOLD.
LIKE GETTING THAT BACK HERE IN A HURRY WAS THE MOST IMPORTANT THING IN THE WORLD.

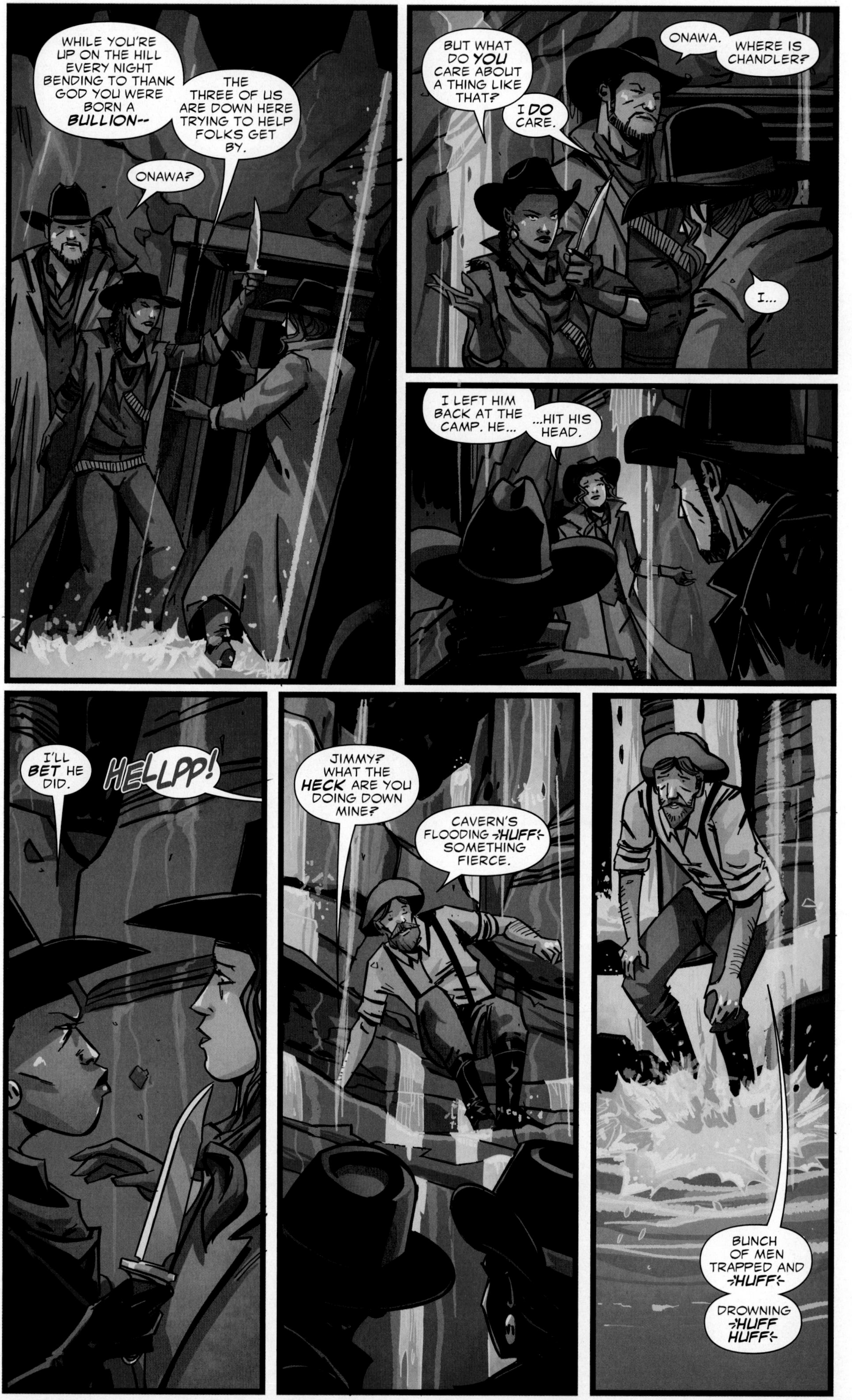

WHILE YOU'RE UP ON THE HILL EVERY NIGHT BENDING TO THANK GOD YOU WERE BORN A **BULLION**--
THE THREE OF US ARE DOWN HERE TRYING TO HELP FOLKS GET BY.
ONAWA?
BUT WHAT DO **YOU** CARE ABOUT A THING LIKE THAT?
I **DO** CARE.
ONAWA.
WHERE IS CHANDLER?
I...
I LEFT HIM BACK AT THE CAMP. HE...
...HIT HIS HEAD.
I'LL **BET** HE DID.
HELLPP!
JIMMY? WHAT THE **HECK** ARE YOU DOING DOWN MINE?
CAVERN'S FLOODING **HUFF** SOMETHING FIERCE.
BUNCH OF MEN TRAPPED AND **HUFF**
DROWNING **HUFF HUFF**

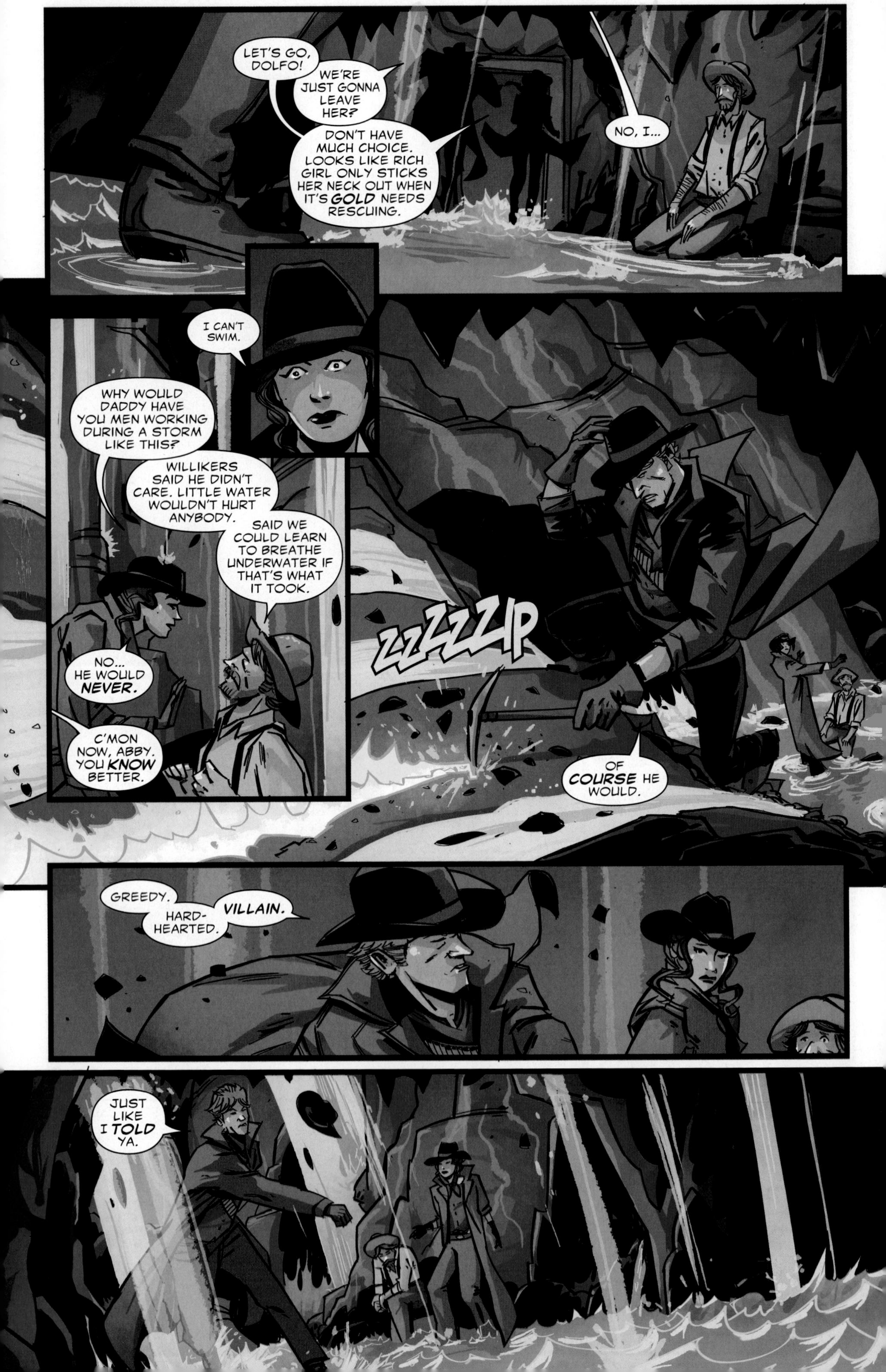
LET'S GO, DOLFO!
WE'RE JUST GONNA LEAVE HER?
DON'T HAVE MUCH CHOICE. LOOKS LIKE RICH GIRL ONLY STICKS HER NECK OUT WHEN IT'S GOLD NEEDS RESCUING.
NO, I...
I CAN'T SWIM.
WHY WOULD DADDY HAVE YOU MEN WORKING DURING A STORM LIKE THIS?
WILLIKERS SAID HE DIDN'T CARE. LITTLE WATER WOULDN'T HURT ANYBODY.
SAID WE COULD LEARN TO BREATHE UNDERWATER IF THAT'S WHAT IT TOOK.
NO... HE WOULD NEVER.
C'MON NOW, ABBY. YOU KNOW BETTER.
ZZZZZIP
OF COURSE HE WOULD.
GREEDY.
HARD-HEARTED.
VILLAIN.
JUST LIKE I TOLD YA.

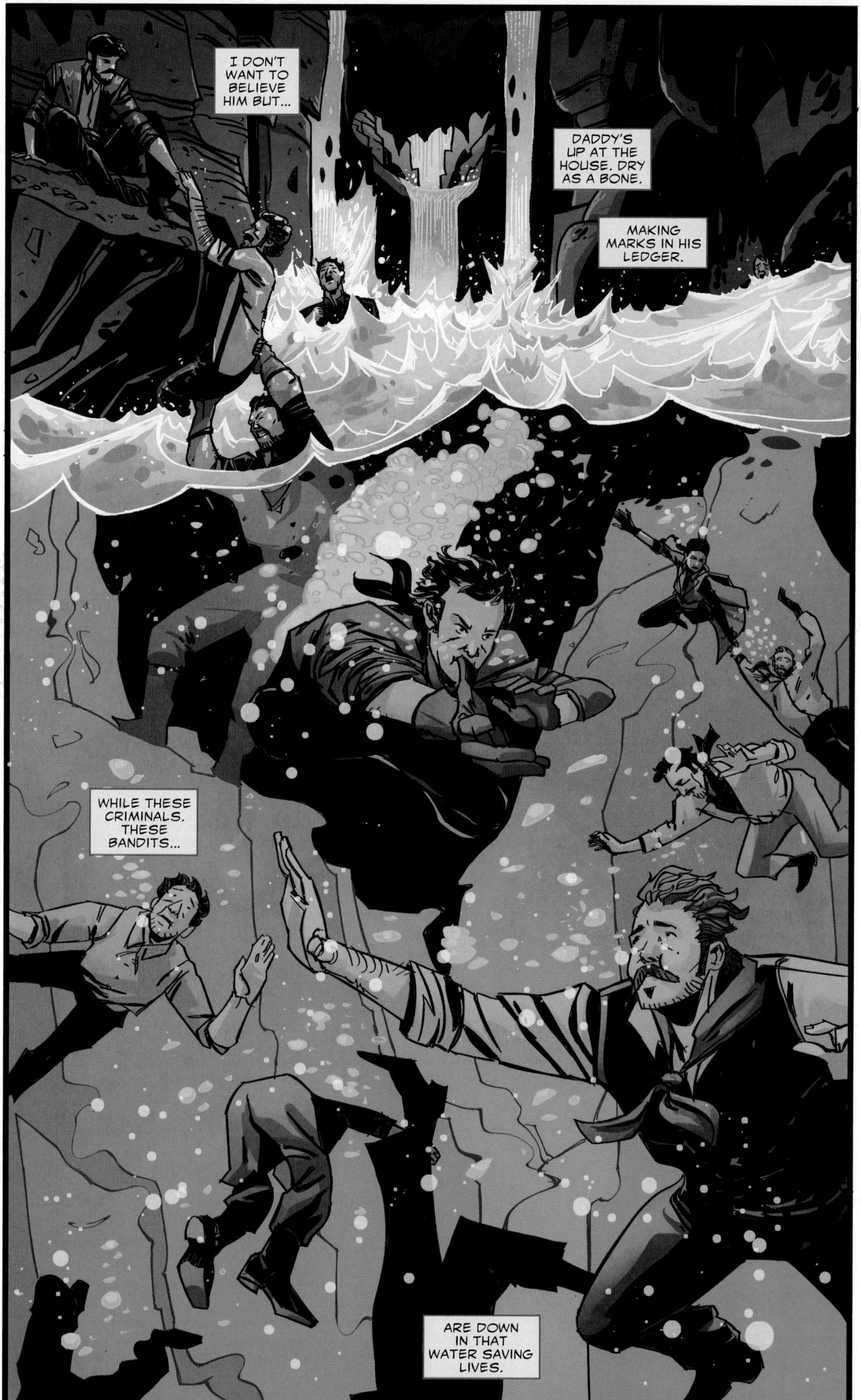
I DON'T WANT TO BELIEVE HIM BUT...
DADDY'S UP AT THE HOUSE. DRY AS A BONE.
MAKING MARKS IN HIS LEDGER.
WHILE THESE CRIMINALS. THESE BANDITS...
ARE DOWN IN THAT WATER SAVING LIVES.

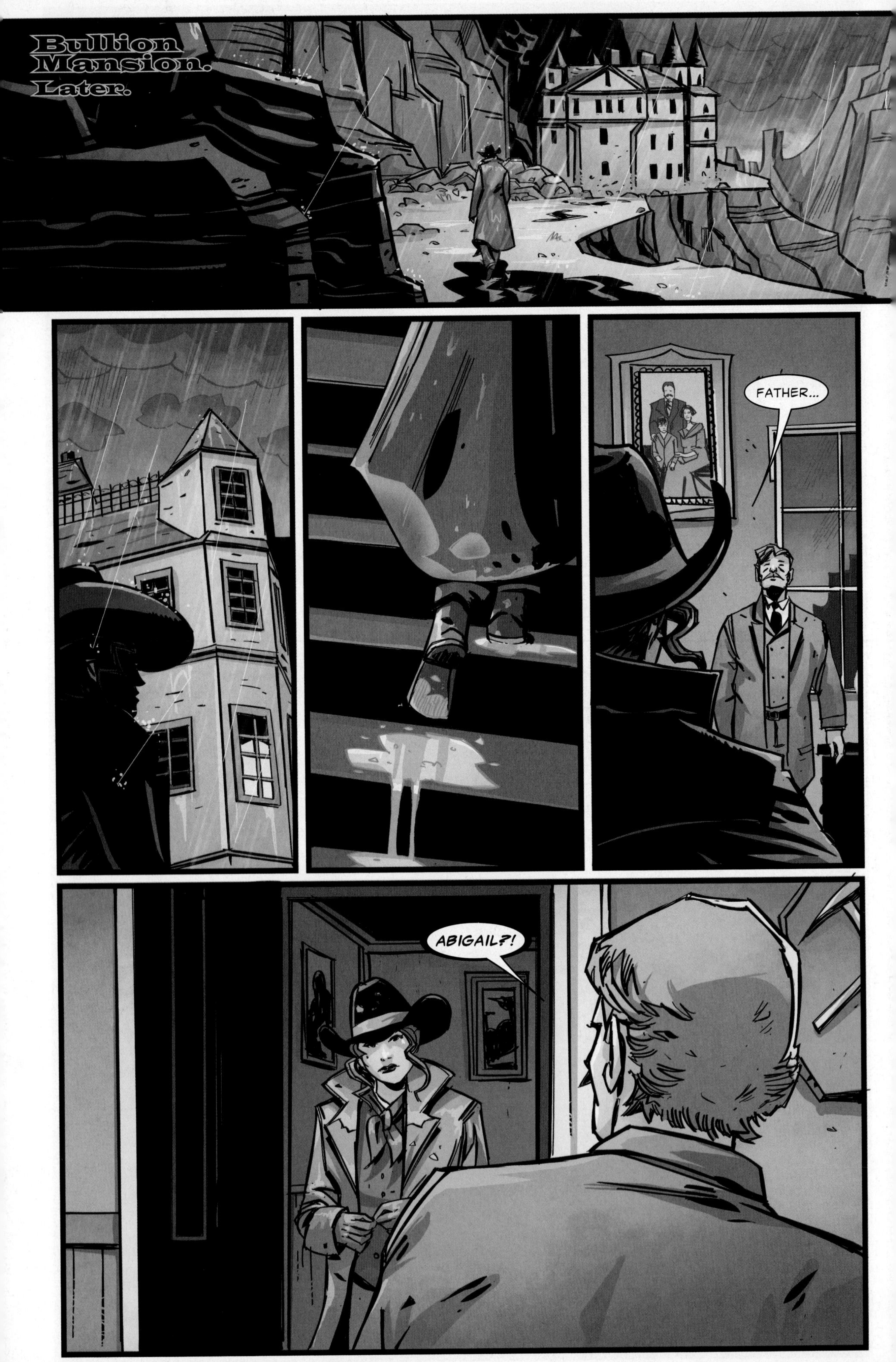
Bullion Mansion. Later.
FATHER...
ABIGAIL?!

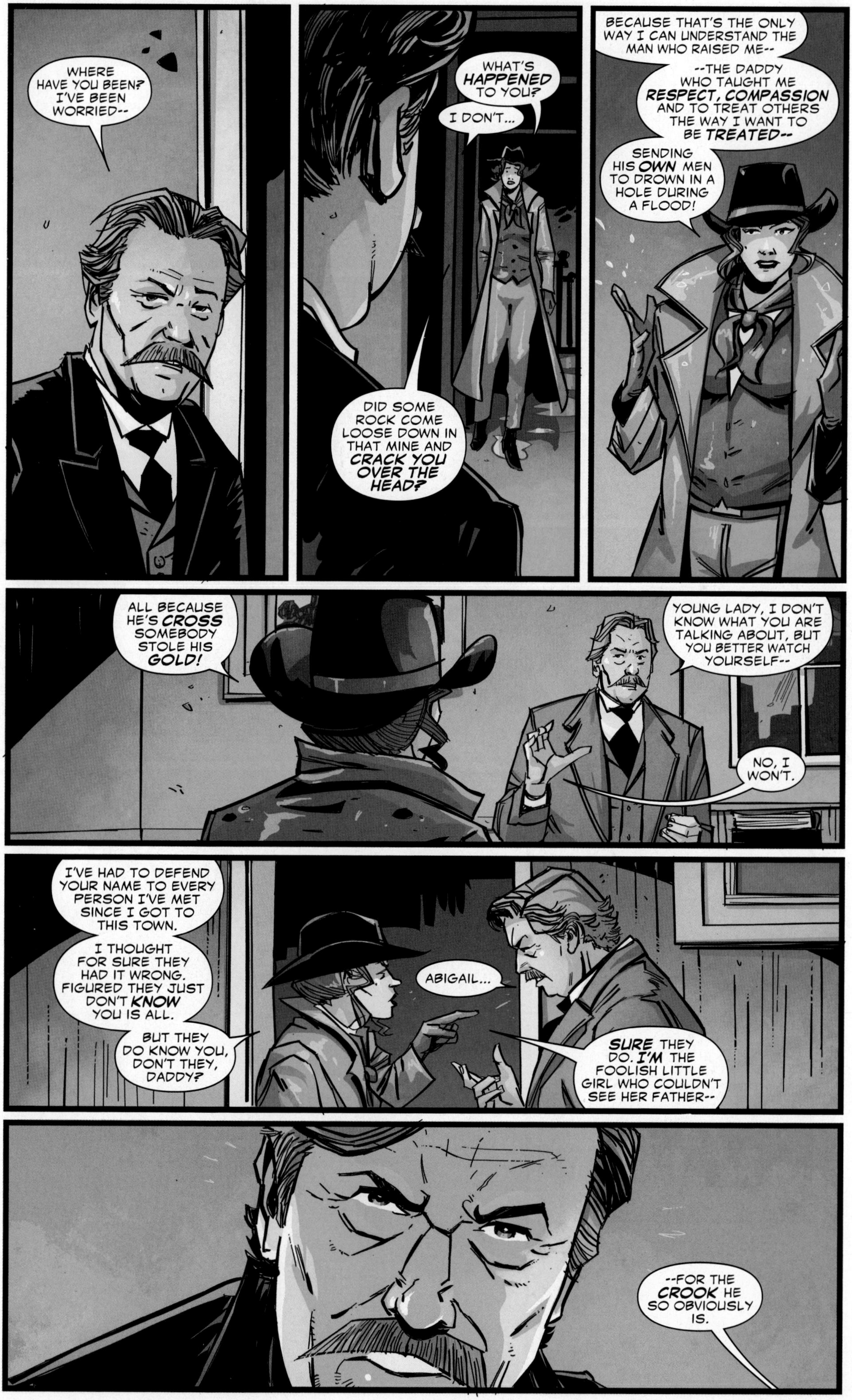
WHERE HAVE YOU BEEN? I'VE BEEN WORRIED--
WHAT'S HAPPENED TO YOU?
I DON'T...
DID SOME ROCK COME LOOSE DOWN IN THAT MINE AND CRACK YOU OVER THE HEAD?
BECAUSE THAT'S THE ONLY WAY I CAN UNDERSTAND THE MAN WHO RAISED ME--
--THE DADDY WHO TAUGHT ME RESPECT, COMPASSION AND TO TREAT OTHERS THE WAY I WANT TO BE TREATED--
SENDING HIS OWN MEN TO DROWN IN A HOLE DURING A FLOOD!
ALL BECAUSE HE'S CROSS SOMEBODY STOLE HIS GOLD!
YOUNG LADY, I DON'T KNOW WHAT YOU ARE TALKING ABOUT, BUT YOU BETTER WATCH YOURSELF--
NO, I WON'T.
I'VE HAD TO DEFEND YOUR NAME TO EVERY PERSON I'VE MET SINCE I GOT TO THIS TOWN.
I THOUGHT FOR SURE THEY HAD IT WRONG. FIGURED THEY JUST DON'T KNOW YOU IS ALL.
BUT THEY DO KNOW YOU, DON'T THEY, DADDY?
ABIGAIL...
SURE THEY DO. I'M THE FOOLISH LITTLE GIRL WHO COULDN'T SEE HER FATHER--
--FOR THE CROOK HE SO OBVIOUSLY IS.

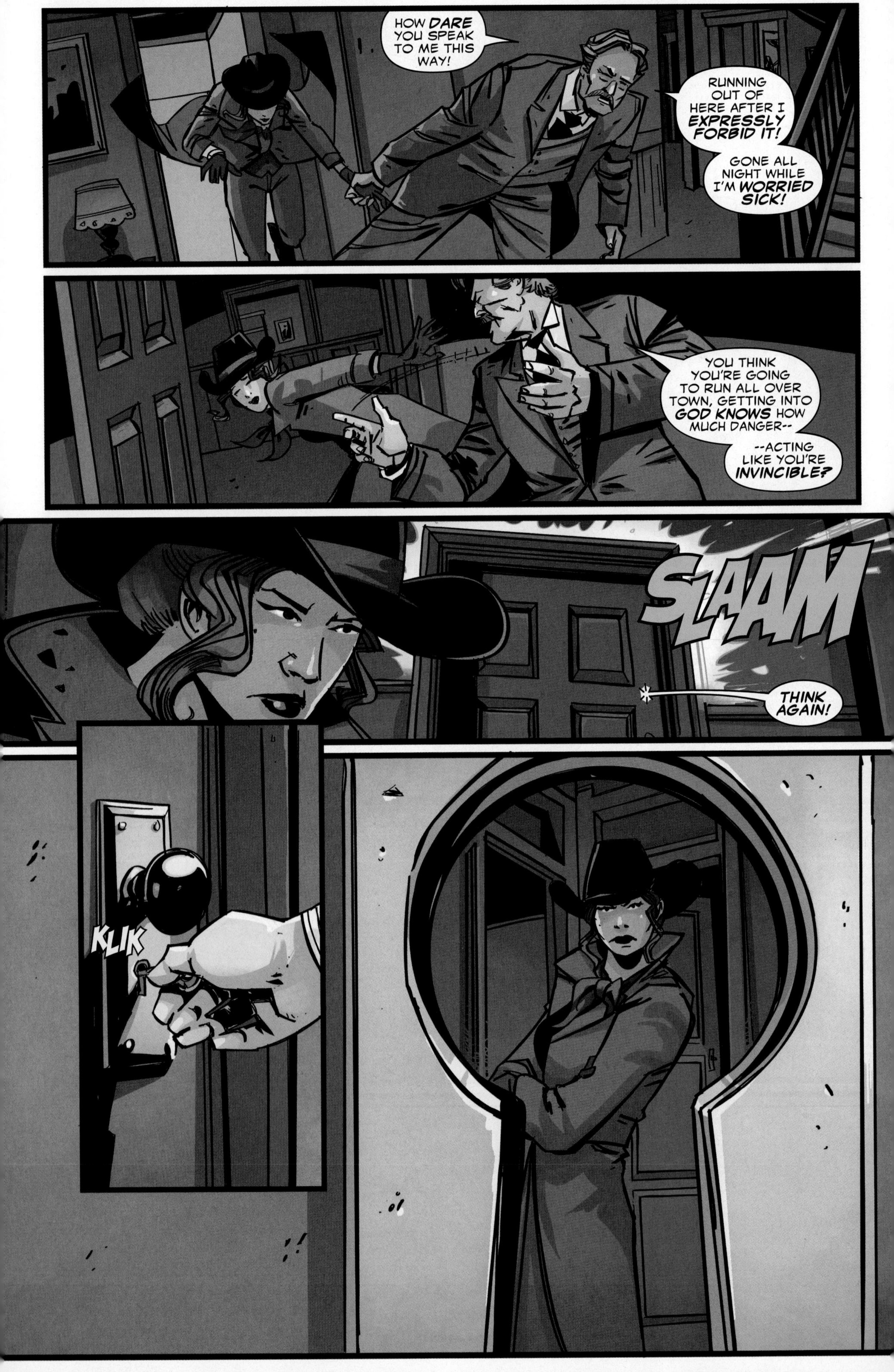
HOW DARE YOU SPEAK TO ME THIS WAY!
RUNNING OUT OF HERE AFTER I EXPRESSLY FORBID IT!
GONE ALL NIGHT WHILE I'M WORRIED SICK!
YOU THINK YOU'RE GOING TO RUN ALL OVER TOWN, GETTING INTO GOD KNOWS HOW MUCH DANGER--
--ACTING LIKE YOU'RE INVINCIBLE?
SLAAM
THINK AGAIN!
KLIK

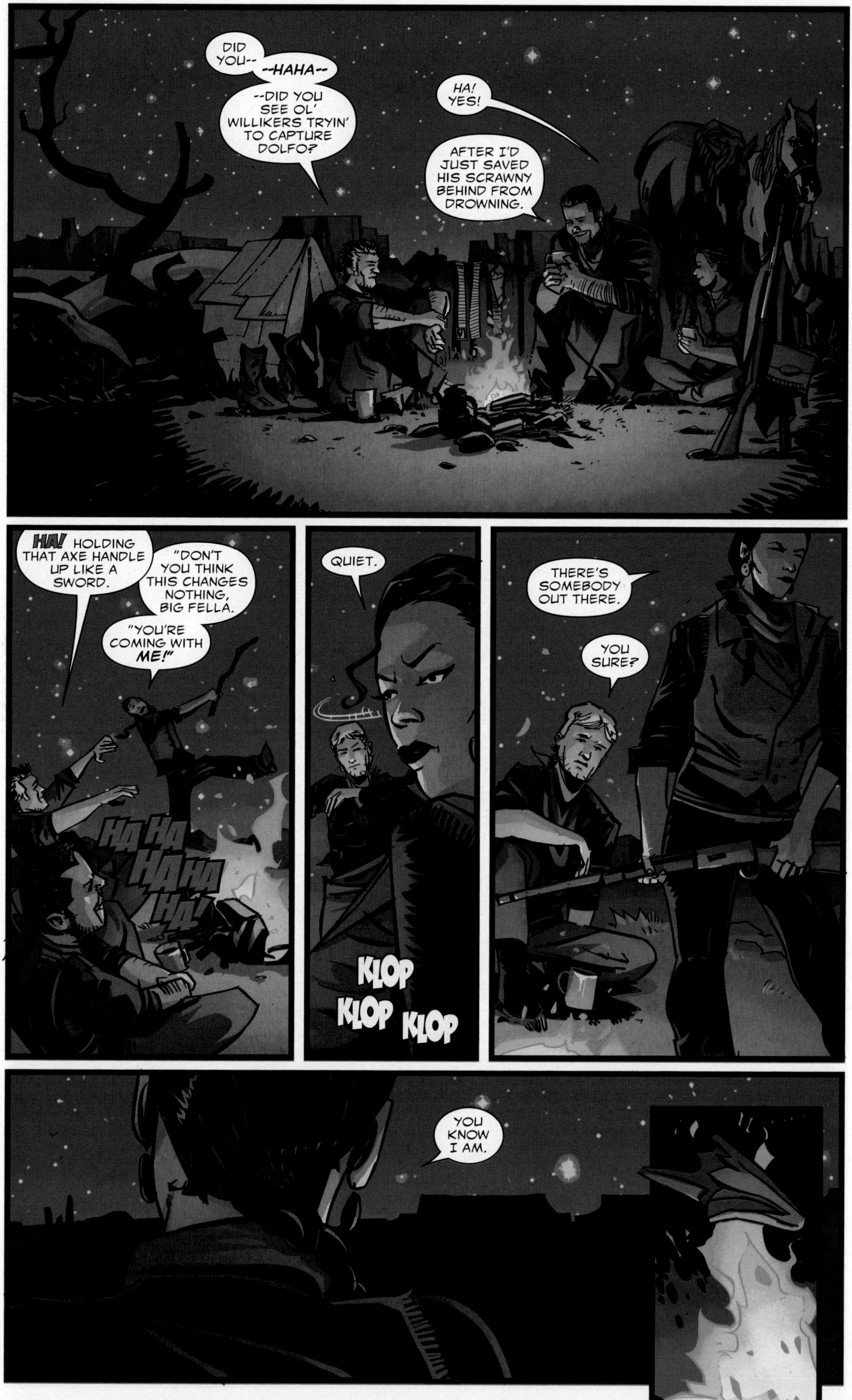
DID YOU-- --HAHA-- --DID YOU SEE OL' WILLIKERS TRYIN' TO CAPTURE DOLFO?
HA! YES!
AFTER I'D JUST SAVED HIS SCRAWNY BEHIND FROM DROWNING.
HA! HOLDING THAT AXE HANDLE UP LIKE A SWORD.
"DON'T YOU THINK THIS CHANGES NOTHING, BIG FELLA.
"YOU'RE COMING WITH ME!"
HA HA HA HA HA!
QUIET.
KLOP KLOP KLOP
THERE'S SOMEBODY OUT THERE.
YOU SURE?
YOU KNOW I AM.

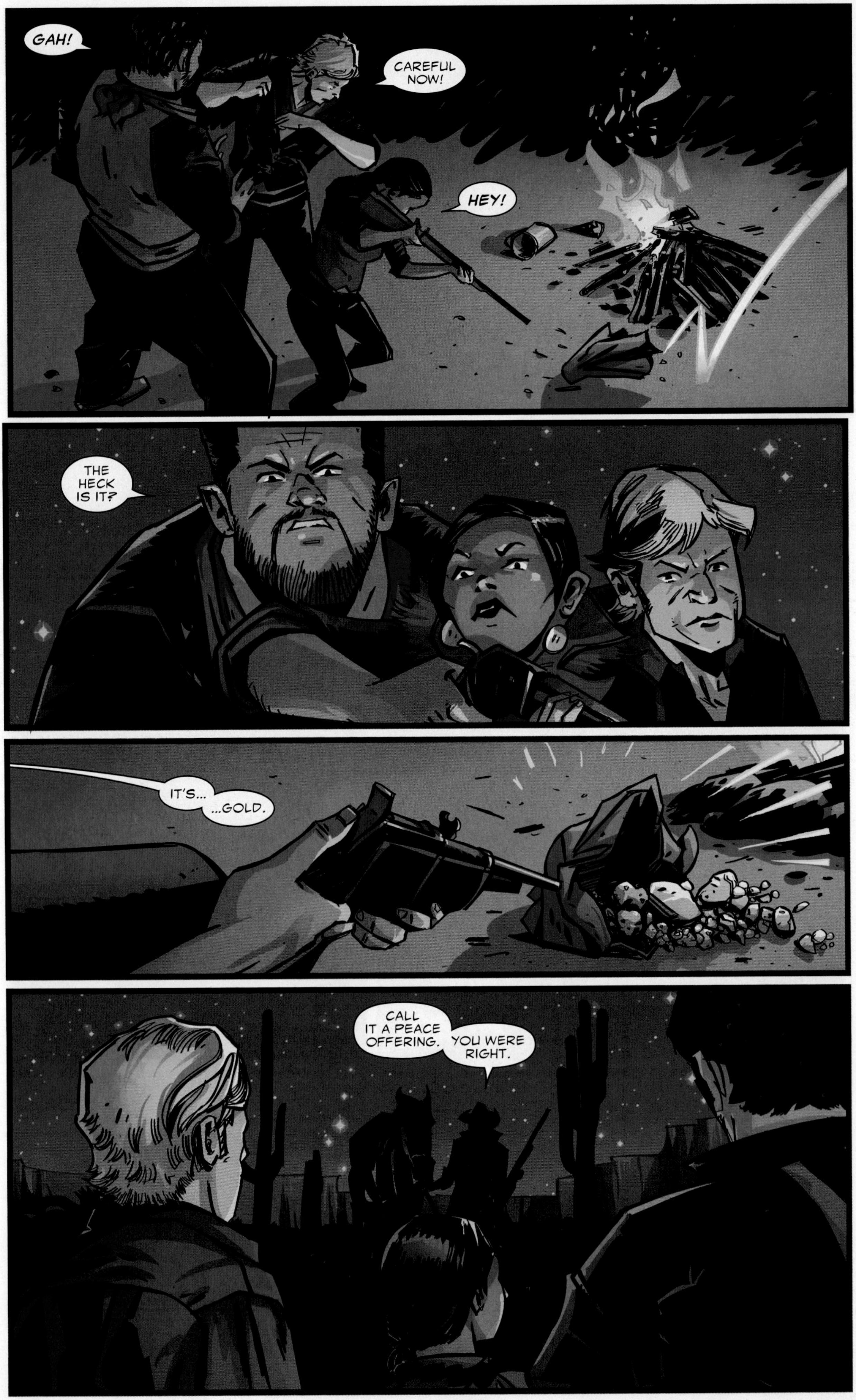
GAH!
CAREFUL NOW!
HEY!
THE HECK IS IT?
IT'S...
...GOLD.
CALL IT A PEACE OFFERING.
YOU WERE RIGHT.

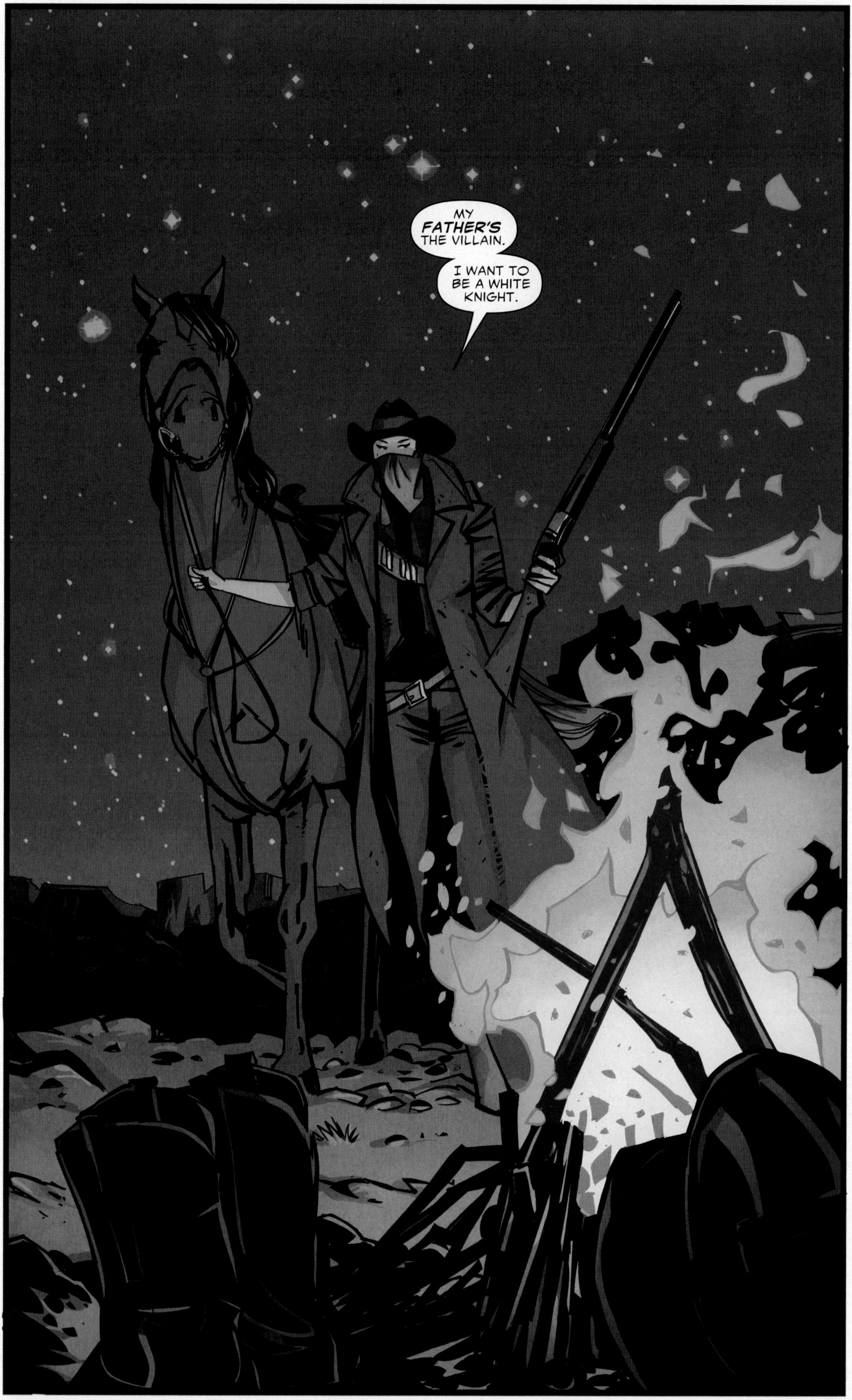
MY FATHER'S THE VILLAIN.
I WANT TO BE A WHITE KNIGHT.

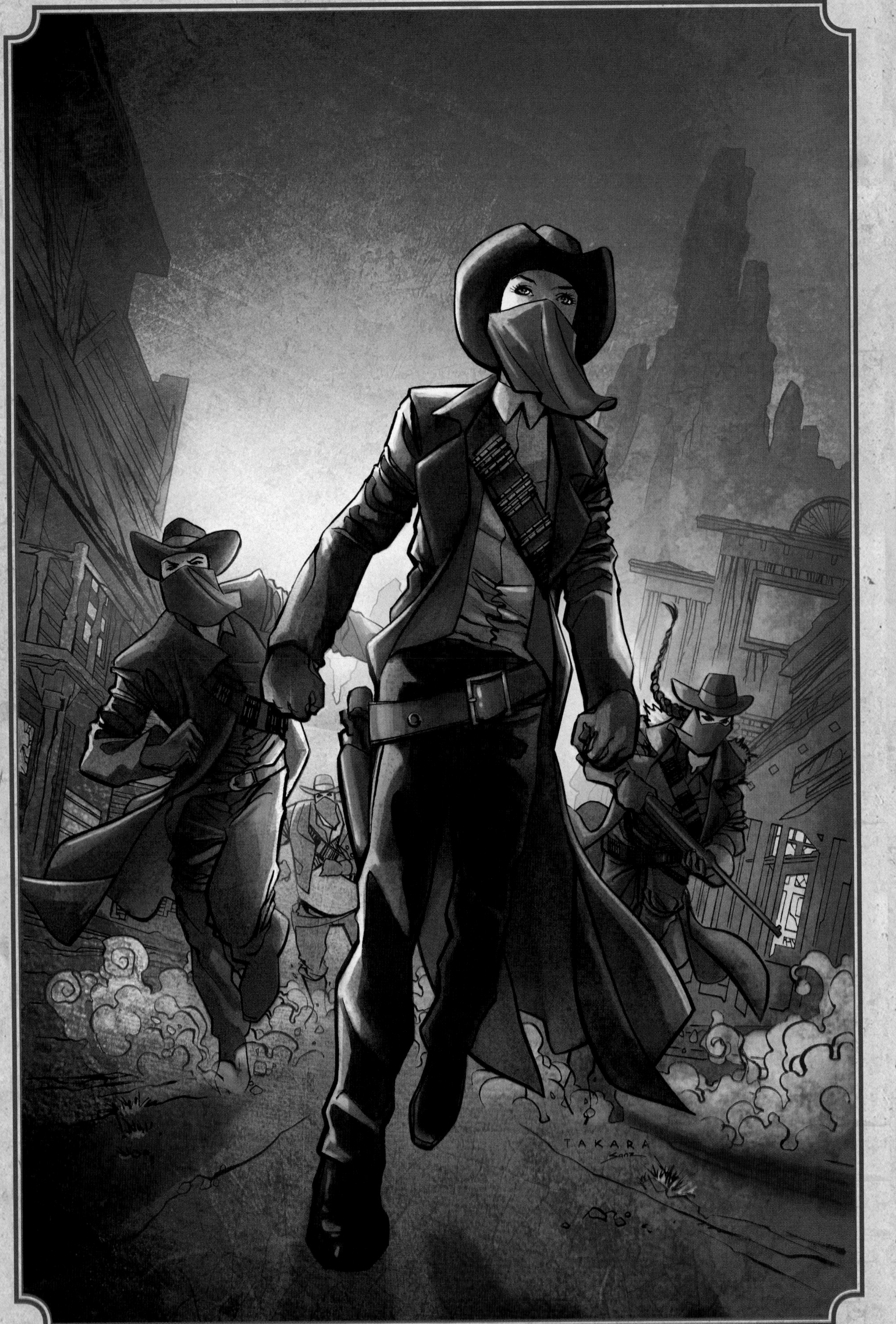
TAKARA

~ 4 ~

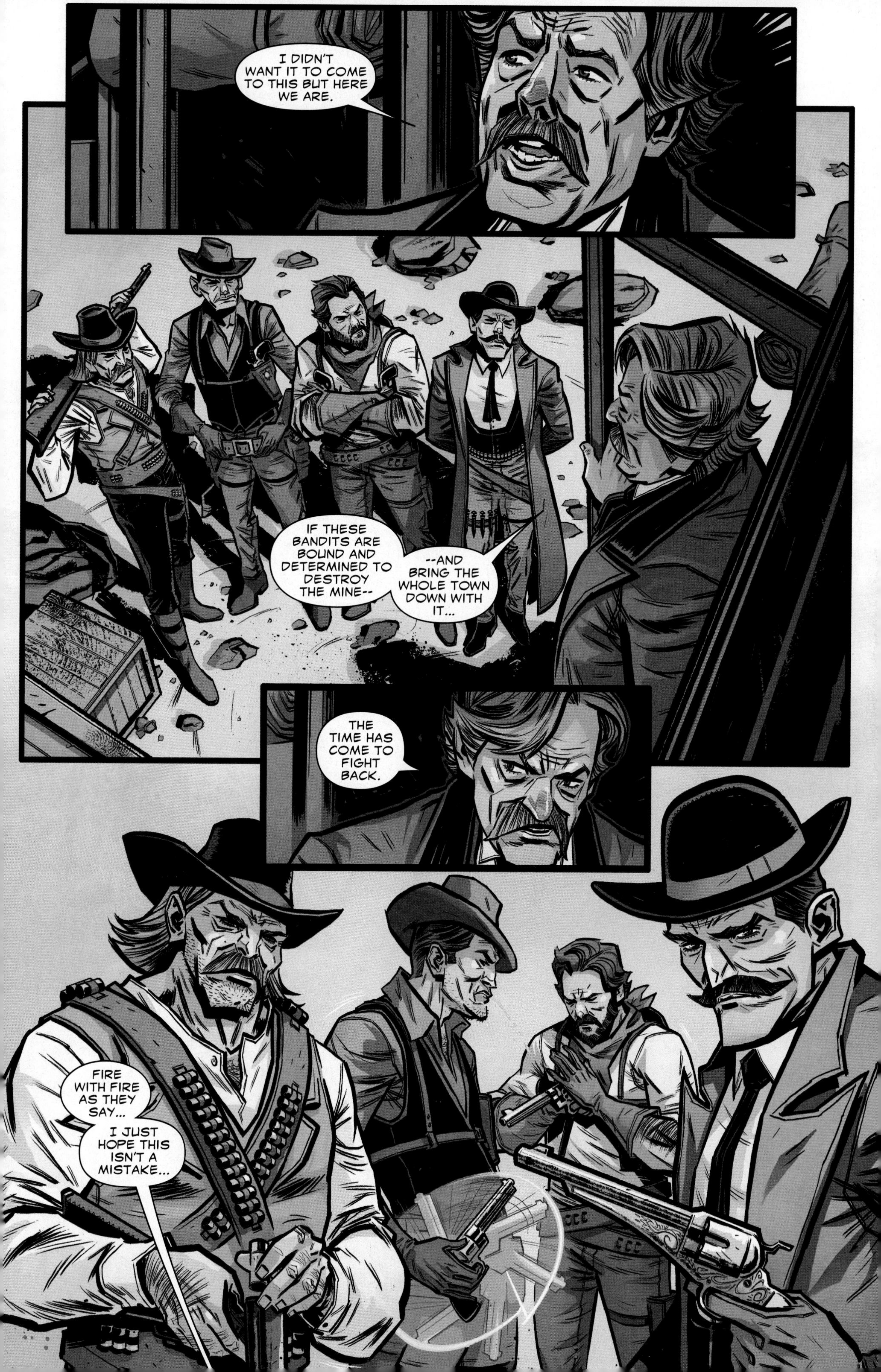
I DIDN'T WANT IT TO COME TO THIS BUT HERE WE ARE.
IF THESE BANDITS ARE BOUND AND DETERMINED TO DESTROY THE MINE--
--AND BRING THE WHOLE TOWN DOWN WITH IT...
THE TIME HAS COME TO FIGHT BACK.
FIRE WITH FIRE AS THEY SAY...
I JUST HOPE THIS ISN'T A MISTAKE...

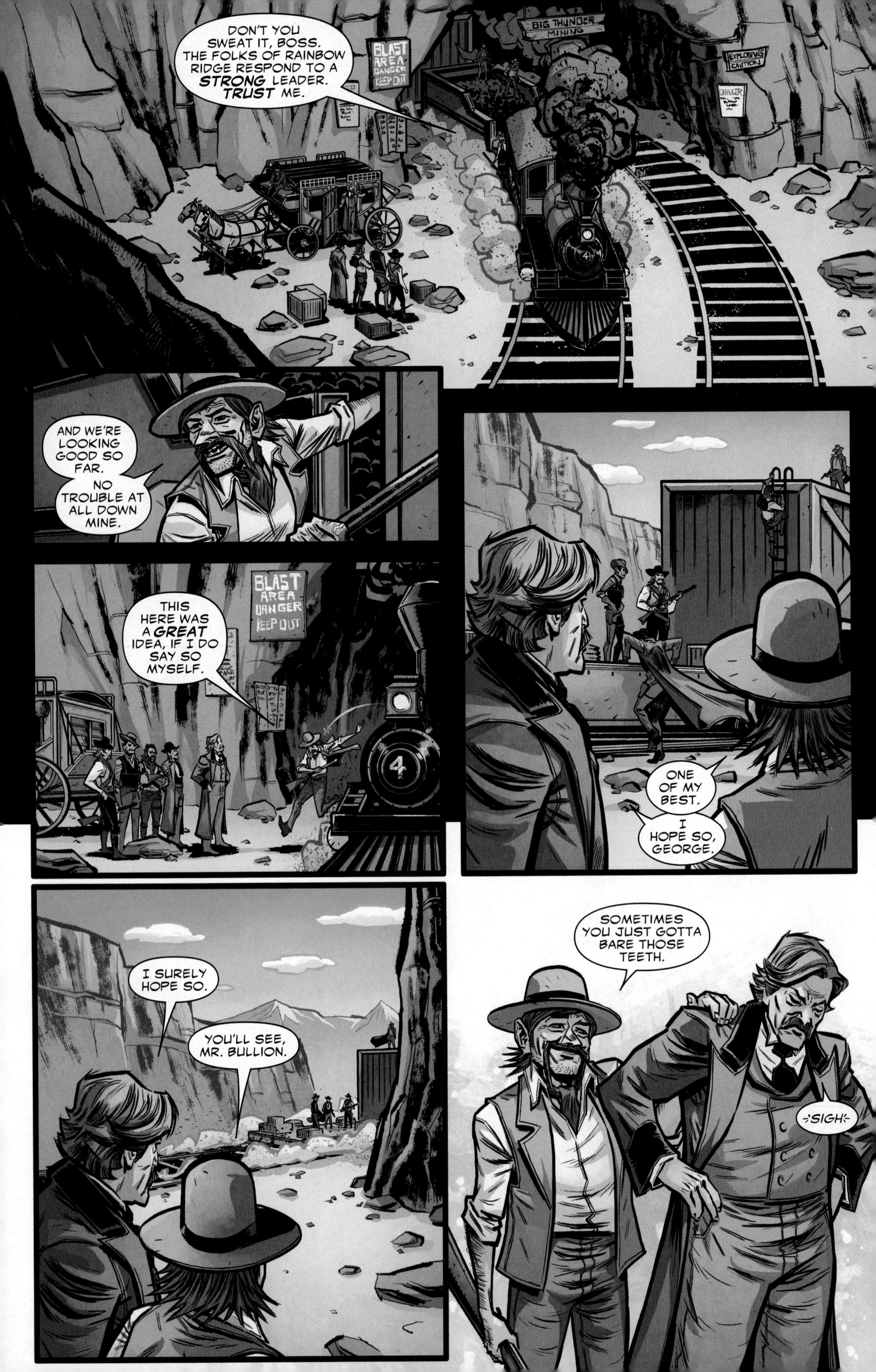
BIG THUNDER MINING
BLAST AREA DANGER KEEP OUT
EXPLOSIVES CAUTION
DANGER
DON'T YOU SWEAT IT, BOSS. THE FOLKS OF RAINBOW RIDGE RESPOND TO A STRONG LEADER. TRUST ME.
AND WE'RE LOOKING GOOD SO FAR.
NO TROUBLE AT ALL DOWN MINE.
THIS HERE WAS A GREAT IDEA, IF I DO SAY SO MYSELF.
4
ONE OF MY BEST.
I HOPE SO, GEORGE.
I SURELY HOPE SO.
YOU'LL SEE, MR. BULLION.
SOMETIMES YOU JUST GOTTA BARE THOSE TEETH.
SIGH

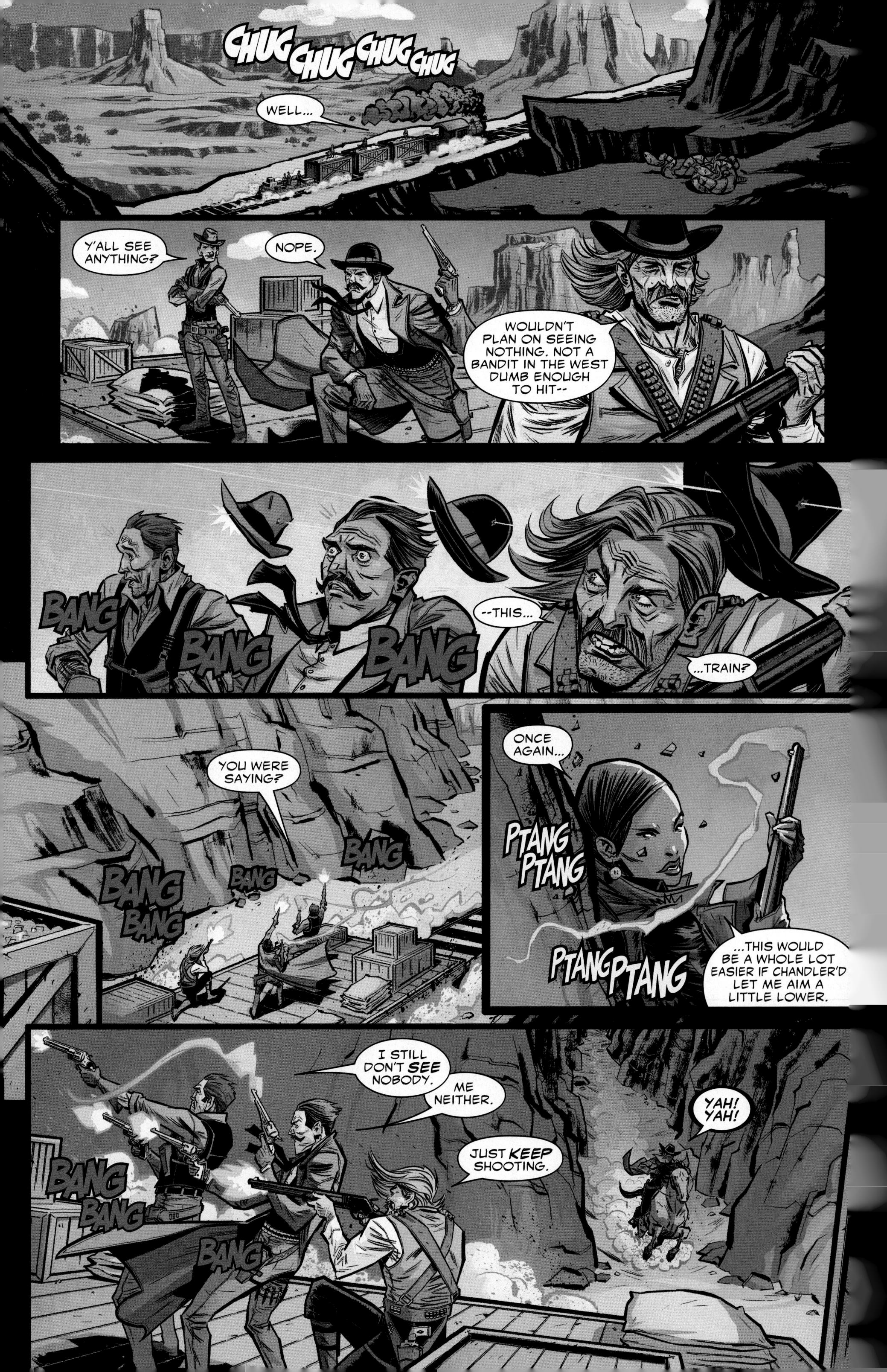

CHUG CHUG CHUG CHUG
WELL...
Y'ALL SEE ANYTHING?
NOPE.
WOULDN'T PLAN ON SEEING NOTHING. NOT A BANDIT IN THE WEST DUMB ENOUGH TO HIT--
BANG
BANG
BANG
--THIS...
...TRAIN?
YOU WERE SAYING?
BANG
BANG
BANG
BANG
ONCE AGAIN...
PTANG PTANG
PTANG PTANG
...THIS WOULD BE A WHOLE LOT EASIER IF CHANDLER'D LET ME AIM A LITTLE LOWER.
I STILL DON'T SEE NOBODY.
ME NEITHER.
JUST KEEP SHOOTING.
YAH! YAH!
BANG
BANG
BANG

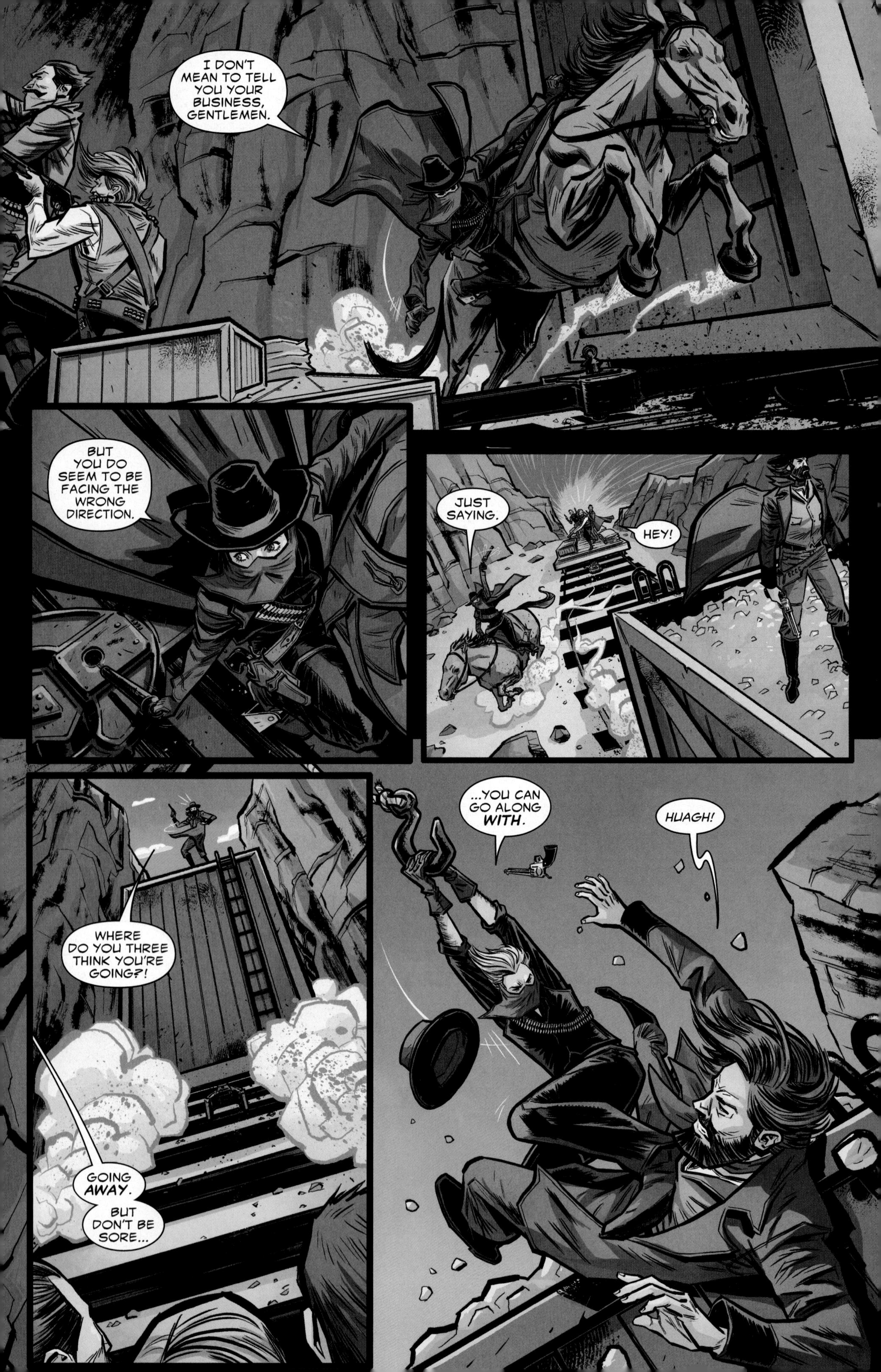
I DON'T MEAN TO TELL YOU YOUR BUSINESS, GENTLEMEN.
BUT YOU DO SEEM TO BE FACING THE WRONG DIRECTION.
JUST SAYING.
HEY!
WHERE DO YOU THREE THINK YOU'RE GOING?!
GOING AWAY.
BUT DON'T BE SORE...
...YOU CAN GO ALONG WITH.
HUAGH!

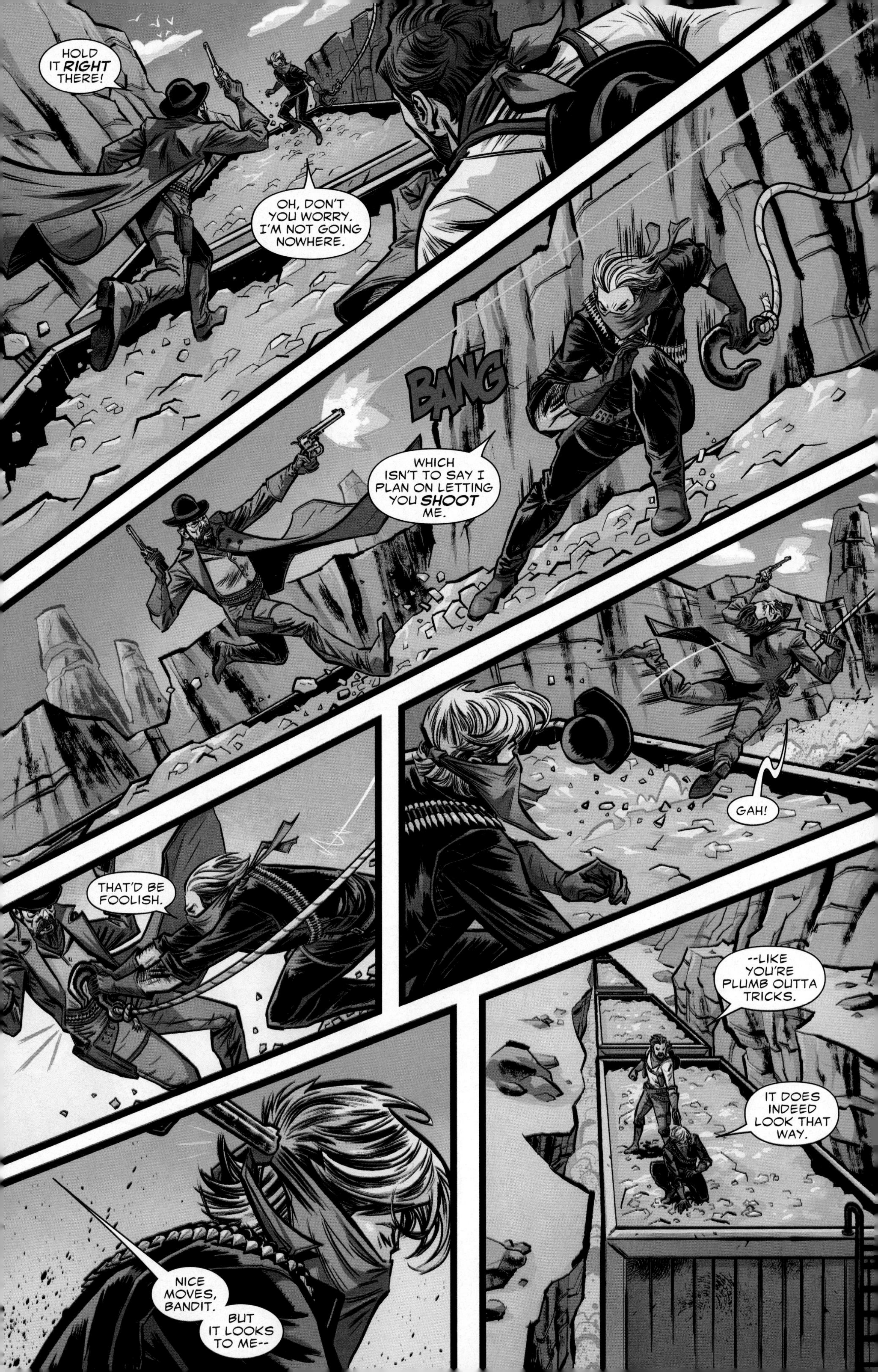
HOLD IT RIGHT THERE!
OH, DON'T YOU WORRY. I'M NOT GOING NOWHERE.
BANG
WHICH ISN'T TO SAY I PLAN ON LETTING YOU SHOOT ME.
THAT'D BE FOOLISH.
GAH!
NICE MOVES, BANDIT.
BUT IT LOOKS TO ME--
--LIKE YOU'RE PLUMB OUTTA TRICKS.
IT DOES INDEED LOOK THAT WAY.

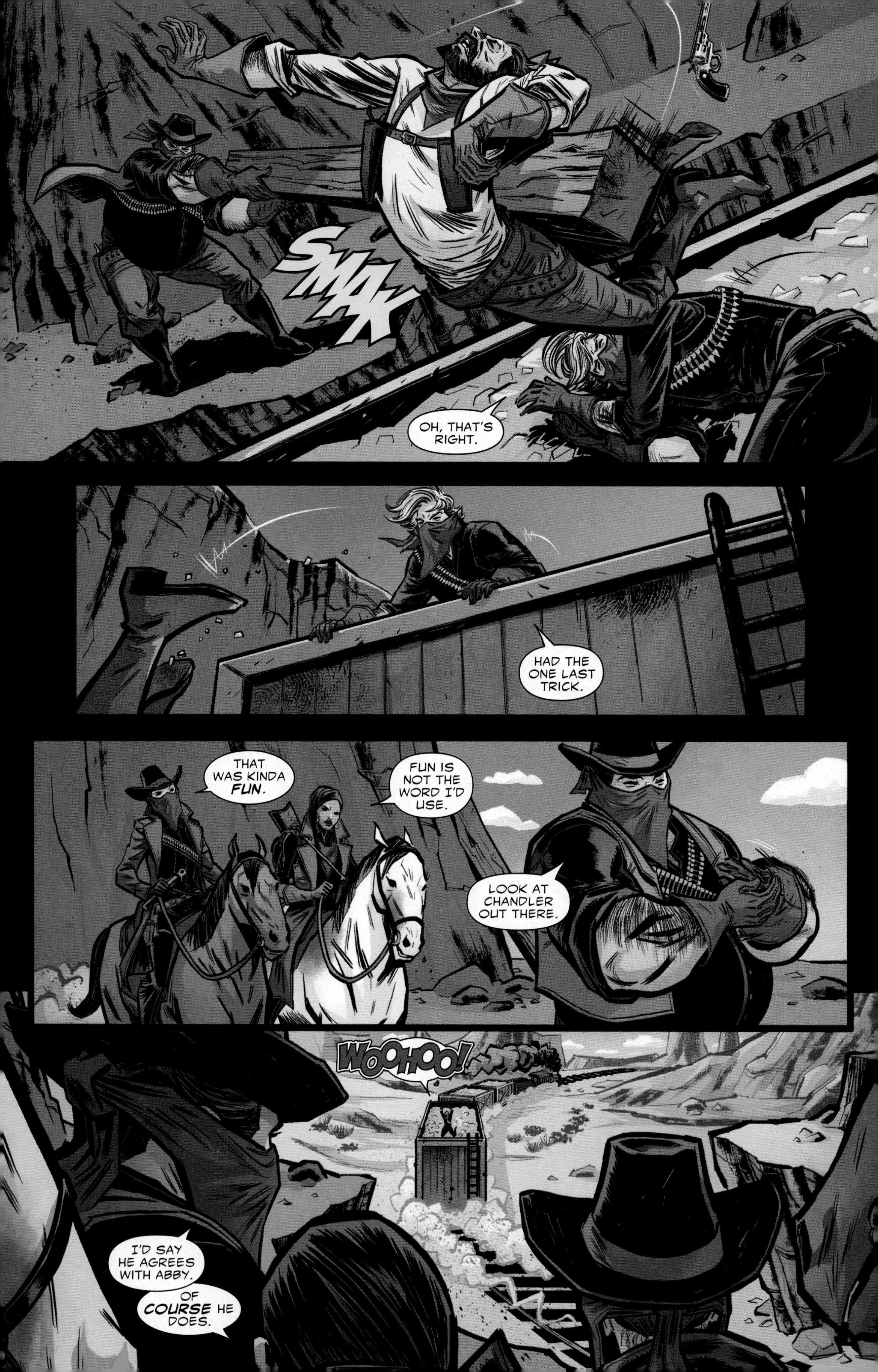
SMAK
OH, THAT'S RIGHT.
HAD THE ONE LAST TRICK.
THAT WAS KINDA *FUN*.
FUN IS NOT THE WORD I'D USE.
LOOK AT CHANDLER OUT THERE.
WOOHOO!
I'D SAY HE AGREES WITH ABBY.
OF *COURSE* HE DOES.

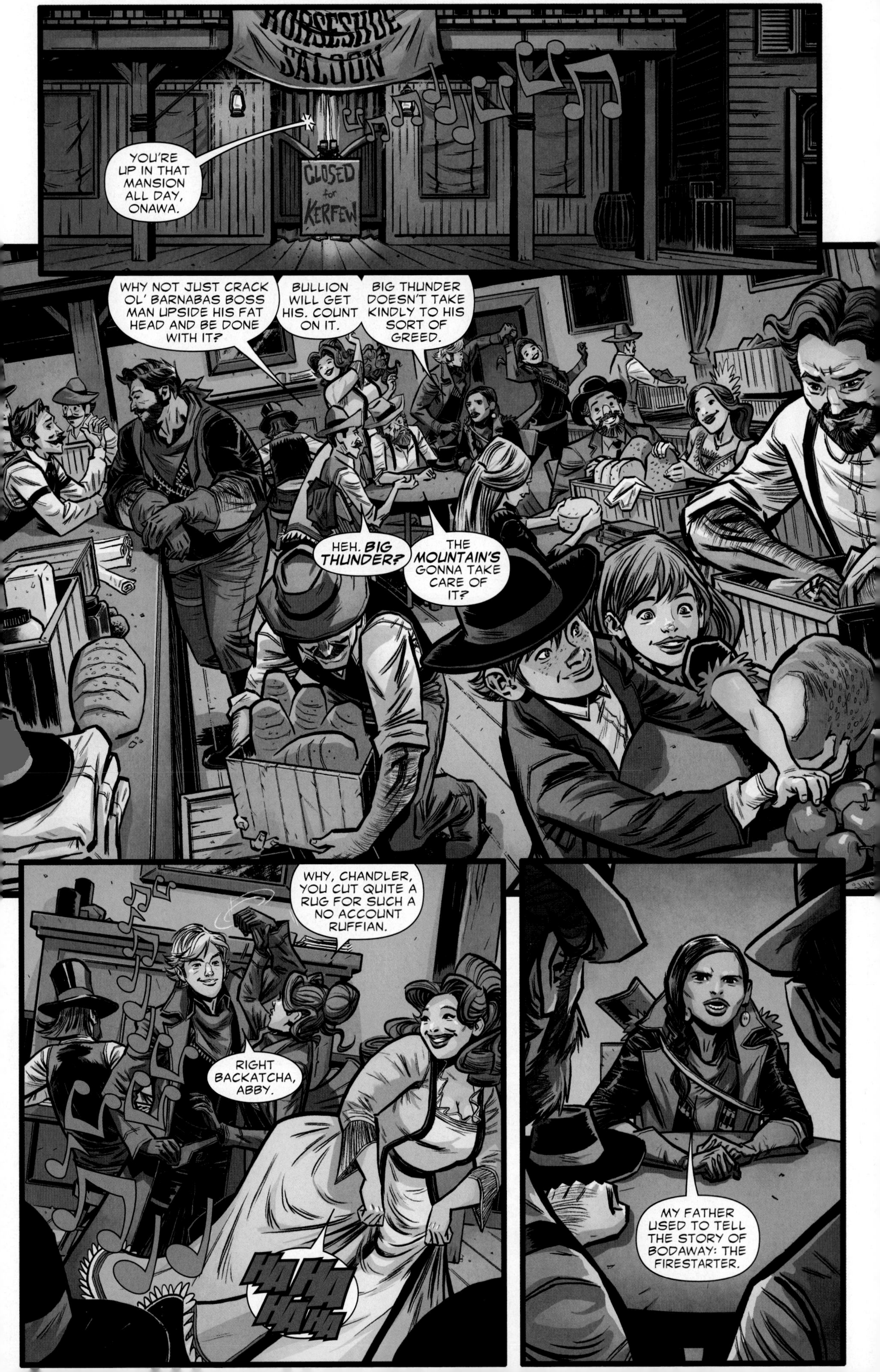
HORSESHOE SALOON
CLOSED for KERFEW
YOU'RE UP IN THAT MANSION ALL DAY, ONAWA.
WHY NOT JUST CRACK OL' BARNABAS BOSS MAN UPSIDE HIS FAT HEAD AND BE DONE WITH IT?
BULLION WILL GET HIS. COUNT ON IT.
BIG THUNDER DOESN'T TAKE KINDLY TO HIS SORT OF GREED.
HEH. BIG THUNDER?
THE MOUNTAIN'S GONNA TAKE CARE OF IT?
WHY, CHANDLER, YOU CUT QUITE A RUG FOR SUCH A NO ACCOUNT RUFFIAN.
RIGHT BACKATCHA, ABBY.
HA HA HA HA
MY FATHER USED TO TELL THE STORY OF BODAWAY: THE FIRESTARTER.

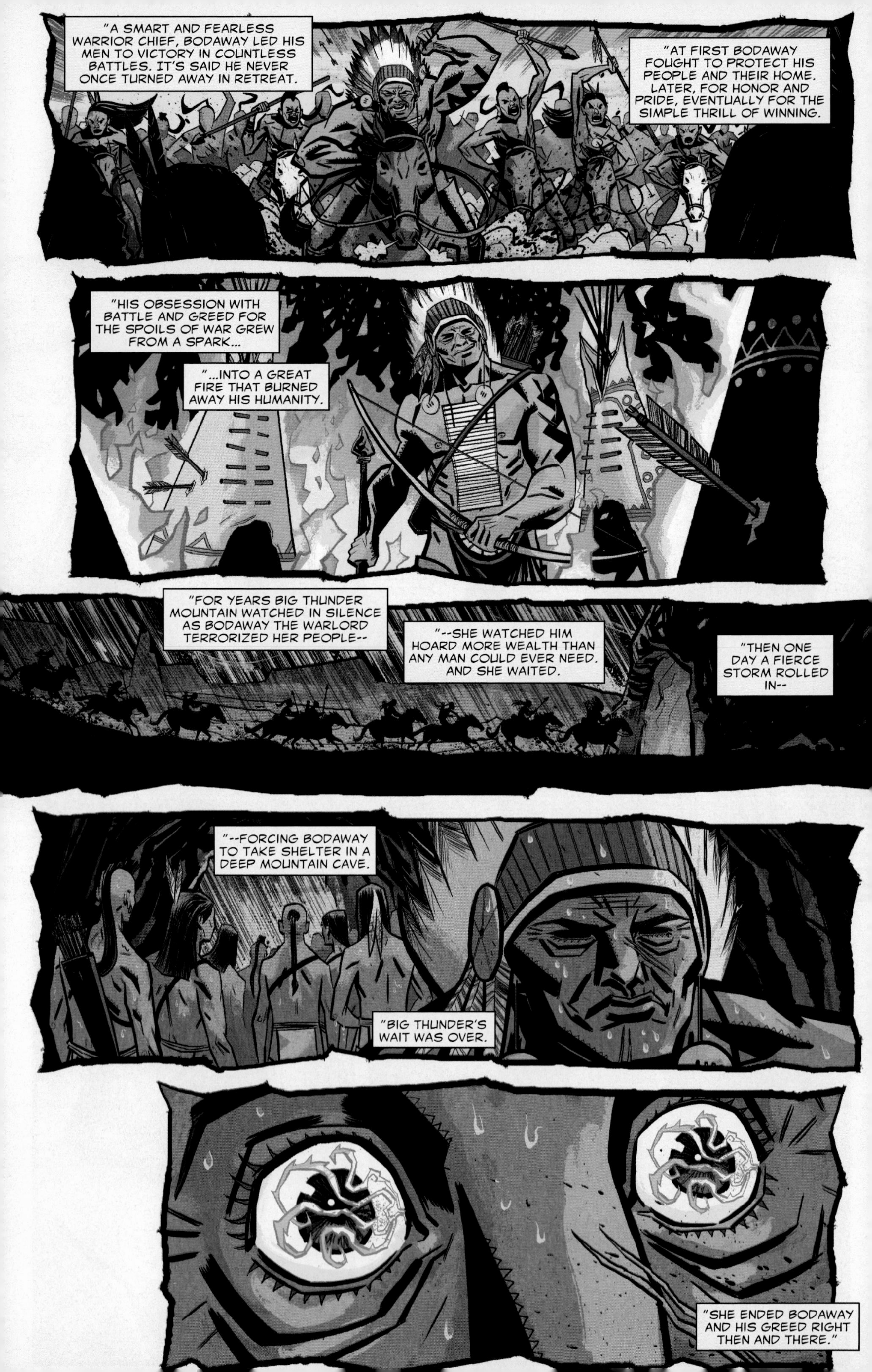
"A SMART AND FEARLESS WARRIOR CHIEF, BODAWAY LED HIS MEN TO VICTORY IN COUNTLESS BATTLES. IT'S SAID HE NEVER ONCE TURNED AWAY IN RETREAT.
"AT FIRST BODAWAY FOUGHT TO PROTECT HIS PEOPLE AND THEIR HOME. LATER, FOR HONOR AND PRIDE, EVENTUALLY FOR THE SIMPLE THRILL OF WINNING.
"HIS OBSESSION WITH BATTLE AND GREED FOR THE SPOILS OF WAR GREW FROM A SPARK...
"...INTO A GREAT FIRE THAT BURNED AWAY HIS HUMANITY.
"FOR YEARS BIG THUNDER MOUNTAIN WATCHED IN SILENCE AS BODAWAY THE WARLORD TERRORIZED HER PEOPLE--
"--SHE WATCHED HIM HOARD MORE WEALTH THAN ANY MAN COULD EVER NEED. AND SHE WAITED.
"THEN ONE DAY A FIERCE STORM ROLLED IN--
"--FORCING BODAWAY TO TAKE SHELTER IN A DEEP MOUNTAIN CAVE.
"BIG THUNDER'S WAIT WAS OVER.
"SHE ENDED BODAWAY AND HIS GREED RIGHT THEN AND THERE."

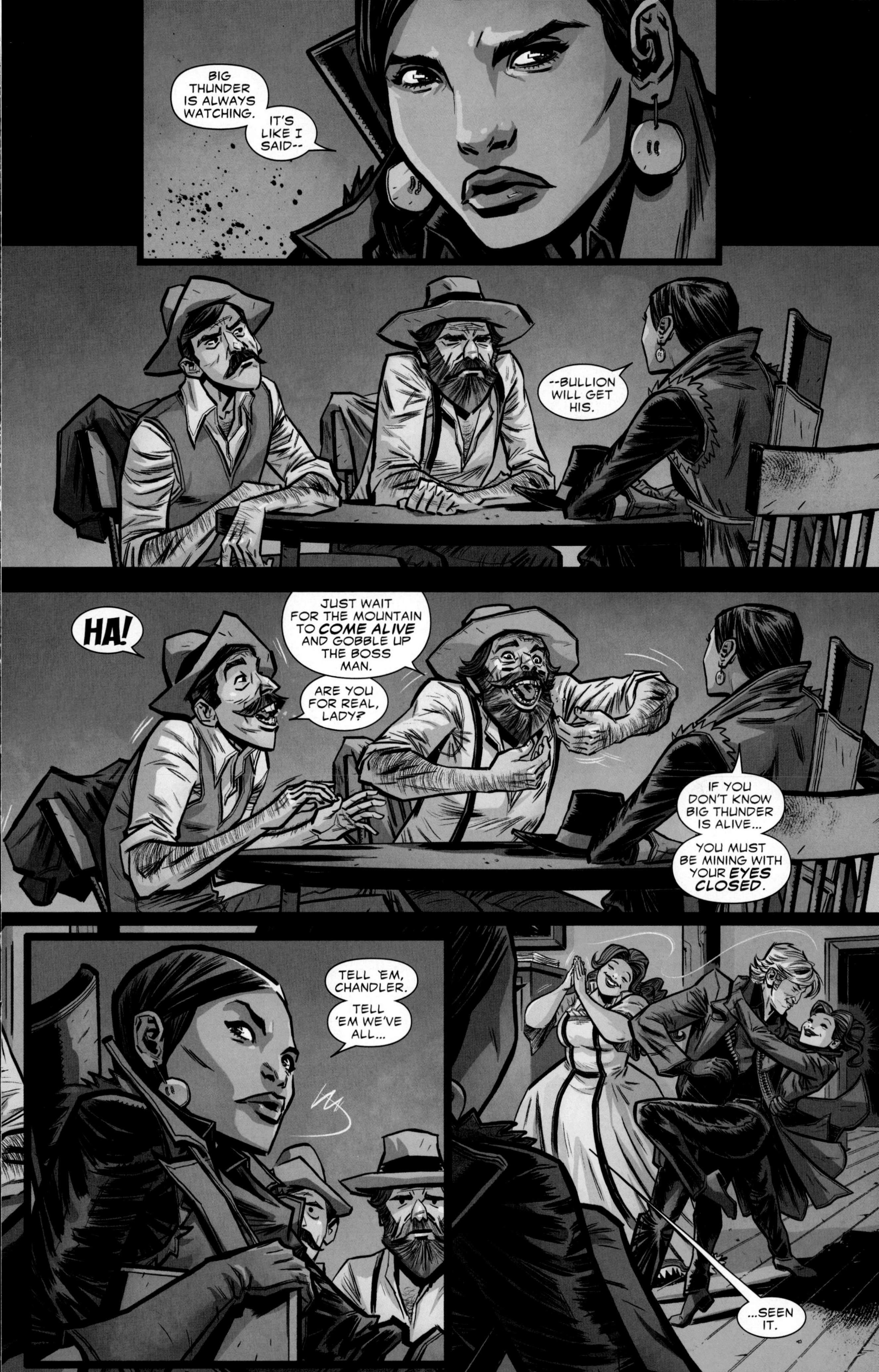

BIG THUNDER IS ALWAYS WATCHING.
IT'S LIKE I SAID--
--BULLION WILL GET HIS.
HA!
JUST WAIT FOR THE MOUNTAIN TO **COME ALIVE** AND GOBBLE UP THE BOSS MAN.
ARE YOU FOR REAL, LADY?
IF YOU DON'T KNOW BIG THUNDER IS ALIVE...
YOU MUST BE MINING WITH YOUR **EYES CLOSED**.
TELL 'EM, CHANDLER.
TELL 'EM WE'VE ALL...
...SEEN IT.

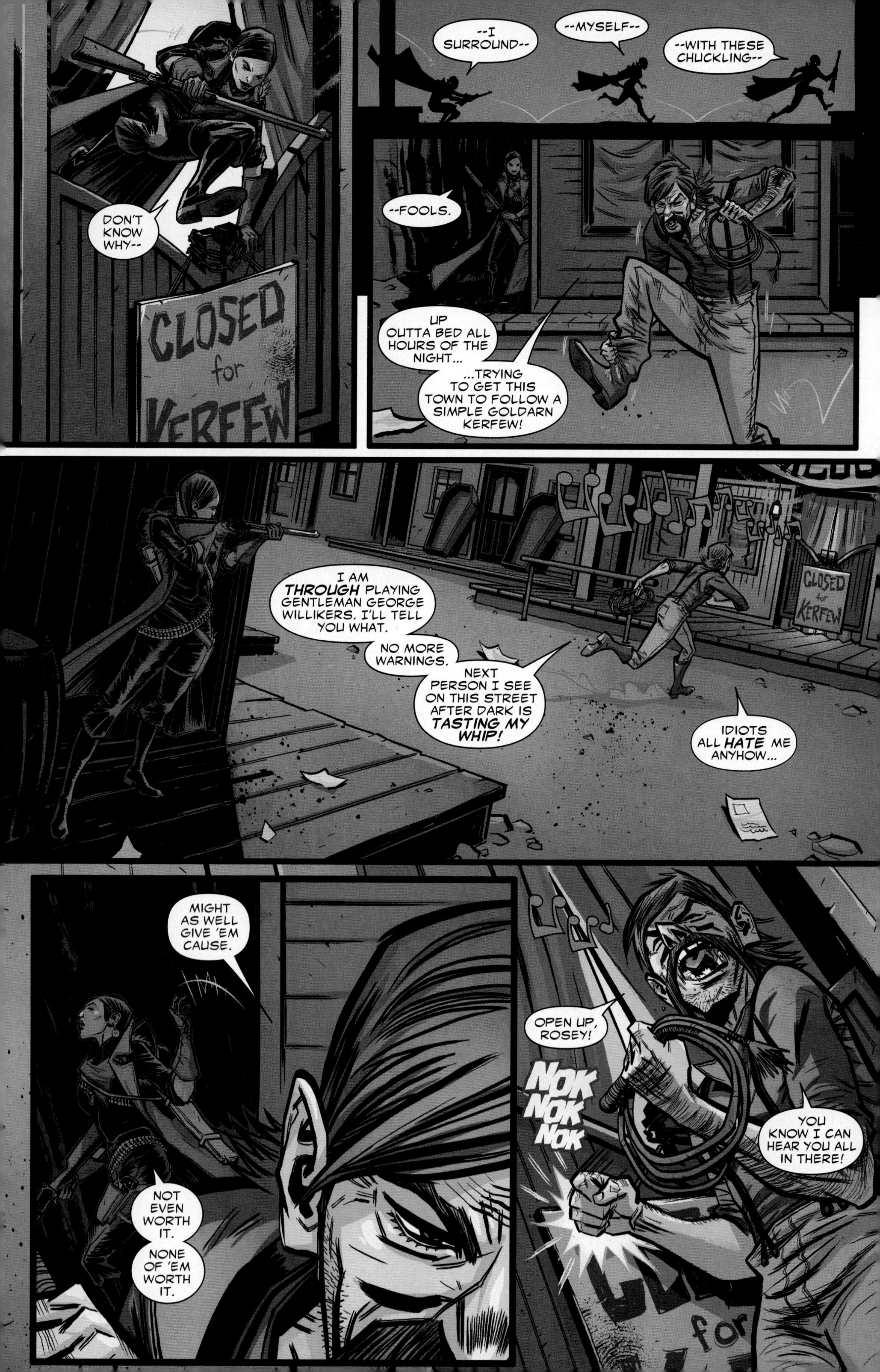
DON'T KNOW WHY--
CLOSED for KERFEW
--I SURROUND--
--MYSELF--
--WITH THESE CHUCKLING--
--FOOLS.
UP OUTTA BED ALL HOURS OF THE NIGHT...
...TRYING TO GET THIS TOWN TO FOLLOW A SIMPLE GOLDARN KERFEW!
I AM **THROUGH** PLAYING GENTLEMAN GEORGE WILLIKERS. I'LL TELL YOU WHAT.
NO MORE WARNINGS.
NEXT PERSON I SEE ON THIS STREET AFTER DARK IS ***TASTING MY WHIP!***
CLOSED for KERFEW
IDIOTS ALL **HATE** ME ANYHOW...
MIGHT AS WELL GIVE 'EM CAUSE.
NOT EVEN WORTH IT.
NONE OF 'EM WORTH IT.
OPEN UP, ROSEY!
NOK NOK NOK
YOU KNOW I CAN HEAR YOU ALL IN THERE!

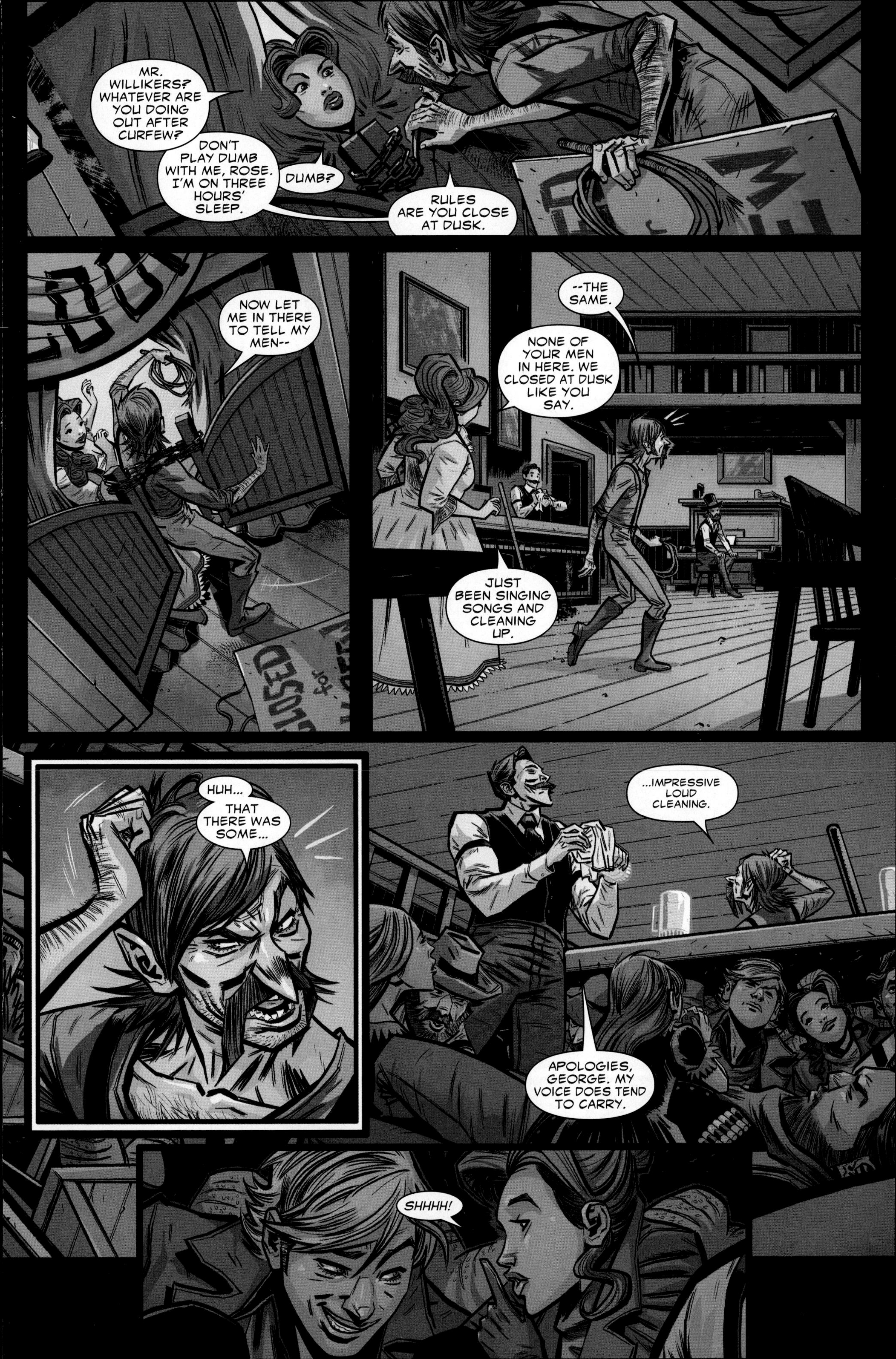
MR. WILLIKERS? WHATEVER ARE YOU DOING OUT AFTER CURFEW?
DON'T PLAY DUMB WITH ME, ROSE. I'M ON THREE HOURS' SLEEP.
DUMB?
RULES ARE YOU CLOSE AT DUSK.
NOW LET ME IN THERE TO TELL MY MEN--
--THE SAME.
NONE OF YOUR MEN IN HERE. WE CLOSED AT DUSK LIKE YOU SAY.
JUST BEEN SINGING SONGS AND CLEANING UP.
CLOSED
HUH... THAT THERE WAS SOME...
...IMPRESSIVE LOUD CLEANING.
APOLOGIES, GEORGE. MY VOICE DOES TEND TO CARRY.
SHHHH!

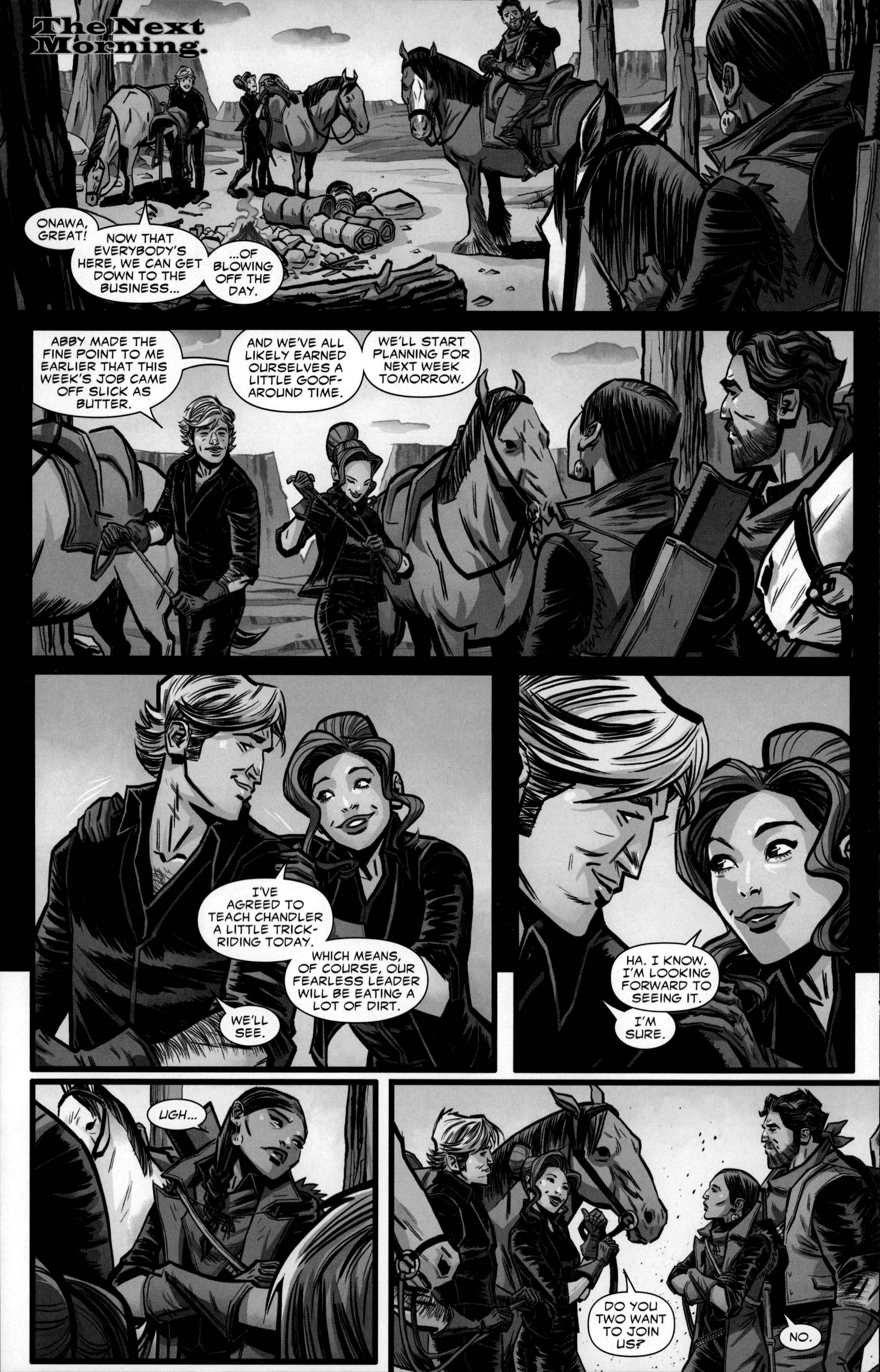

The Next Morning.
ONAWA, GREAT!
NOW THAT EVERYBODY'S HERE, WE CAN GET DOWN TO THE BUSINESS...
...OF BLOWING OFF THE DAY.
ABBY MADE THE FINE POINT TO ME EARLIER THAT THIS WEEK'S JOB CAME OFF SLICK AS BUTTER.
AND WE'VE ALL LIKELY EARNED OURSELVES A LITTLE GOOF-AROUND TIME.
WE'LL START PLANNING FOR NEXT WEEK TOMORROW.
I'VE AGREED TO TEACH CHANDLER A LITTLE TRICK-RIDING TODAY.
WHICH MEANS, OF COURSE, OUR FEARLESS LEADER WILL BE EATING A LOT OF DIRT.
WE'LL SEE.
HA. I KNOW. I'M LOOKING FORWARD TO SEEING IT.
I'M SURE.
UGH...
DO YOU TWO WANT TO JOIN US?
NO.

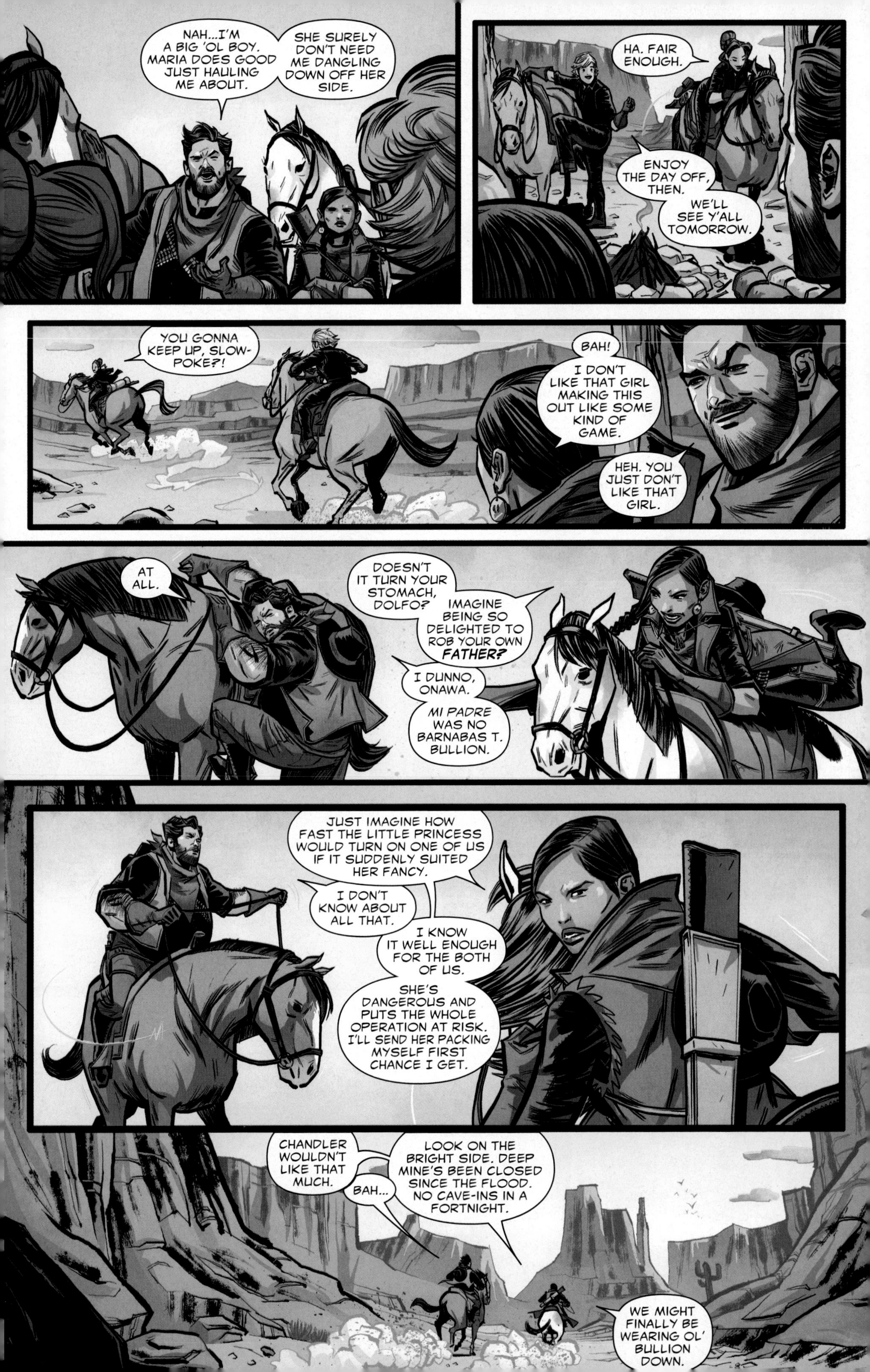

NAH...I'M A BIG 'OL BOY. MARIA DOES GOOD JUST HAULING ME ABOUT.
SHE SURELY DON'T NEED ME DANGLING DOWN OFF HER SIDE.
HA. FAIR ENOUGH.
ENJOY THE DAY OFF, THEN.
WE'LL SEE Y'ALL TOMORROW.
YOU GONNA KEEP UP, SLOW-POKE?!
BAH!
I DON'T LIKE THAT GIRL MAKING THIS OUT LIKE SOME KIND OF GAME.
HEH. YOU JUST DON'T LIKE THAT GIRL.
AT ALL.
DOESN'T IT TURN YOUR STOMACH, DOLFO?
IMAGINE BEING SO DELIGHTED TO ROB YOUR OWN ***FATHER?***
I DUNNO, ONAWA.
MI PADRE WAS NO BARNABAS T. BULLION.
JUST IMAGINE HOW FAST THE LITTLE PRINCESS WOULD TURN ON ONE OF US IF IT SUDDENLY SUITED HER FANCY.
I DON'T KNOW ABOUT ALL THAT.
I KNOW IT WELL ENOUGH FOR THE BOTH OF US.
SHE'S DANGEROUS AND PUTS THE WHOLE OPERATION AT RISK. I'LL SEND HER PACKING MYSELF FIRST CHANCE I GET.
CHANDLER WOULDN'T LIKE THAT MUCH.
BAH...
LOOK ON THE BRIGHT SIDE. DEEP MINE'S BEEN CLOSED SINCE THE FLOOD. NO CAVE-INS IN A FORTNIGHT.
WE MIGHT FINALLY BE WEARING OL' BULLION DOWN.

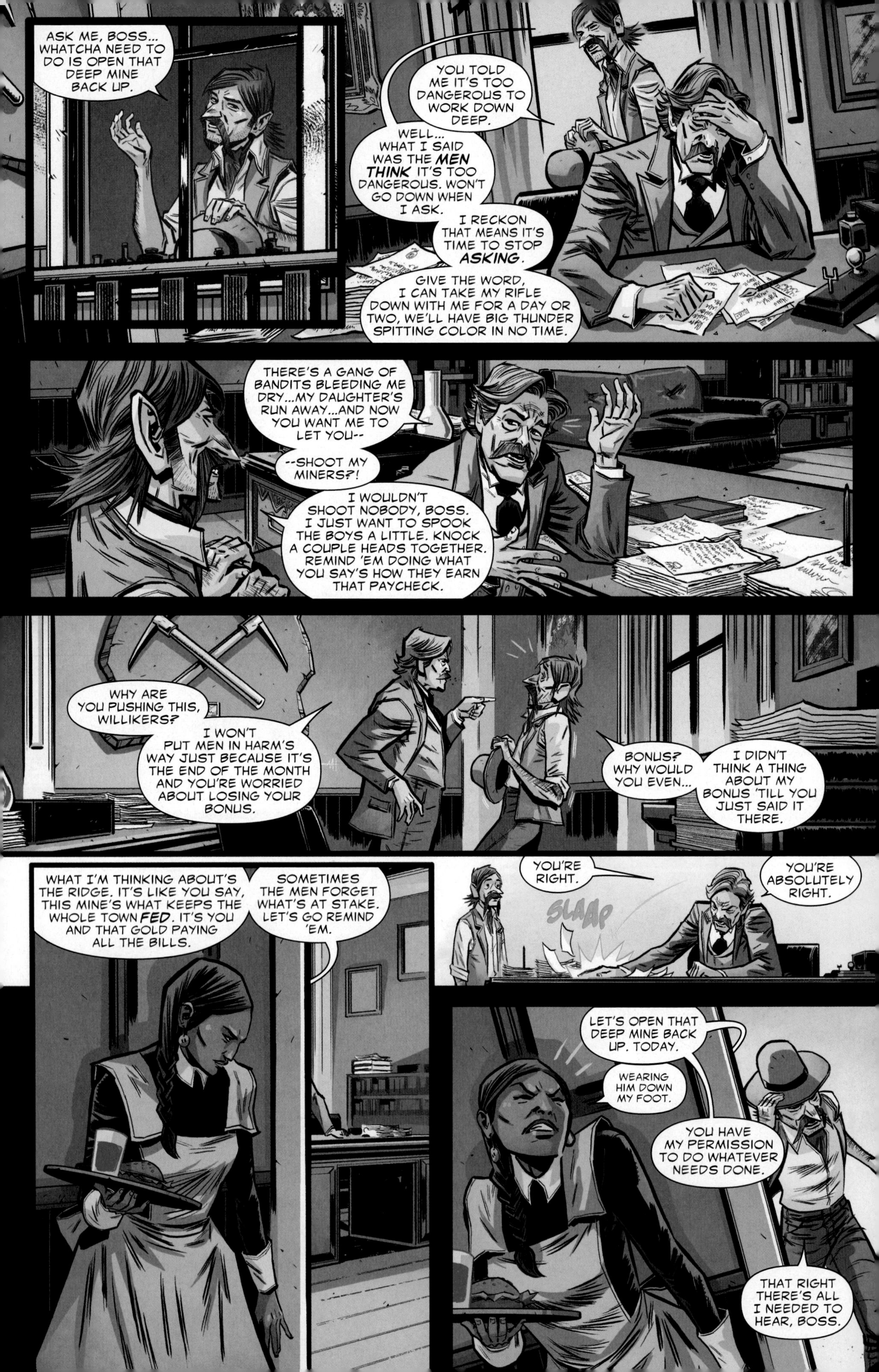

ASK ME, BOSS... WHATCHA NEED TO DO IS OPEN THAT DEEP MINE BACK UP.
YOU TOLD ME IT'S TOO DANGEROUS TO WORK DOWN DEEP.
WELL... WHAT I SAID WAS THE MEN THINK IT'S TOO DANGEROUS. WON'T GO DOWN WHEN I ASK.
I RECKON THAT MEANS IT'S TIME TO STOP ASKING.
GIVE THE WORD, I CAN TAKE MY RIFLE DOWN WITH ME FOR A DAY OR TWO, WE'LL HAVE BIG THUNDER SPITTING COLOR IN NO TIME.
THERE'S A GANG OF BANDITS BLEEDING ME DRY...MY DAUGHTER'S RUN AWAY...AND NOW YOU WANT ME TO LET YOU--
--SHOOT MY MINERS?!
I WOULDN'T SHOOT NOBODY, BOSS. I JUST WANT TO SPOOK THE BOYS A LITTLE. KNOCK A COUPLE HEADS TOGETHER. REMIND 'EM DOING WHAT YOU SAY'S HOW THEY EARN THAT PAYCHECK.
WHY ARE YOU PUSHING THIS, WILLIKERS?
I WON'T PUT MEN IN HARM'S WAY JUST BECAUSE IT'S THE END OF THE MONTH AND YOU'RE WORRIED ABOUT LOSING YOUR BONUS.
BONUS? WHY WOULD YOU EVEN...
I DIDN'T THINK A THING ABOUT MY BONUS 'TILL YOU JUST SAID IT THERE.
WHAT I'M THINKING ABOUT'S THE RIDGE. IT'S LIKE YOU SAY, THIS MINE'S WHAT KEEPS THE WHOLE TOWN FED. IT'S YOU AND THAT GOLD PAYING ALL THE BILLS.
SOMETIMES THE MEN FORGET WHAT'S AT STAKE. LET'S GO REMIND 'EM.
YOU'RE RIGHT.
SLAAP
YOU'RE ABSOLUTELY RIGHT.
LET'S OPEN THAT DEEP MINE BACK UP. TODAY.
WEARING HIM DOWN MY FOOT.
YOU HAVE MY PERMISSION TO DO WHATEVER NEEDS DONE.
THAT RIGHT THERE'S ALL I NEEDED TO HEAR, BOSS.

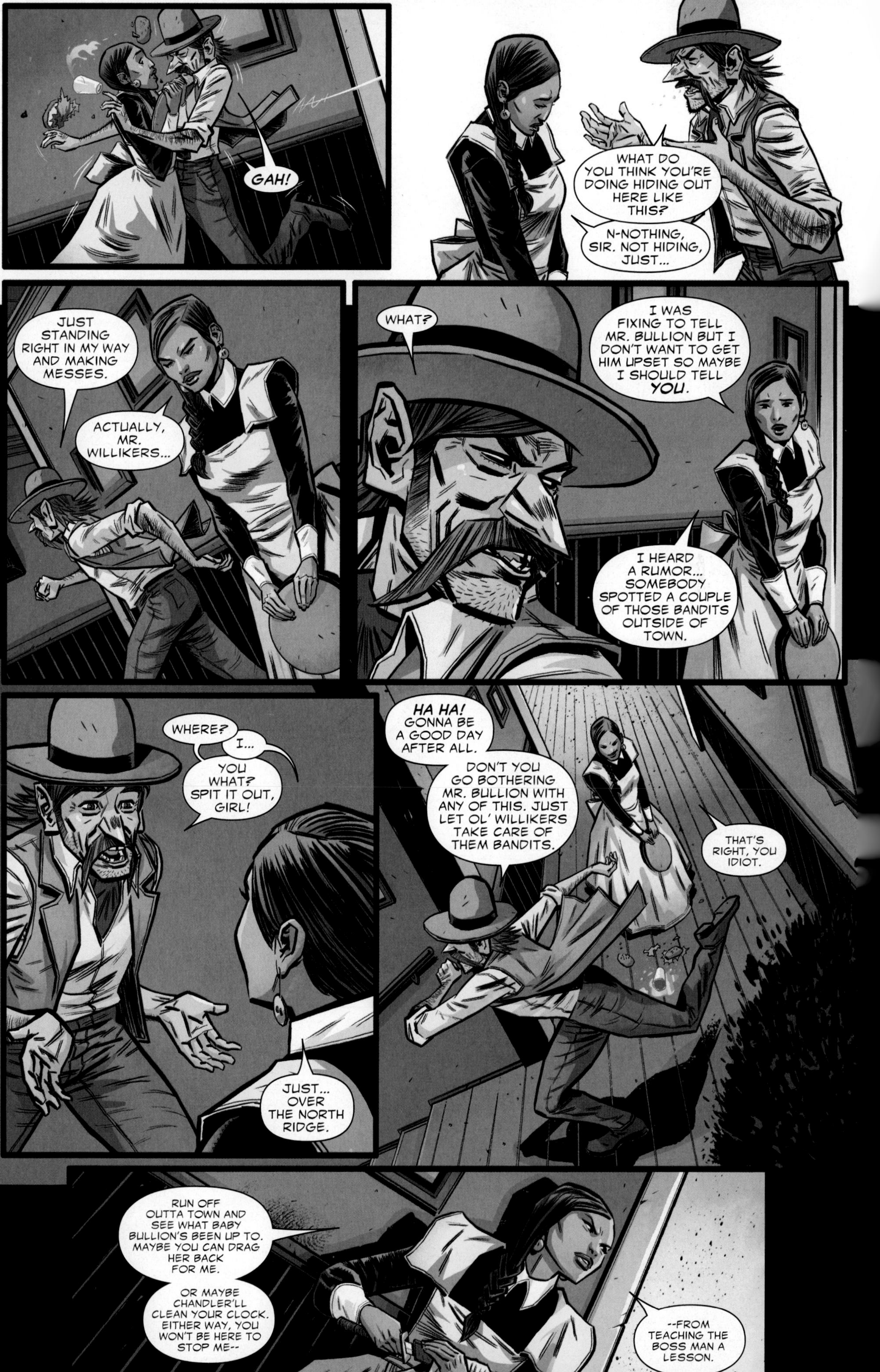
GAH!
WHAT DO YOU THINK YOU'RE DOING HIDING OUT HERE LIKE THIS?
N-NOTHING, SIR. NOT HIDING, JUST...
JUST STANDING RIGHT IN MY WAY AND MAKING MESSES.
ACTUALLY, MR. WILLIKERS...
WHAT?
I WAS FIXING TO TELL MR. BULLION BUT I DON'T WANT TO GET HIM UPSET SO MAYBE I SHOULD TELL YOU.
I HEARD A RUMOR... SOMEBODY SPOTTED A COUPLE OF THOSE BANDITS OUTSIDE OF TOWN.
WHERE?
I...
YOU WHAT? SPIT IT OUT, GIRL!
JUST... OVER THE NORTH RIDGE.
HA HA! GONNA BE A GOOD DAY AFTER ALL.
DON'T YOU GO BOTHERING MR. BULLION WITH ANY OF THIS. JUST LET OL' WILLIKERS TAKE CARE OF THEM BANDITS.
THAT'S RIGHT, YOU IDIOT.
RUN OFF OUTTA TOWN AND SEE WHAT BABY BULLION'S BEEN UP TO. MAYBE YOU CAN DRAG HER BACK FOR ME.
OR MAYBE CHANDLER'LL CLEAN YOUR CLOCK. EITHER WAY, YOU WON'T BE HERE TO STOP ME--
--FROM TEACHING THE BOSS MAN A LESSON.

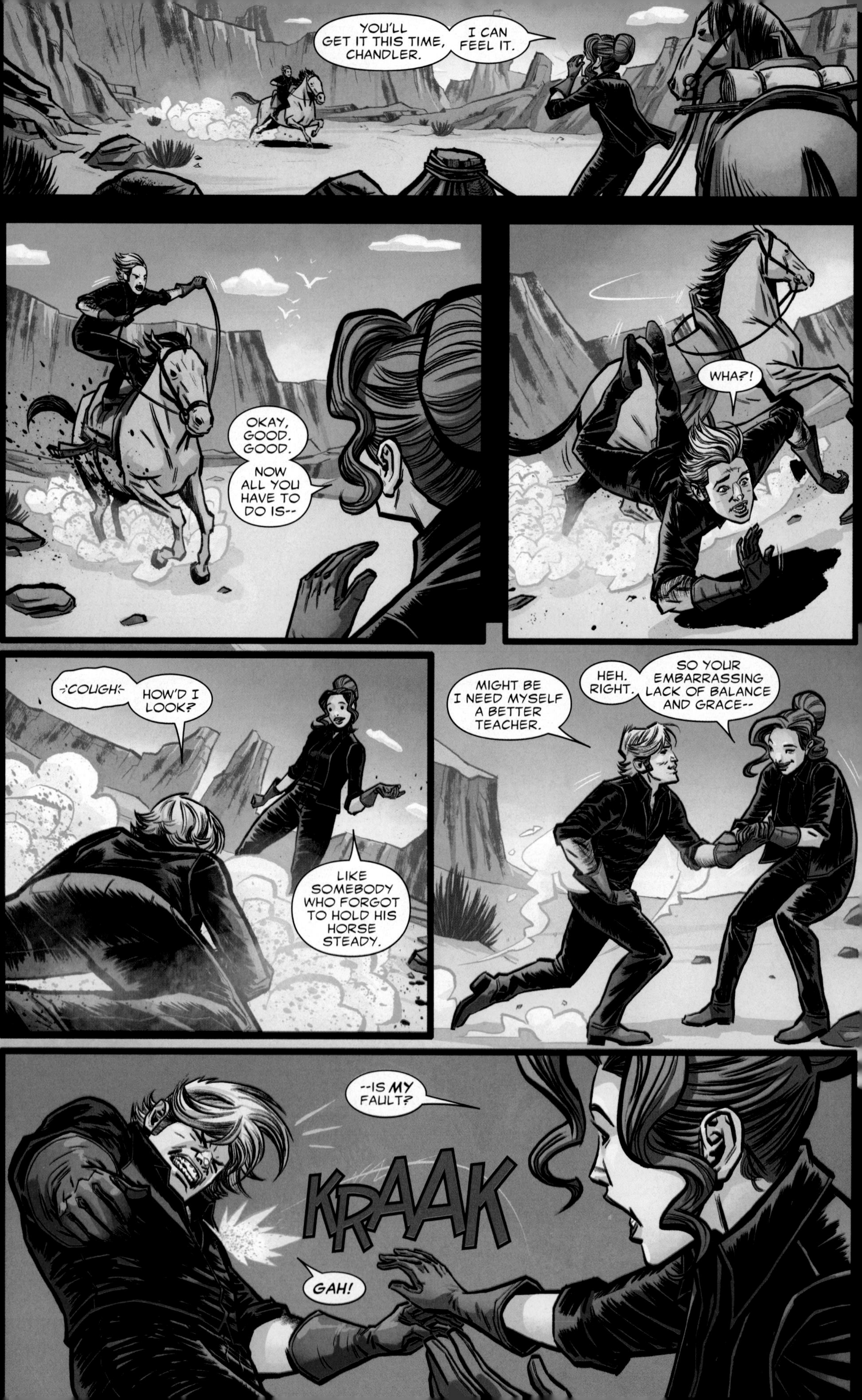
YOU'LL GET IT THIS TIME, CHANDLER.
I CAN FEEL IT.
OKAY, GOOD. GOOD.
NOW ALL YOU HAVE TO DO IS--
WHA?!
COUGH
HOW'D I LOOK?
LIKE SOMEBODY WHO FORGOT TO HOLD HIS HORSE STEADY.
MIGHT BE I NEED MYSELF A BETTER TEACHER.
HEH. RIGHT.
SO YOUR EMBARRASSING LACK OF BALANCE AND GRACE--
--IS MY FAULT?
KRAAAK
GAH!

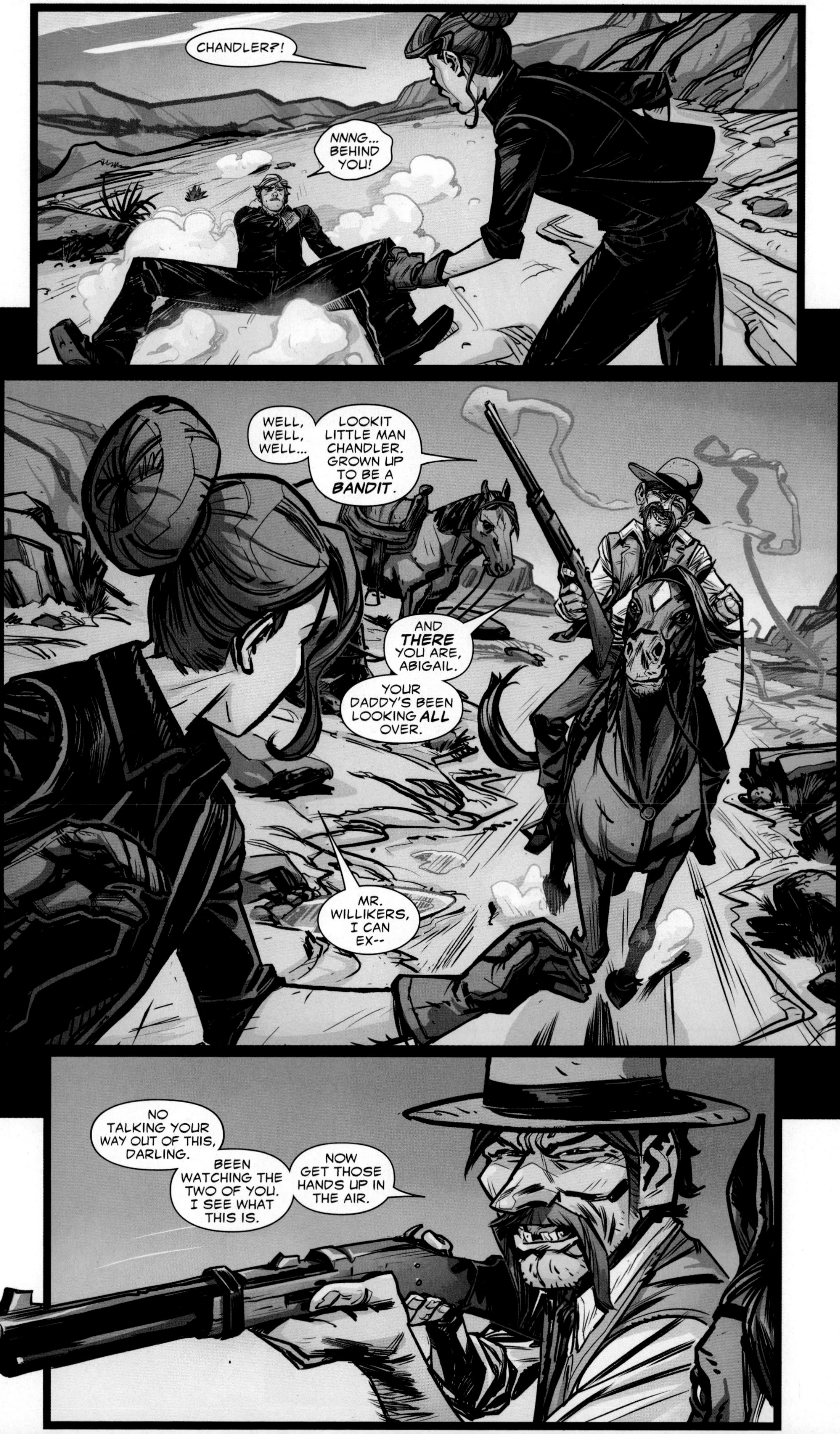
CHANDLER?!
NNNG... BEHIND YOU!
WELL, WELL, WELL...
LOOKIT LITTLE MAN CHANDLER. GROWN UP TO BE A **BANDIT**.
AND **THERE** YOU ARE, ABIGAIL.
YOUR DADDY'S BEEN LOOKING **ALL** OVER.
MR. WILLIKERS, I CAN EX--
NO TALKING YOUR WAY OUT OF THIS, DARLING.
BEEN WATCHING THE TWO OF YOU. I SEE WHAT THIS IS.
NOW GET THOSE HANDS UP IN THE AIR.

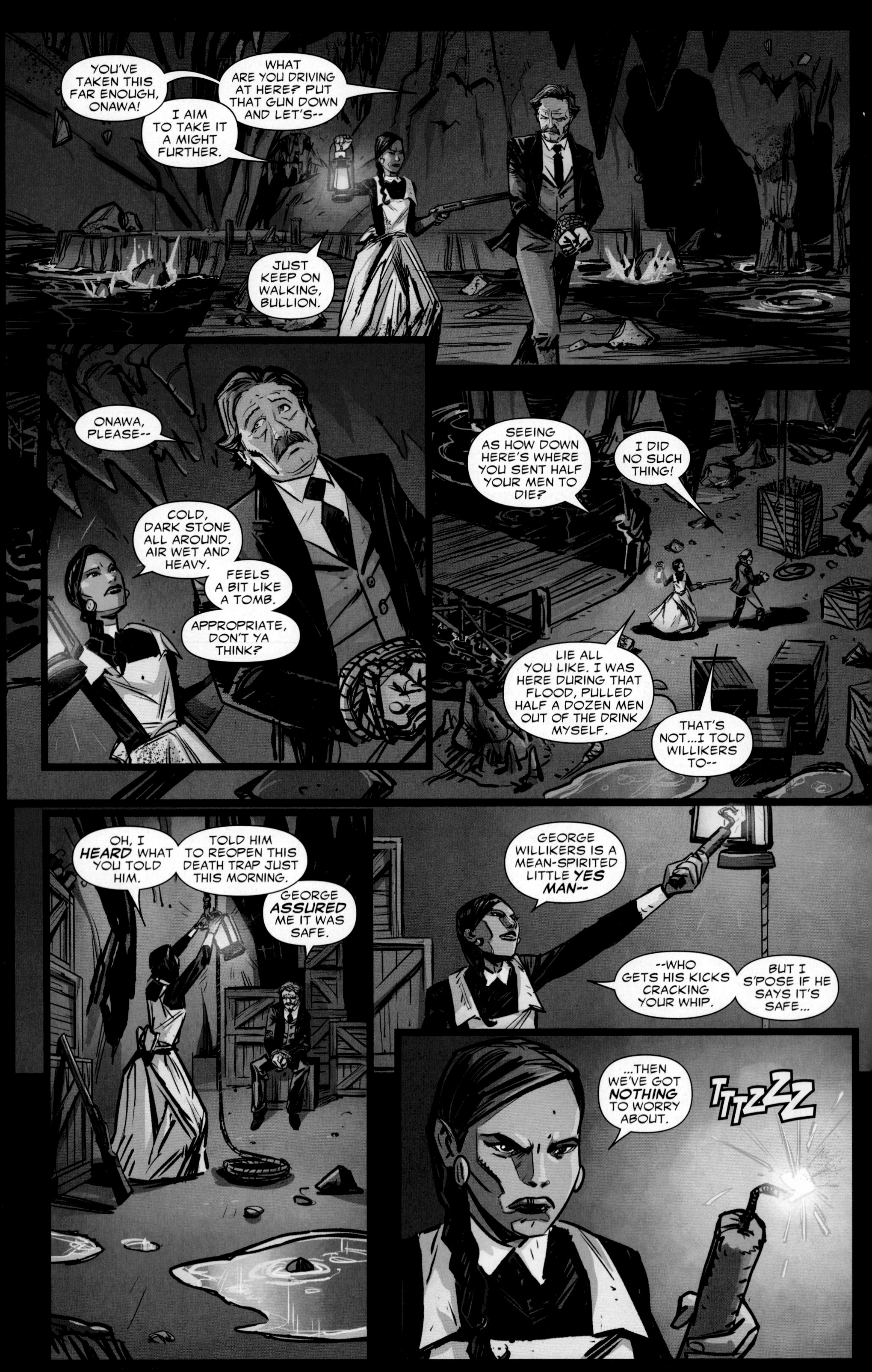
YOU'VE TAKEN THIS FAR ENOUGH, ONAWA!
WHAT ARE YOU DRIVING AT HERE? PUT THAT GUN DOWN AND LET'S--
I AIM TO TAKE IT A MIGHT FURTHER.
JUST KEEP ON WALKING, BULLION.
ONAWA, PLEASE--
COLD, DARK STONE ALL AROUND. AIR WET AND HEAVY.
FEELS A BIT LIKE A TOMB.
APPROPRIATE, DON'T YA THINK?
SEEING AS HOW DOWN HERE'S WHERE YOU SENT HALF YOUR MEN TO DIE?
I DID NO SUCH THING!
LIE ALL YOU LIKE. I WAS HERE DURING THAT FLOOD, PULLED HALF A DOZEN MEN OUT OF THE DRINK MYSELF.
THAT'S NOT...I TOLD WILLIKERS TO--
OH, I HEARD WHAT YOU TOLD HIM.
TOLD HIM TO REOPEN THIS DEATH TRAP JUST THIS MORNING.
GEORGE ASSURED ME IT WAS SAFE.
GEORGE WILLIKERS IS A MEAN-SPIRITED LITTLE YES MAN--
--WHO GETS HIS KICKS CRACKING YOUR WHIP.
BUT I S'POSE IF HE SAYS IT'S SAFE...
...THEN WE'VE GOT NOTHING TO WORRY ABOUT.
TTTZZZZ

ONAWA, STOP THIS!

WHAT'S THAT?

ALL I DID WAS LIGHT THIS HERE WATERLOGGED STICK OF DYNAMITE--

--IN WHAT YOUR *BEST MAN* ASSURES US IS THE SAFEST GOLD MINE IN THE WEST.

TTZZZ

EACH ONE OF YOUR MINERS DOES THE SAME--

TTZZZ

--A DOZEN TIMES BEFORE LUNCH.

FFFTTSSS

WHAT'S THE MATTER, BOSS MAN?

DID YOUR PRECIOUS MINE TURN SCARY ALL THE SUDDEN?

NOW YOU'RE DOWN IN IT?

YOU'RE INSANE!

YOU SIT BACK DOWN!

HUAGH!

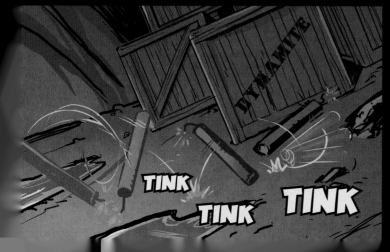

DYNAMITE

TINK

TINK

TINK

TTZZZ

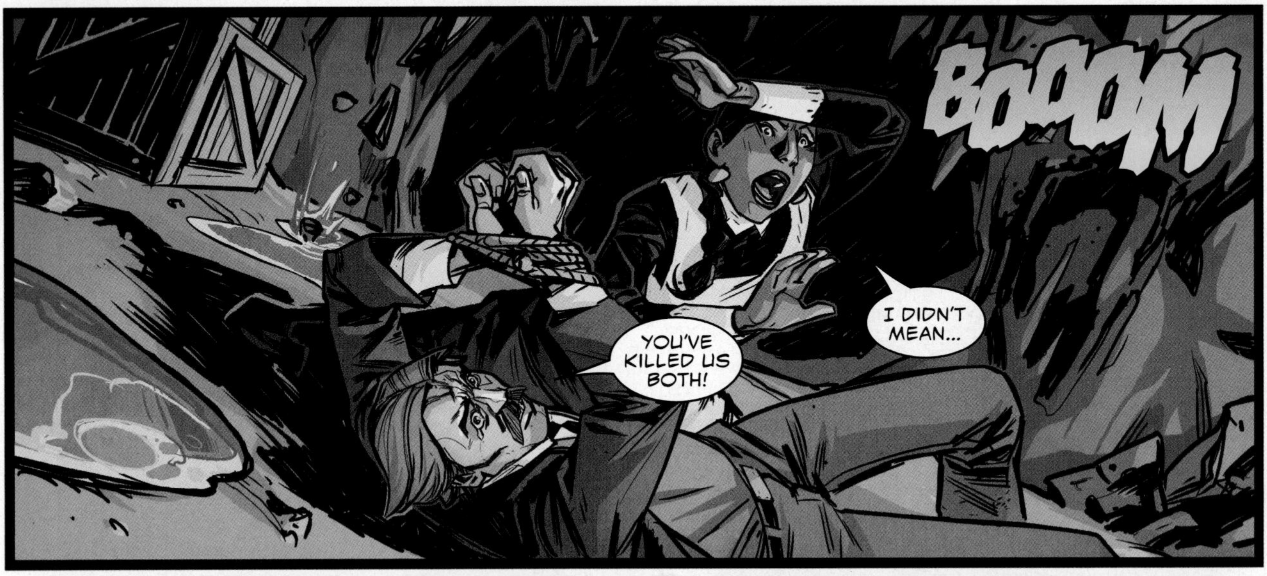
BOOOM
YOU'VE KILLED US BOTH!
I DIDN'T MEAN...

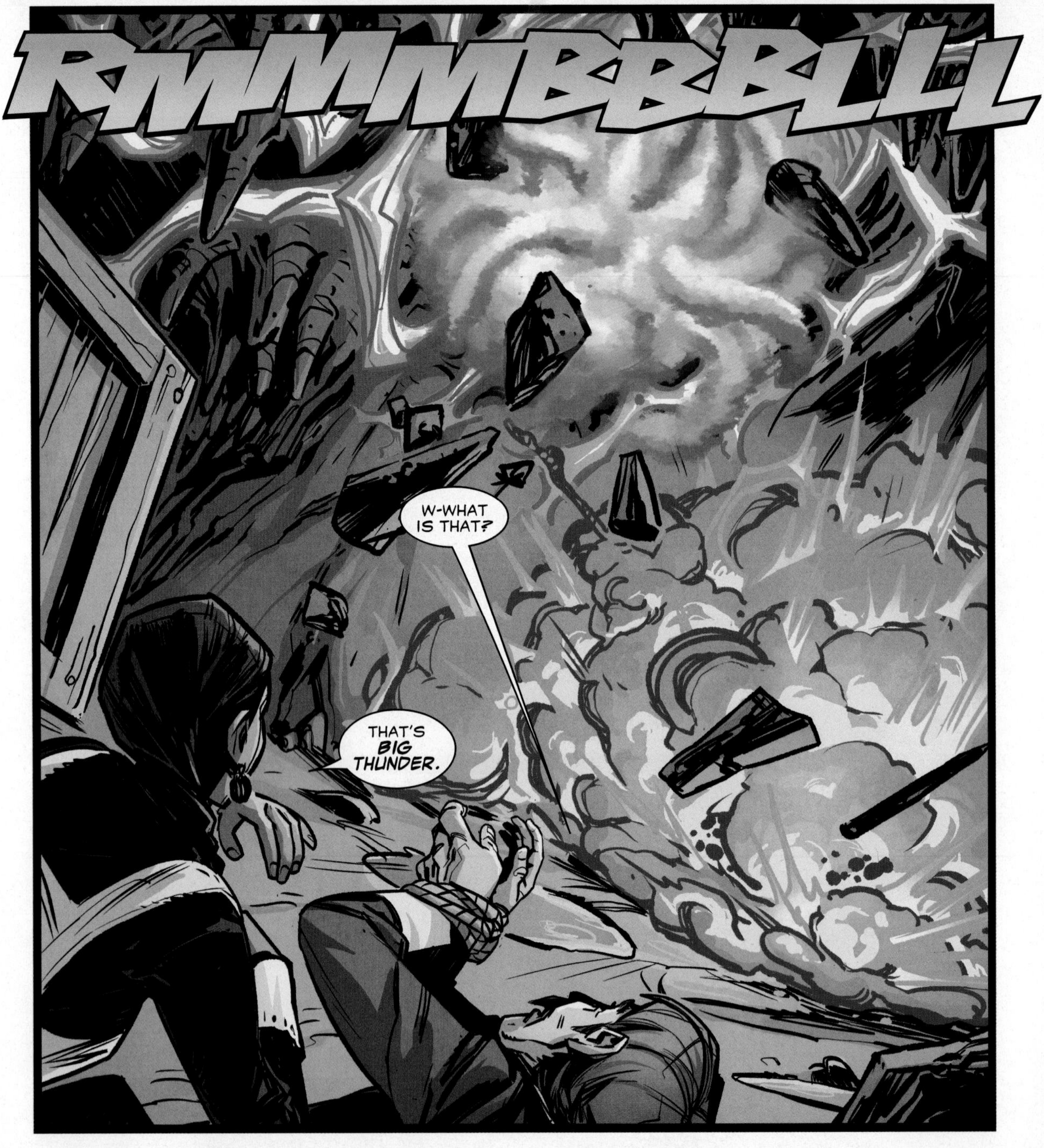
RMMMBBBLLL
W-WHAT IS THAT?
THAT'S BIG THUNDER.

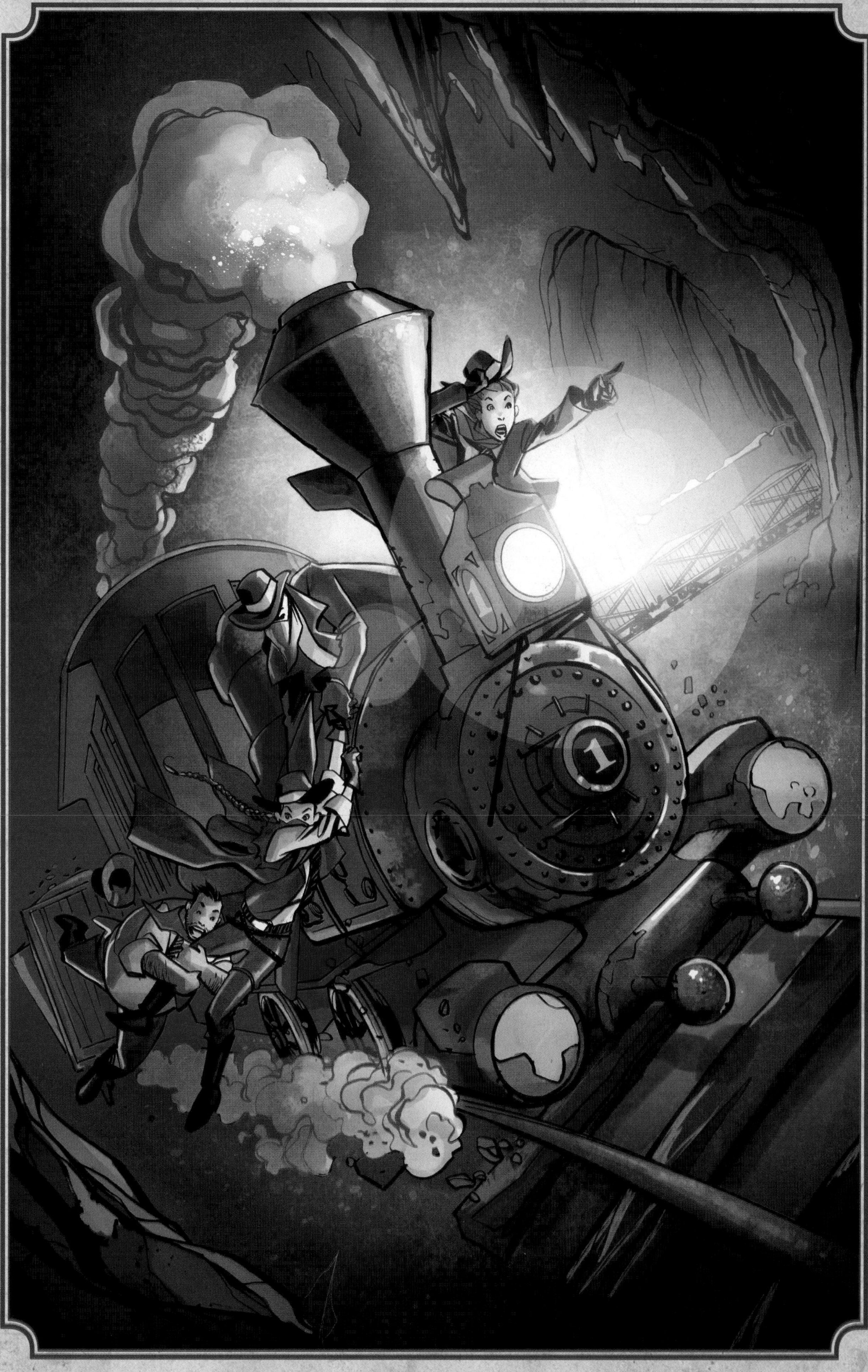

~ 5 ~

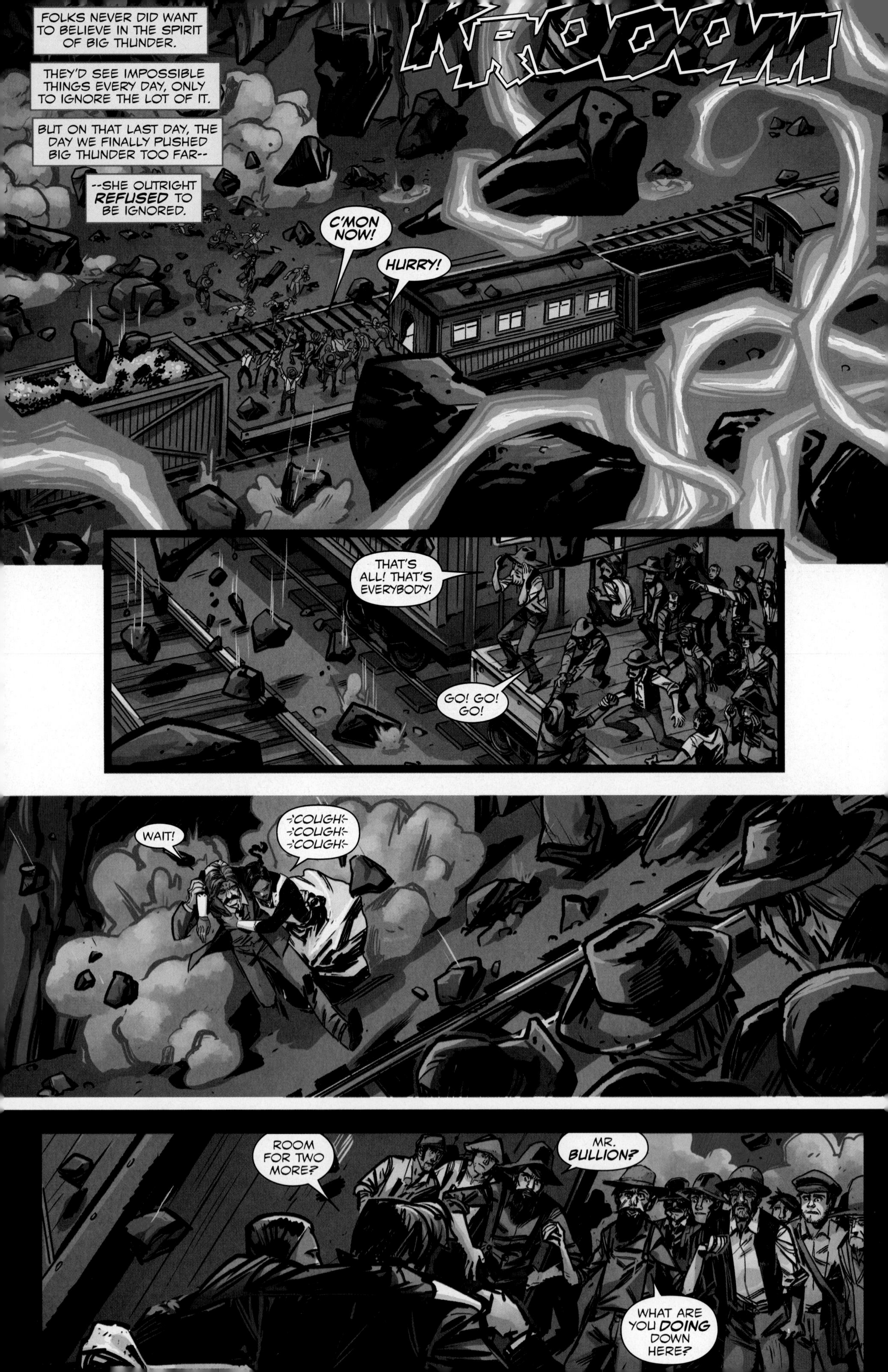
FOLKS NEVER DID WANT TO BELIEVE IN THE SPIRIT OF BIG THUNDER.
THEY'D SEE IMPOSSIBLE THINGS EVERY DAY, ONLY TO IGNORE THE LOT OF IT.
BUT ON THAT LAST DAY, THE DAY WE FINALLY PUSHED BIG THUNDER TOO FAR--
KRADOOM
--SHE OUTRIGHT REFUSED TO BE IGNORED.
C'MON NOW!
HURRY!
THAT'S ALL! THAT'S EVERYBODY!
GO! GO! GO!
WAIT!
COUGH COUGH COUGH
ROOM FOR TWO MORE?
MR. BULLION?
WHAT ARE YOU DOING DOWN HERE?

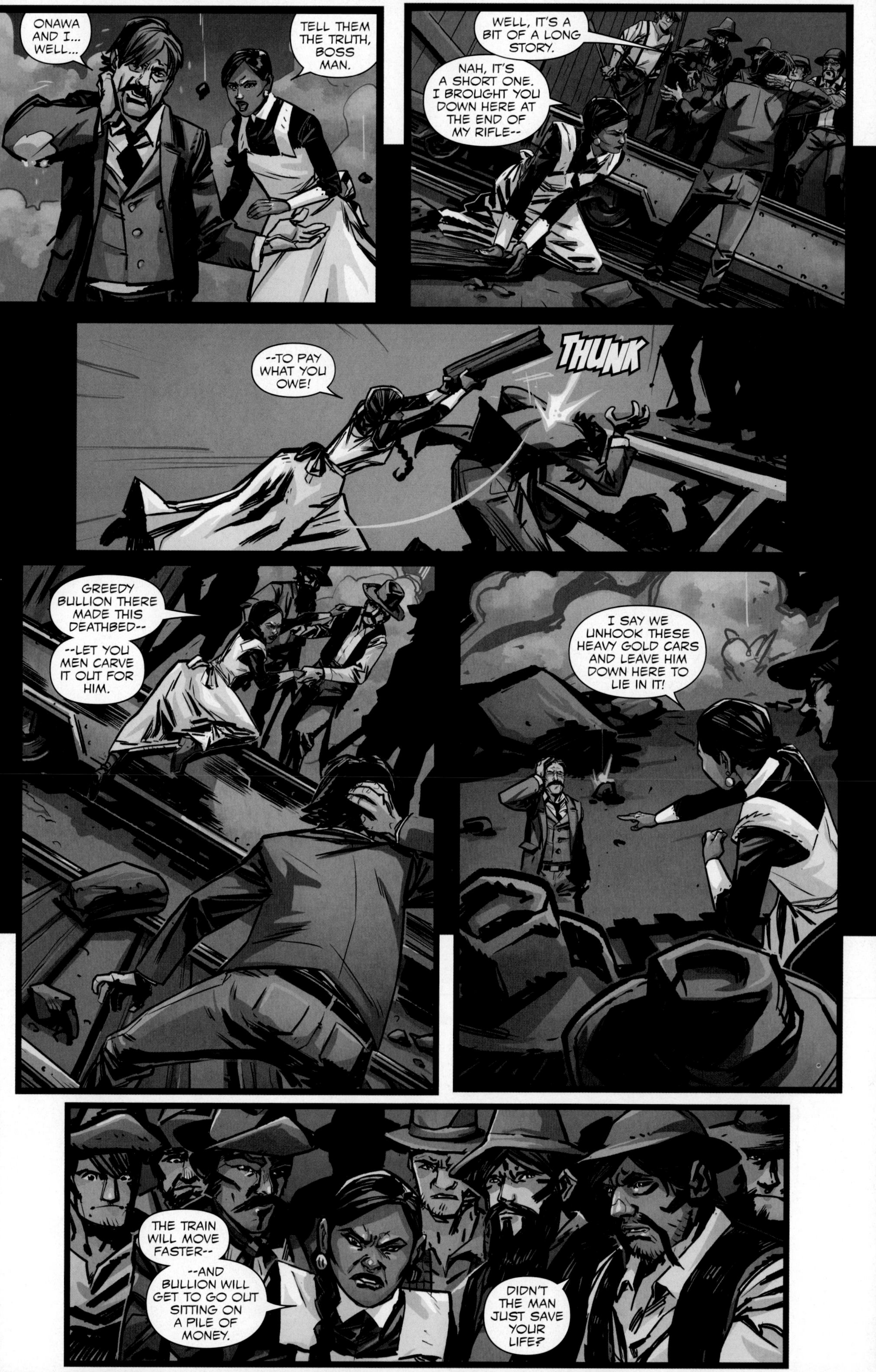
ONAWA AND I... WELL...
TELL THEM THE TRUTH, BOSS MAN.
WELL, IT'S A BIT OF A LONG STORY.
NAH, IT'S A SHORT ONE. I BROUGHT YOU DOWN HERE AT THE END OF MY RIFLE--
--TO PAY WHAT YOU OWE!
THUNK
GREEDY BULLION THERE MADE THIS DEATHBED--
--LET YOU MEN CARVE IT OUT FOR HIM.
I SAY WE UNHOOK THESE HEAVY GOLD CARS AND LEAVE HIM DOWN HERE TO LIE IN IT!
THE TRAIN WILL MOVE FASTER--
--AND BULLION WILL GET TO GO OUT SITTING ON A PILE OF MONEY.
DIDN'T THE MAN JUST SAVE YOUR LIFE?

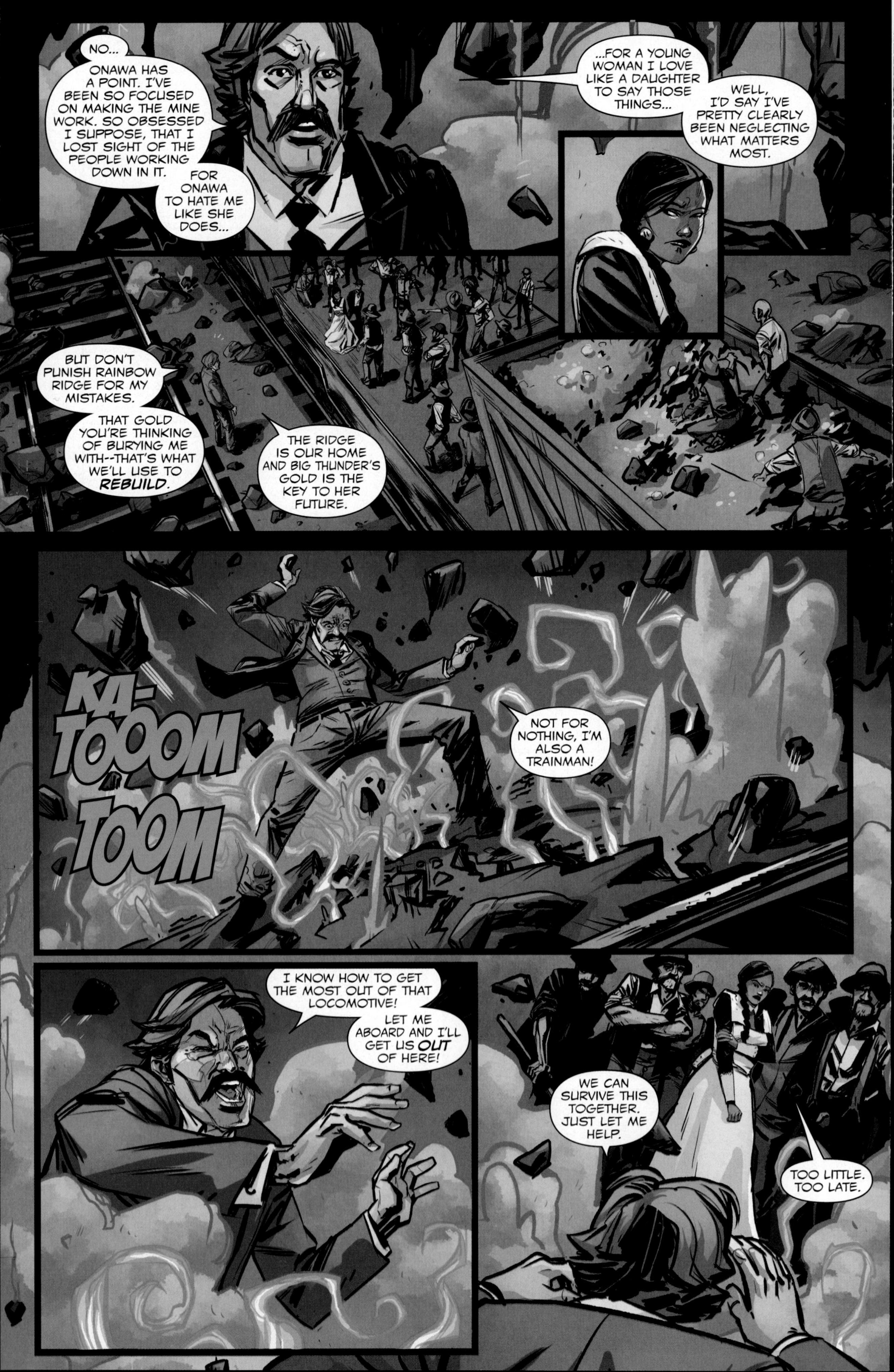
NO...
ONAWA HAS A POINT. I'VE BEEN SO FOCUSED ON MAKING THE MINE WORK. SO OBSESSED I SUPPOSE, THAT I LOST SIGHT OF THE PEOPLE WORKING DOWN IN IT.
FOR ONAWA TO HATE ME LIKE SHE DOES...
...FOR A YOUNG WOMAN I LOVE LIKE A DAUGHTER TO SAY THOSE THINGS...
WELL, I'D SAY I'VE PRETTY CLEARLY BEEN NEGLECTING WHAT MATTERS MOST.
BUT DON'T PUNISH RAINBOW RIDGE FOR MY MISTAKES.
THAT GOLD YOU'RE THINKING OF BURYING ME WITH--THAT'S WHAT WE'LL USE TO REBUILD.
THE RIDGE IS OUR HOME AND BIG THUNDER'S GOLD IS THE KEY TO HER FUTURE.
KA-TOOOM TOOM
NOT FOR NOTHING, I'M ALSO A TRAINMAN!
I KNOW HOW TO GET THE MOST OUT OF THAT LOCOMOTIVE!
LET ME ABOARD AND I'LL GET US OUT OF HERE!
WE CAN SURVIVE THIS TOGETHER. JUST LET ME HELP.
TOO LITTLE. TOO LATE.

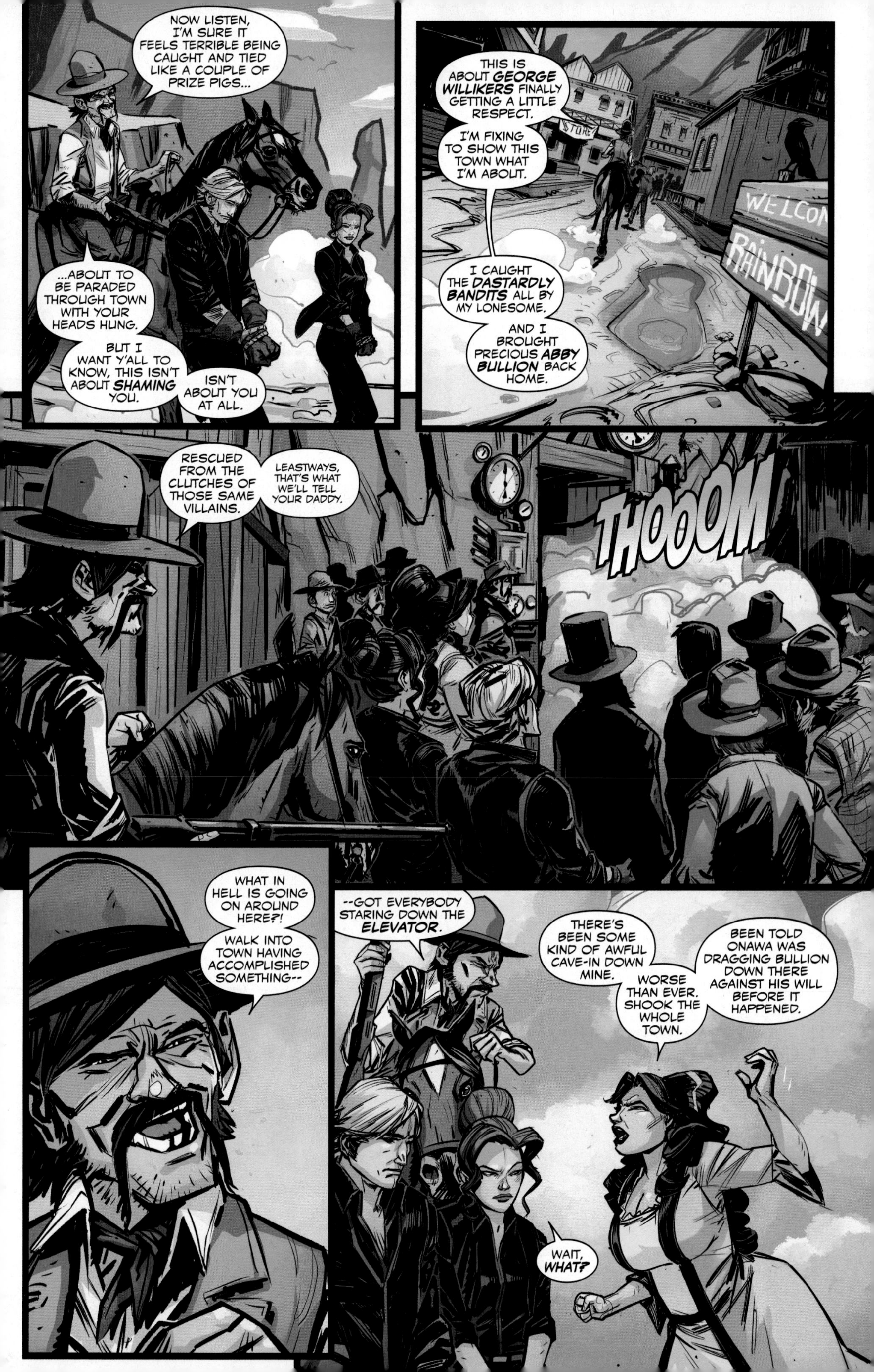
NOW LISTEN, I'M SURE IT FEELS TERRIBLE BEING CAUGHT AND TIED LIKE A COUPLE OF PRIZE PIGS...
...ABOUT TO BE PARADED THROUGH TOWN WITH YOUR HEADS HUNG.
BUT I WANT Y'ALL TO KNOW, THIS ISN'T ABOUT SHAMING YOU.
ISN'T ABOUT YOU AT ALL.
THIS IS ABOUT GEORGE WILLIKERS FINALLY GETTING A LITTLE RESPECT.
I'M FIXING TO SHOW THIS TOWN WHAT I'M ABOUT.
STORE
WELCO
RAINBOW
I CAUGHT THE DASTARDLY BANDITS ALL BY MY LONESOME.
AND I BROUGHT PRECIOUS ABBY BULLION BACK HOME.
RESCUED FROM THE CLUTCHES OF THOSE SAME VILLAINS.
LEASTWAYS, THAT'S WHAT WE'LL TELL YOUR DADDY.
THOOOM
WHAT IN HELL IS GOING ON AROUND HERE?!
WALK INTO TOWN HAVING ACCOMPLISHED SOMETHING--
--GOT EVERYBODY STARING DOWN THE ELEVATOR.
THERE'S BEEN SOME KIND OF AWFUL CAVE-IN DOWN MINE.
WORSE THAN EVER. SHOOK THE WHOLE TOWN.
BEEN TOLD ONAWA WAS DRAGGING BULLION DOWN THERE AGAINST HIS WILL BEFORE IT HAPPENED.
WAIT, WHAT?

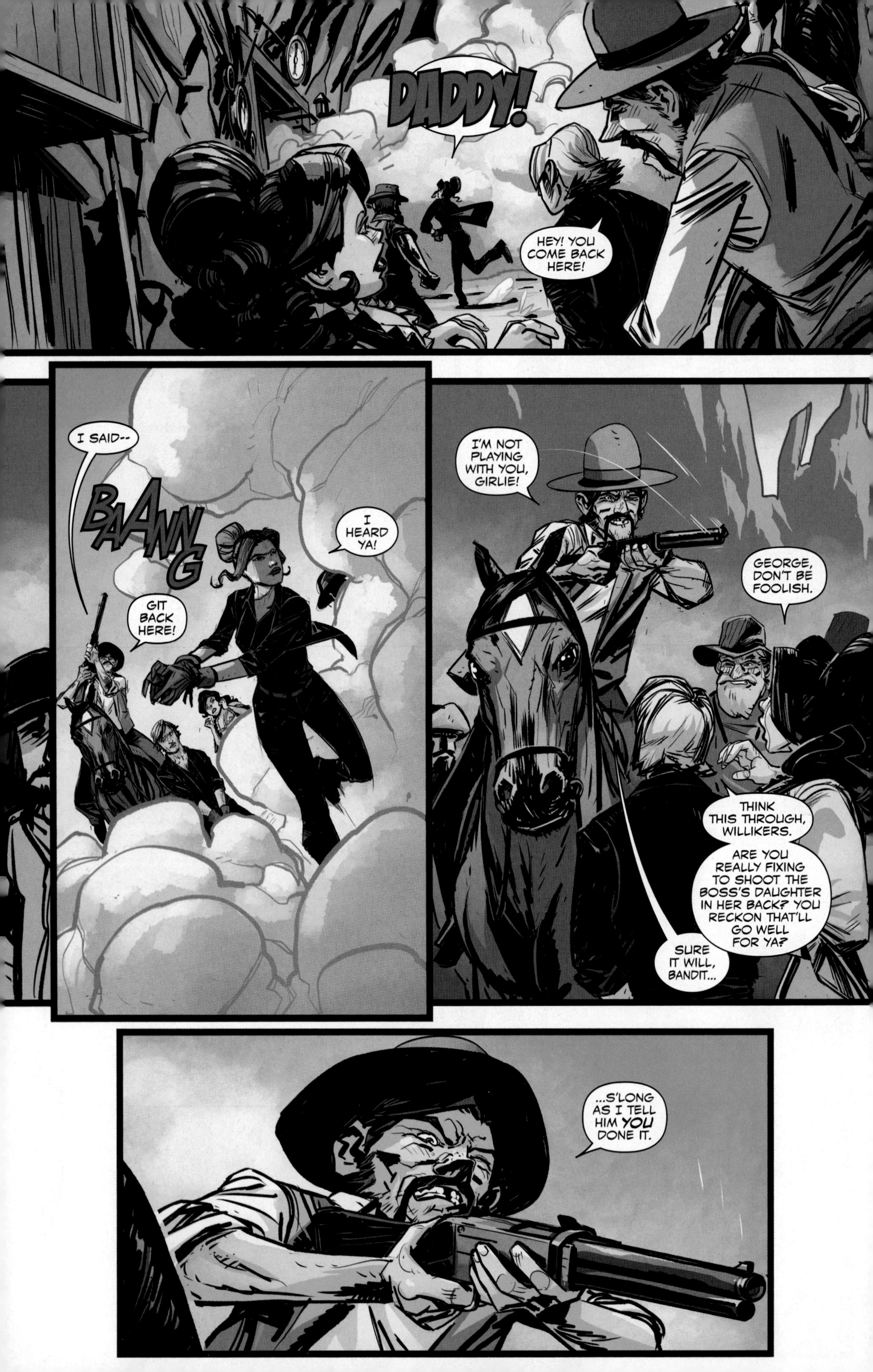
DADDY!
HEY! YOU COME BACK HERE!
I SAID--
BAANNG
GIT BACK HERE!
I HEARD YA!
I'M NOT PLAYING WITH YOU, GIRLIE!
GEORGE, DON'T BE FOOLISH.
THINK THIS THROUGH, WILLIKERS.
ARE YOU REALLY FIXING TO SHOOT THE BOSS'S DAUGHTER IN HER BACK? YOU RECKON THAT'LL GO WELL FOR YA?
SURE IT WILL, BANDIT...
...S'LONG AS I TELL HIM YOU DONE IT.

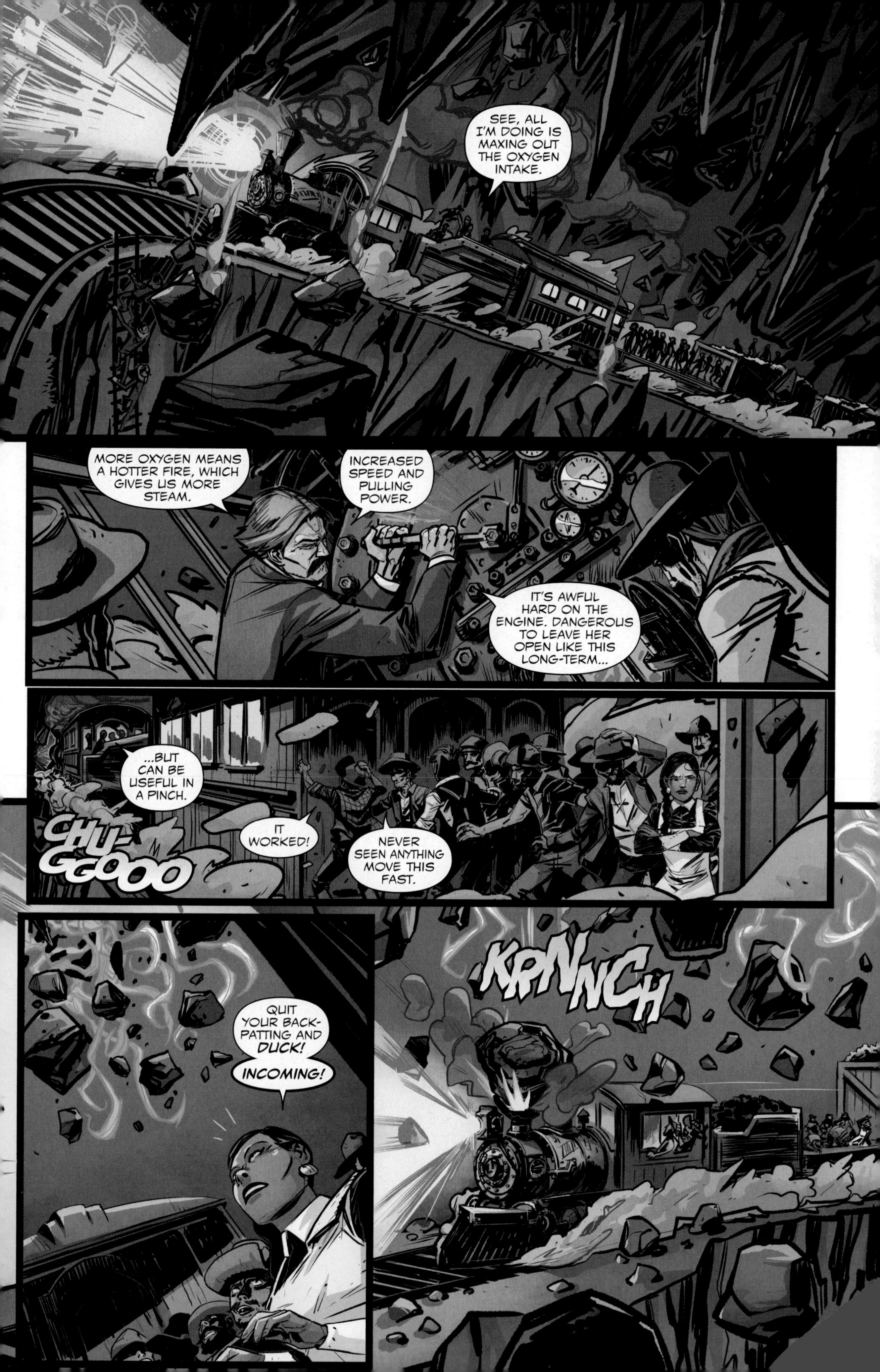
SEE, ALL I'M DOING IS MAXING OUT THE OXYGEN INTAKE.
MORE OXYGEN MEANS A HOTTER FIRE, WHICH GIVES US MORE STEAM.
INCREASED SPEED AND PULLING POWER.
IT'S AWFUL HARD ON THE ENGINE. DANGEROUS TO LEAVE HER OPEN LIKE THIS LONG-TERM...
...BUT CAN BE USEFUL IN A PINCH.
CHU-GGOOO
IT WORKED!
NEVER SEEN ANYTHING MOVE THIS FAST.
QUIT YOUR BACK-PATTING AND DUCK!
INCOMING!
KRNNCH

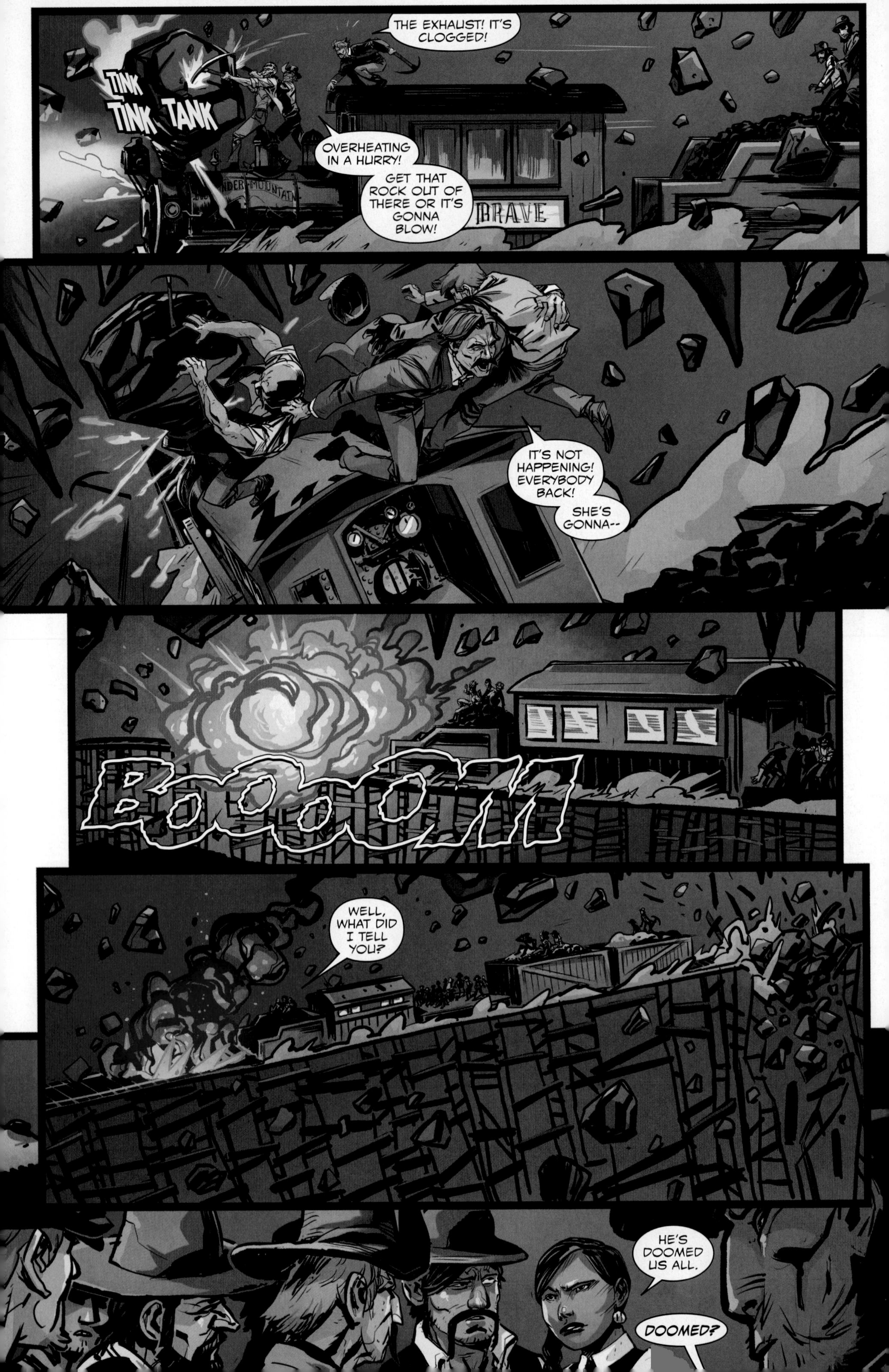
THE EXHAUST! IT'S CLOGGED!
TINK TINK TANK
OVERHEATING IN A HURRY!
GET THAT ROCK OUT OF THERE OR IT'S GONNA BLOW!
BRAVE
IT'S NOT HAPPENING! EVERYBODY BACK!
SHE'S GONNA--
BOOOOM
WELL, WHAT DID I TELL YOU?
HE'S DOOMED US ALL.
DOOMED?

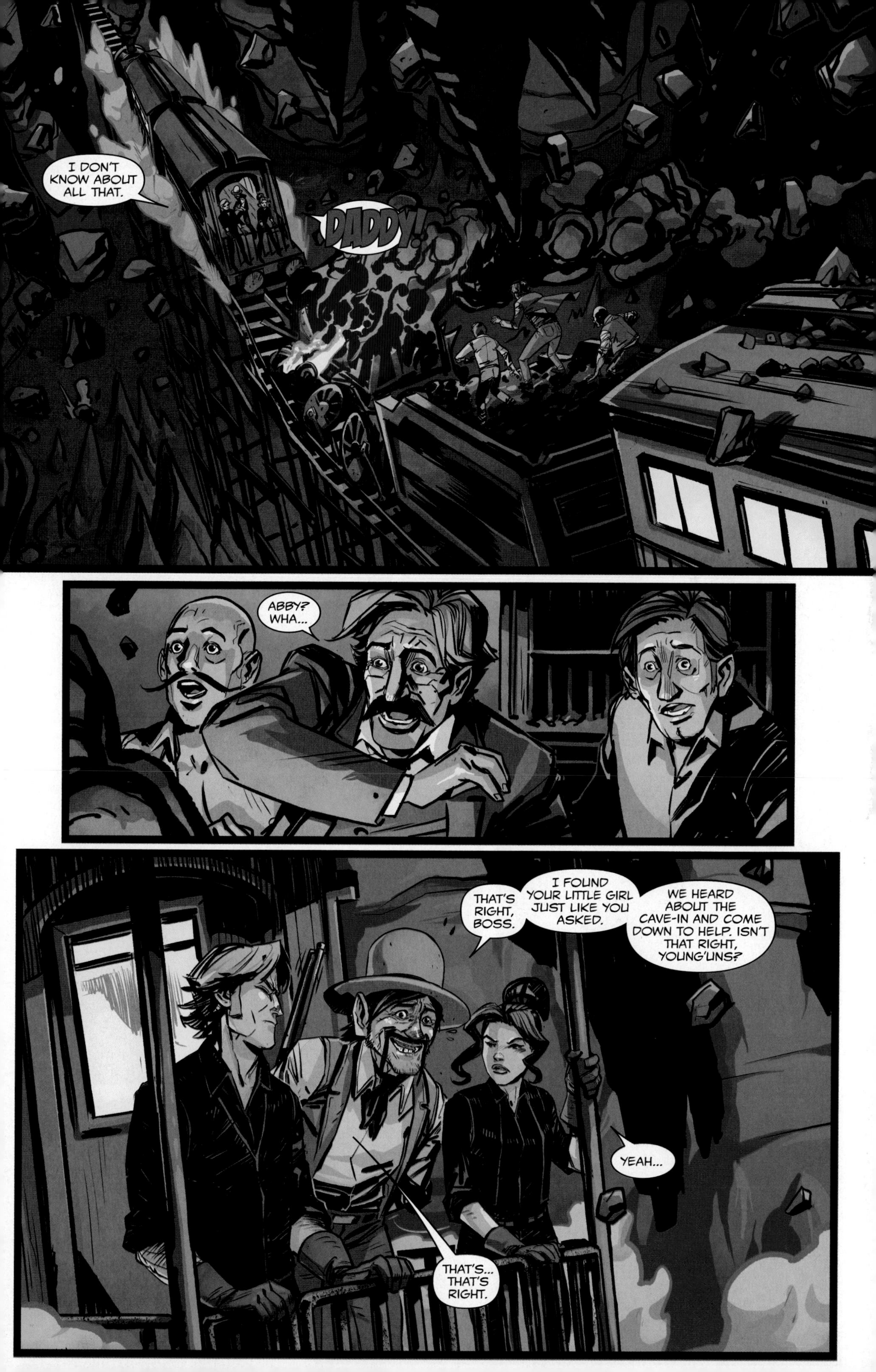
I DON'T KNOW ABOUT ALL THAT.
DADDY!
ABBY? WHA...
THAT'S RIGHT, BOSS.
I FOUND YOUR LITTLE GIRL JUST LIKE YOU ASKED.
WE HEARD ABOUT THE CAVE-IN AND COME DOWN TO HELP. ISN'T THAT RIGHT, YOUNG'UNS?
YEAH...
THAT'S... THAT'S RIGHT.

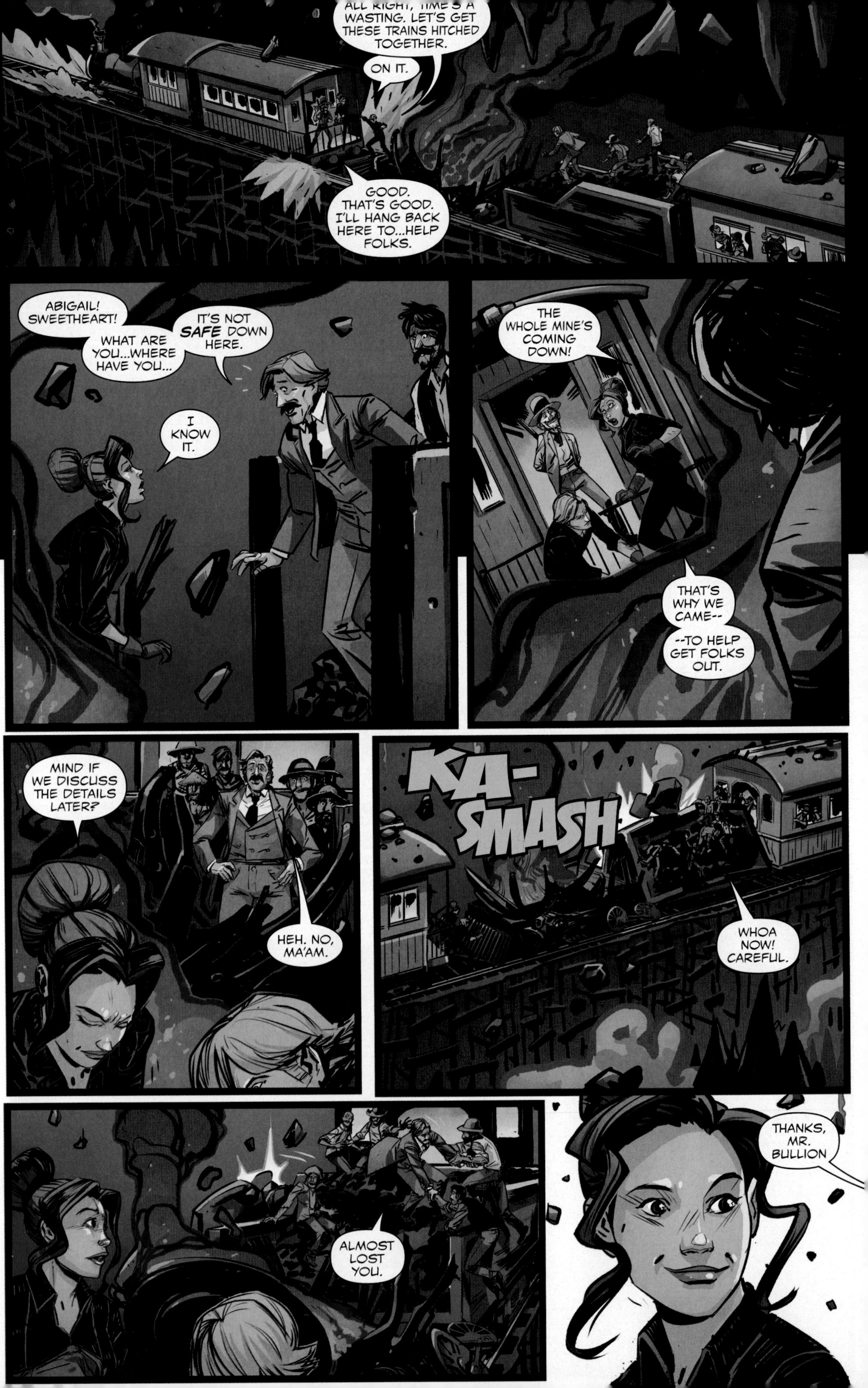
ALL RIGHT, TIME'S A WASTING. LET'S GET THESE TRAINS HITCHED TOGETHER.
ON IT.
GOOD. THAT'S GOOD. I'LL HANG BACK HERE TO...HELP FOLKS.
ABIGAIL! SWEETHEART!
WHAT ARE YOU...WHERE HAVE YOU...
IT'S NOT SAFE DOWN HERE.
I KNOW IT.
THE WHOLE MINE'S COMING DOWN!
THAT'S WHY WE CAME--
--TO HELP GET FOLKS OUT.
MIND IF WE DISCUSS THE DETAILS LATER?
HEH. NO, MA'AM.
KA-SMASH
WHOA NOW! CAREFUL.
ALMOST LOST YOU.
THANKS, MR. BULLION

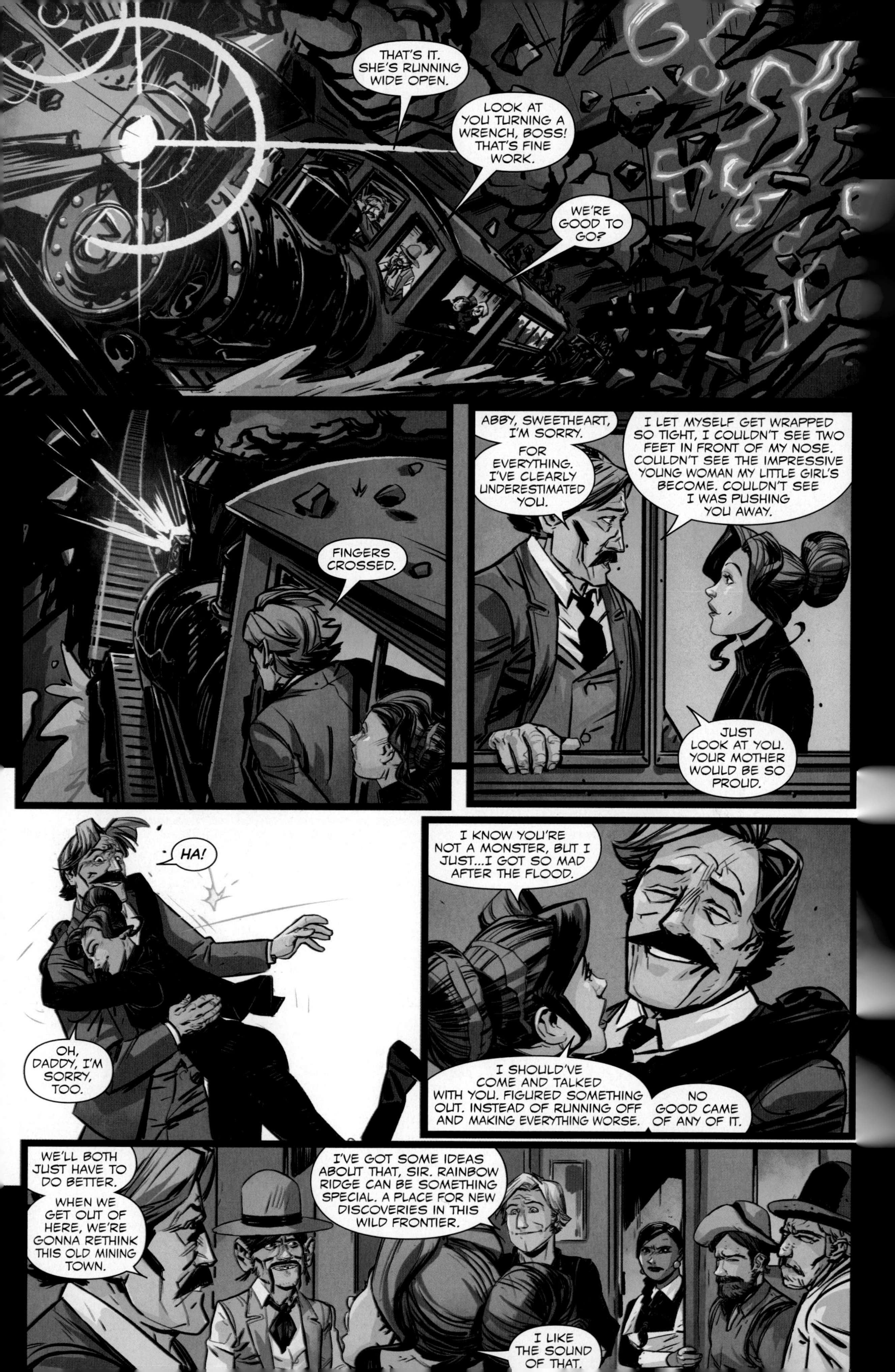
THAT'S IT. SHE'S RUNNING WIDE OPEN.
LOOK AT YOU TURNING A WRENCH, BOSS! THAT'S FINE WORK.
WE'RE GOOD TO GO?
FINGERS CROSSED.
ABBY, SWEETHEART, I'M SORRY.
FOR EVERYTHING. I'VE CLEARLY UNDERESTIMATED YOU.
I LET MYSELF GET WRAPPED SO TIGHT, I COULDN'T SEE TWO FEET IN FRONT OF MY NOSE. COULDN'T SEE THE IMPRESSIVE YOUNG WOMAN MY LITTLE GIRL'S BECOME. COULDN'T SEE I WAS PUSHING YOU AWAY.
JUST LOOK AT YOU. YOUR MOTHER WOULD BE SO PROUD.
HA!
OH, DADDY, I'M SORRY, TOO.
I KNOW YOU'RE NOT A MONSTER, BUT I JUST...I GOT SO MAD AFTER THE FLOOD.
I SHOULD'VE COME AND TALKED WITH YOU. FIGURED SOMETHING OUT. INSTEAD OF RUNNING OFF AND MAKING EVERYTHING WORSE.
NO GOOD CAME OF ANY OF IT.
WE'LL BOTH JUST HAVE TO DO BETTER.
WHEN WE GET OUT OF HERE, WE'RE GONNA RETHINK THIS OLD MINING TOWN.
I'VE GOT SOME IDEAS ABOUT THAT, SIR. RAINBOW RIDGE CAN BE SOMETHING SPECIAL. A PLACE FOR NEW DISCOVERIES IN THIS WILD FRONTIER.
I LIKE THE SOUND OF THAT.

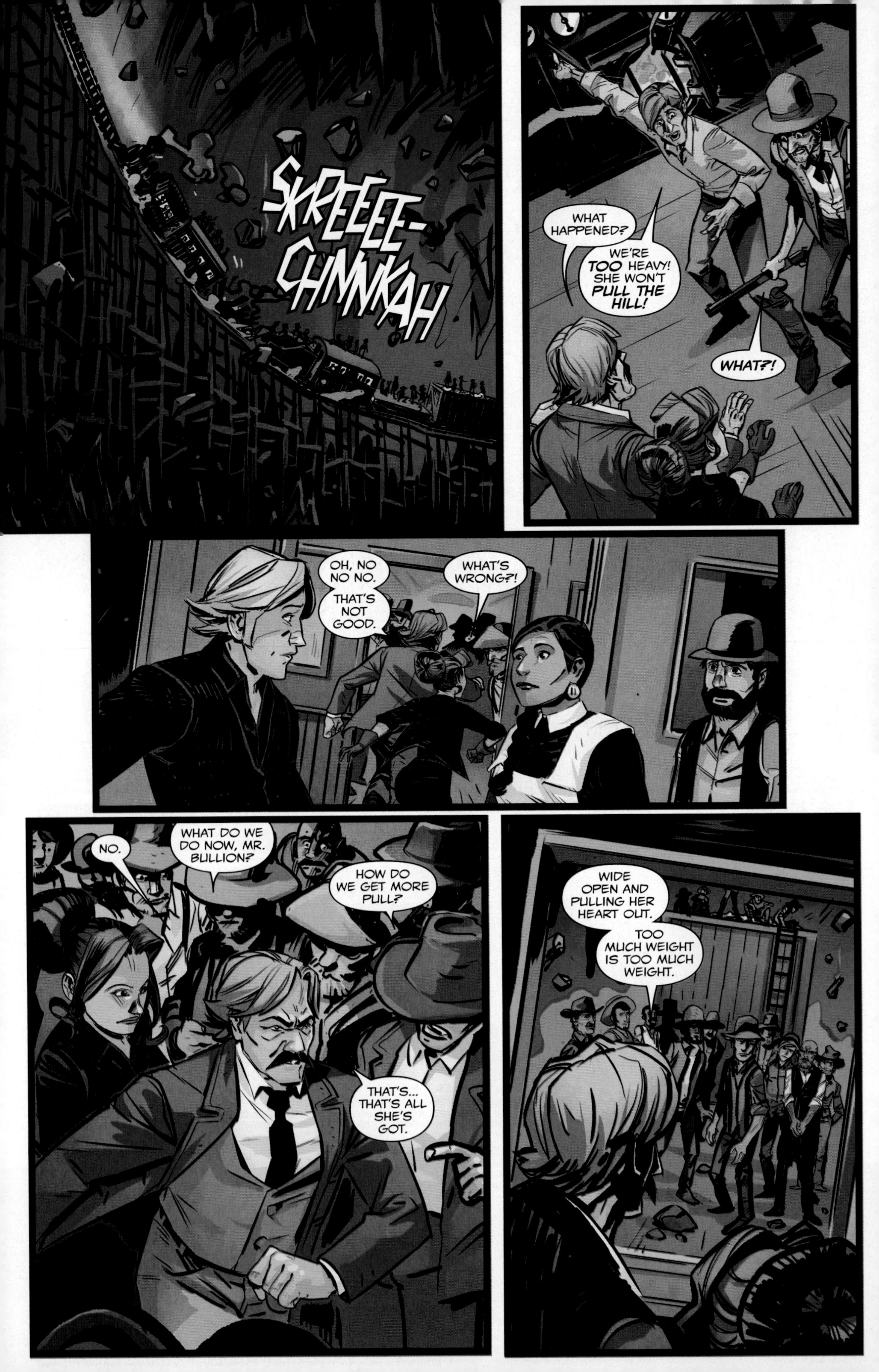
SKREEEE-CHNNKAH
WHAT HAPPENED?
WE'RE TOO HEAVY! SHE WON'T PULL THE HILL!
WHAT?!
OH, NO NO NO.
THAT'S NOT GOOD.
WHAT'S WRONG?!
NO.
WHAT DO WE DO NOW, MR. BULLION?
HOW DO WE GET MORE PULL?
THAT'S... THAT'S ALL SHE'S GOT.
WIDE OPEN AND PULLING HER HEART OUT.
TOO MUCH WEIGHT IS TOO MUCH WEIGHT.

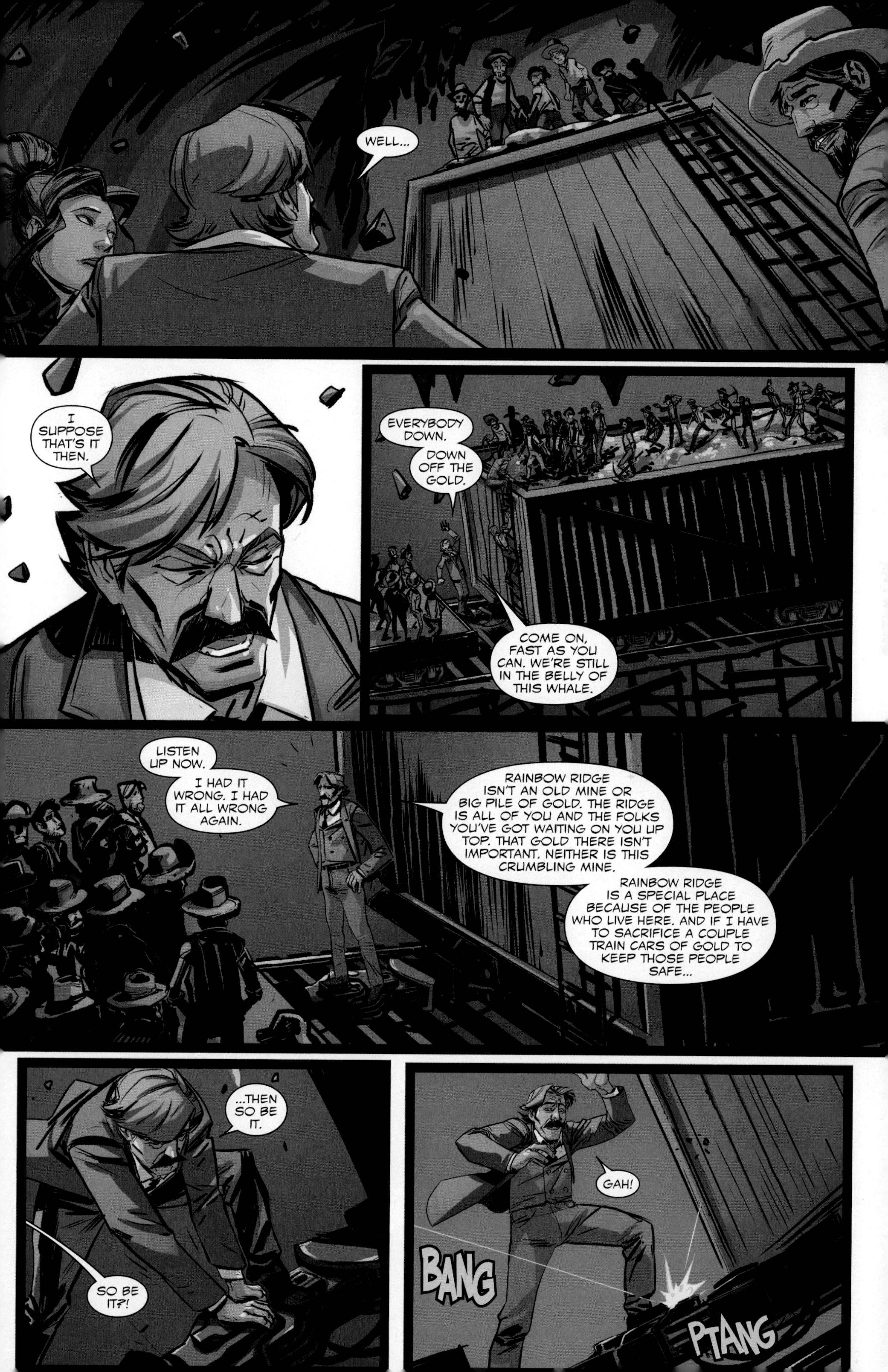
WELL...
I SUPPOSE THAT'S IT THEN.
EVERYBODY DOWN.
DOWN OFF THE GOLD.
COME ON, FAST AS YOU CAN. WE'RE STILL IN THE BELLY OF THIS WHALE.
LISTEN UP NOW.
I HAD IT WRONG. I HAD IT ALL WRONG AGAIN.
RAINBOW RIDGE ISN'T AN OLD MINE OR BIG PILE OF GOLD. THE RIDGE IS ALL OF YOU AND THE FOLKS YOU'VE GOT WAITING ON YOU UP TOP. THAT GOLD THERE ISN'T IMPORTANT. NEITHER IS THIS CRUMBLING MINE.
RAINBOW RIDGE IS A SPECIAL PLACE BECAUSE OF THE PEOPLE WHO LIVE HERE. AND IF I HAVE TO SACRIFICE A COUPLE TRAIN CARS OF GOLD TO KEEP THOSE PEOPLE SAFE...
...THEN SO BE IT.
SO BE IT?!
GAH!
BANG
PTANG

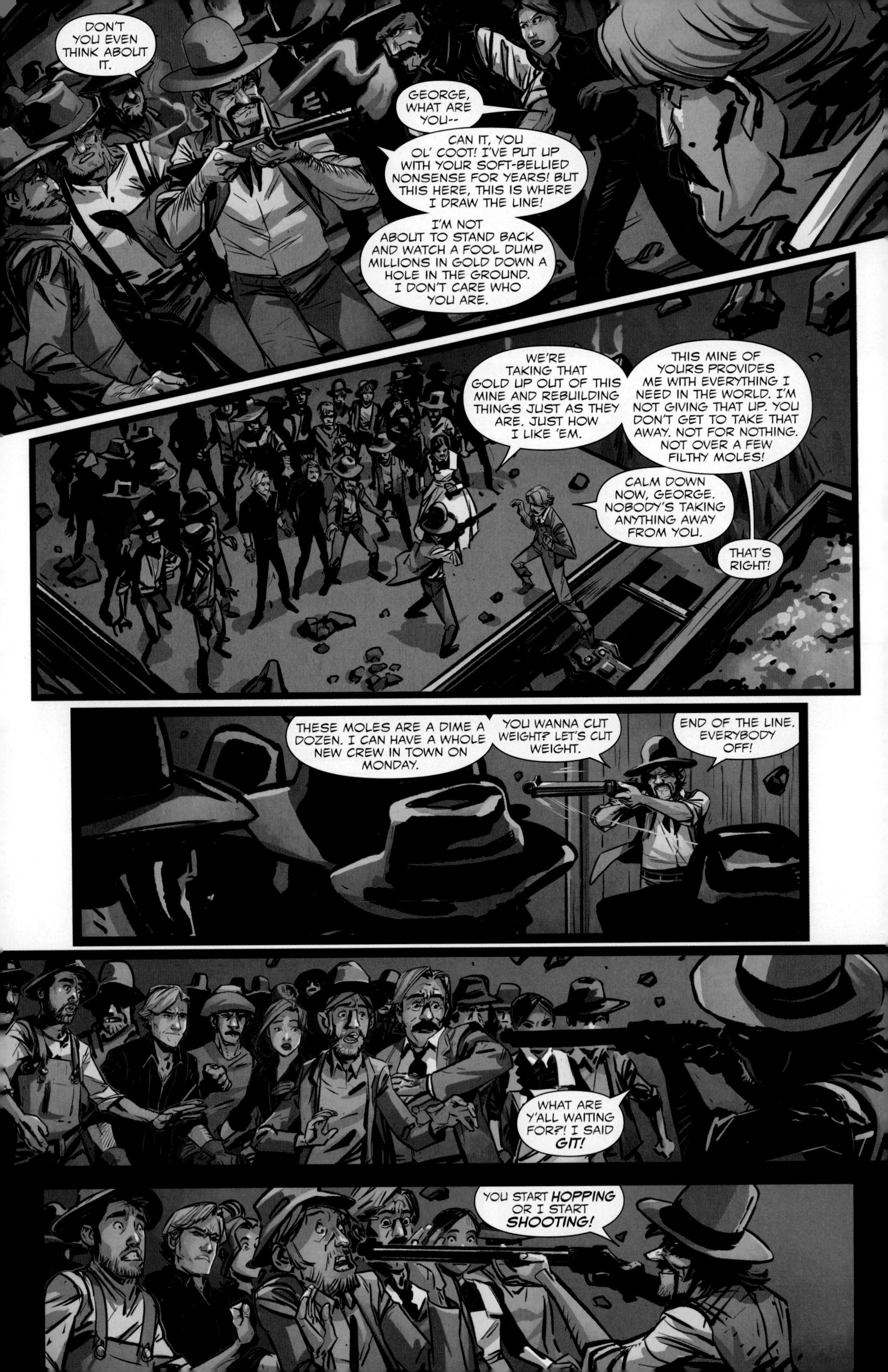
DON'T YOU EVEN THINK ABOUT IT.
GEORGE, WHAT ARE YOU--
CAN IT, YOU OL' COOT! I'VE PUT UP WITH YOUR SOFT-BELLIED NONSENSE FOR YEARS! BUT THIS HERE, THIS IS WHERE I DRAW THE LINE!
I'M NOT ABOUT TO STAND BACK AND WATCH A FOOL DUMP MILLIONS IN GOLD DOWN A HOLE IN THE GROUND. I DON'T CARE WHO YOU ARE.
WE'RE TAKING THAT GOLD UP OUT OF THIS MINE AND REBUILDING THINGS JUST AS THEY ARE. JUST HOW I LIKE 'EM.
THIS MINE OF YOURS PROVIDES ME WITH EVERYTHING I NEED IN THE WORLD. I'M NOT GIVING THAT UP. YOU DON'T GET TO TAKE THAT AWAY. NOT FOR NOTHING. NOT OVER A FEW FILTHY MOLES!
CALM DOWN NOW, GEORGE. NOBODY'S TAKING ANYTHING AWAY FROM YOU.
THAT'S RIGHT!
THESE MOLES ARE A DIME A DOZEN. I CAN HAVE A WHOLE NEW CREW IN TOWN ON MONDAY.
YOU WANNA CUT WEIGHT? LET'S CUT WEIGHT.
END OF THE LINE. EVERYBODY OFF!
WHAT ARE Y'ALL WAITING FOR?! I SAID *GIT!*
YOU START *HOPPING* OR I START *SHOOTING!*

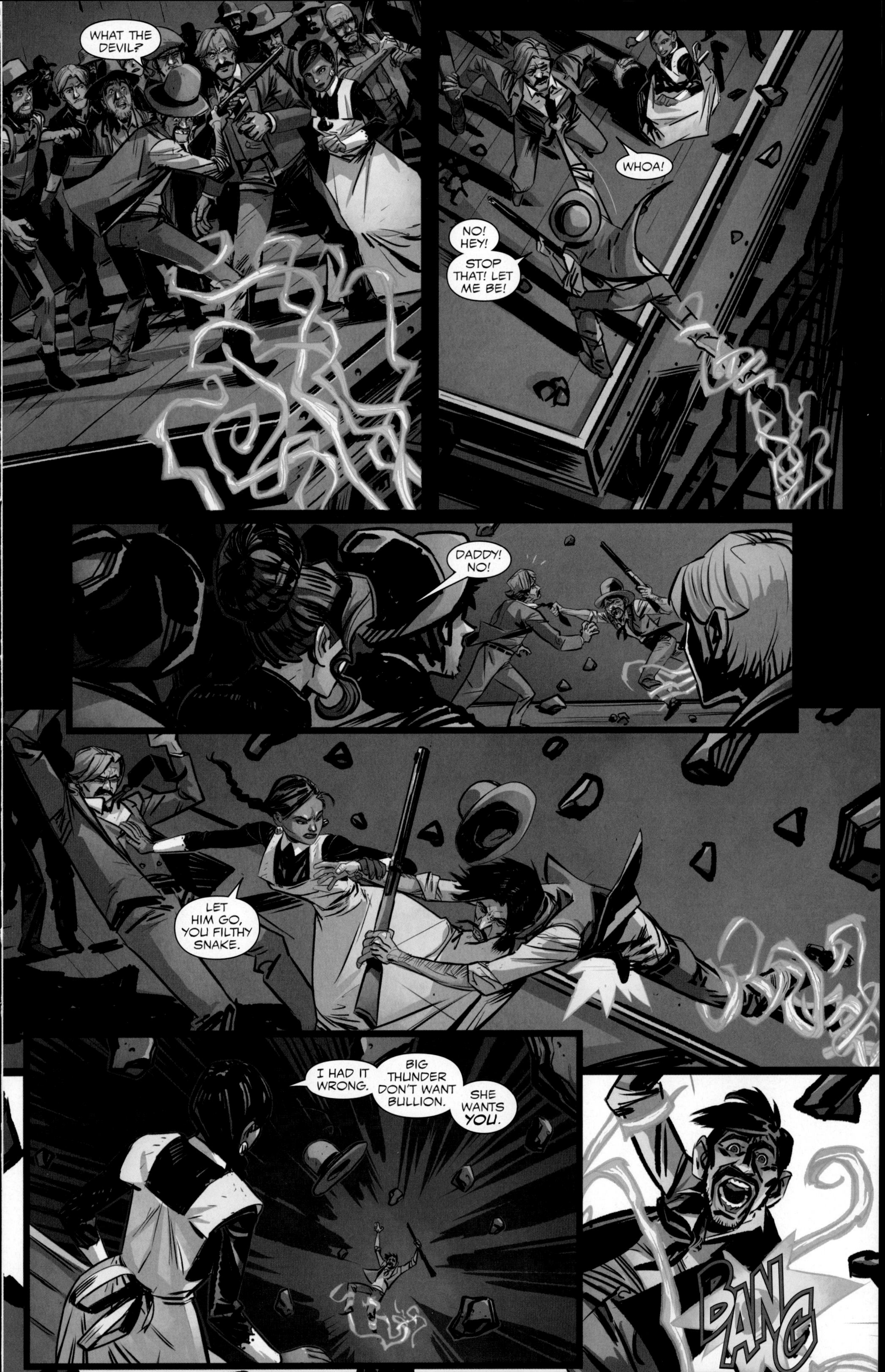
WHAT THE DEVIL?
WHOA!
NO! HEY! STOP THAT! LET ME BE!
DADDY! NO!
LET HIM GO, YOU FILTHY SNAKE.
I HAD IT WRONG.
BIG THUNDER DON'T WANT BULLION.
SHE WANTS YOU.
BANG

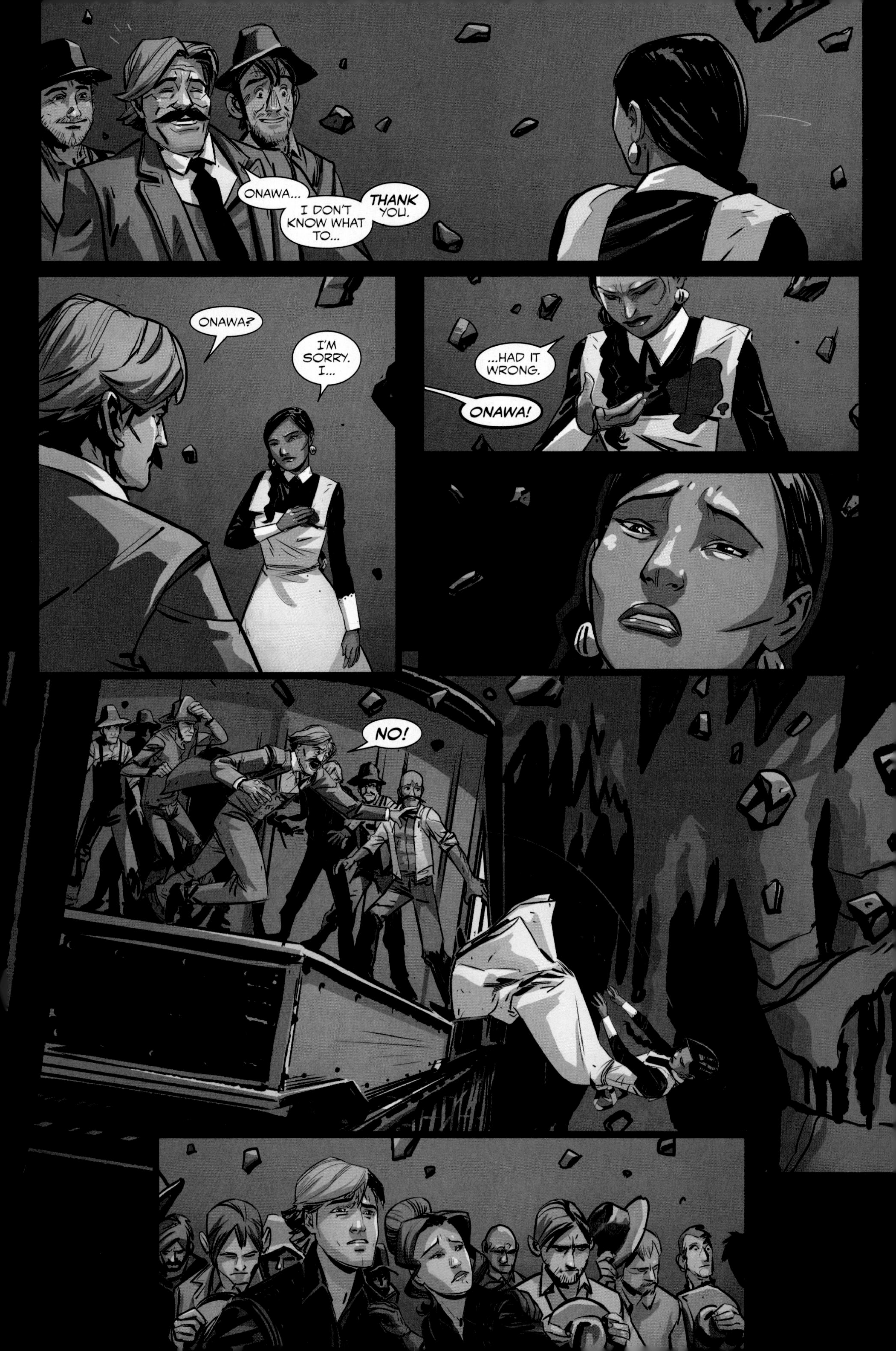
ONAWA... I DON'T KNOW WHAT TO...
THANK YOU.
ONAWA?
I'M SORRY. I...
...HAD IT WRONG.
ONAWA!
NO!

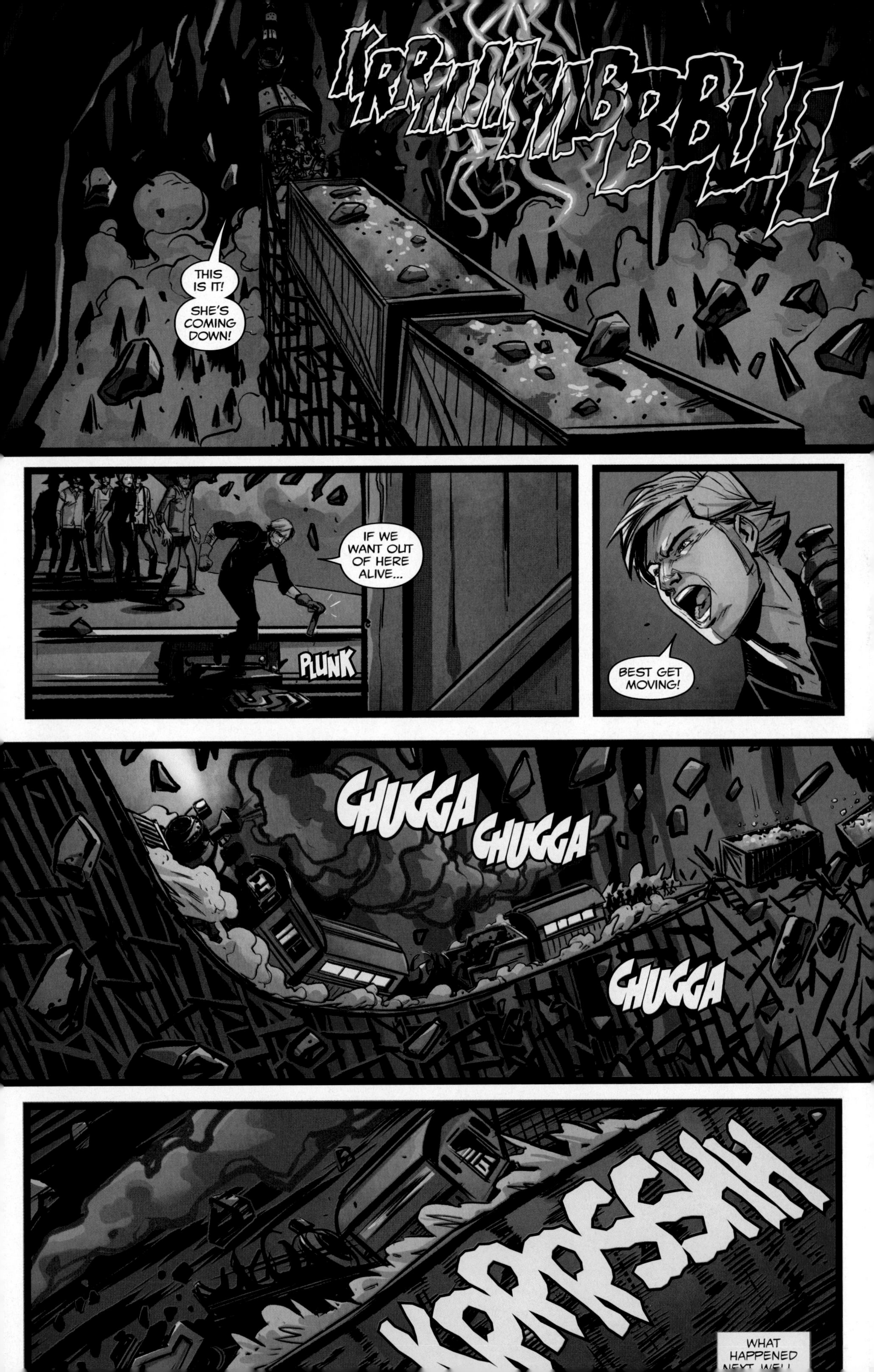
THIS IS IT!
SHE'S COMING DOWN!
IF WE WANT OUT OF HERE ALIVE...
PLUNK
BEST GET MOVING!
CHUGGA
CHUGGA
CHUGGA
WHAT HAPPENED

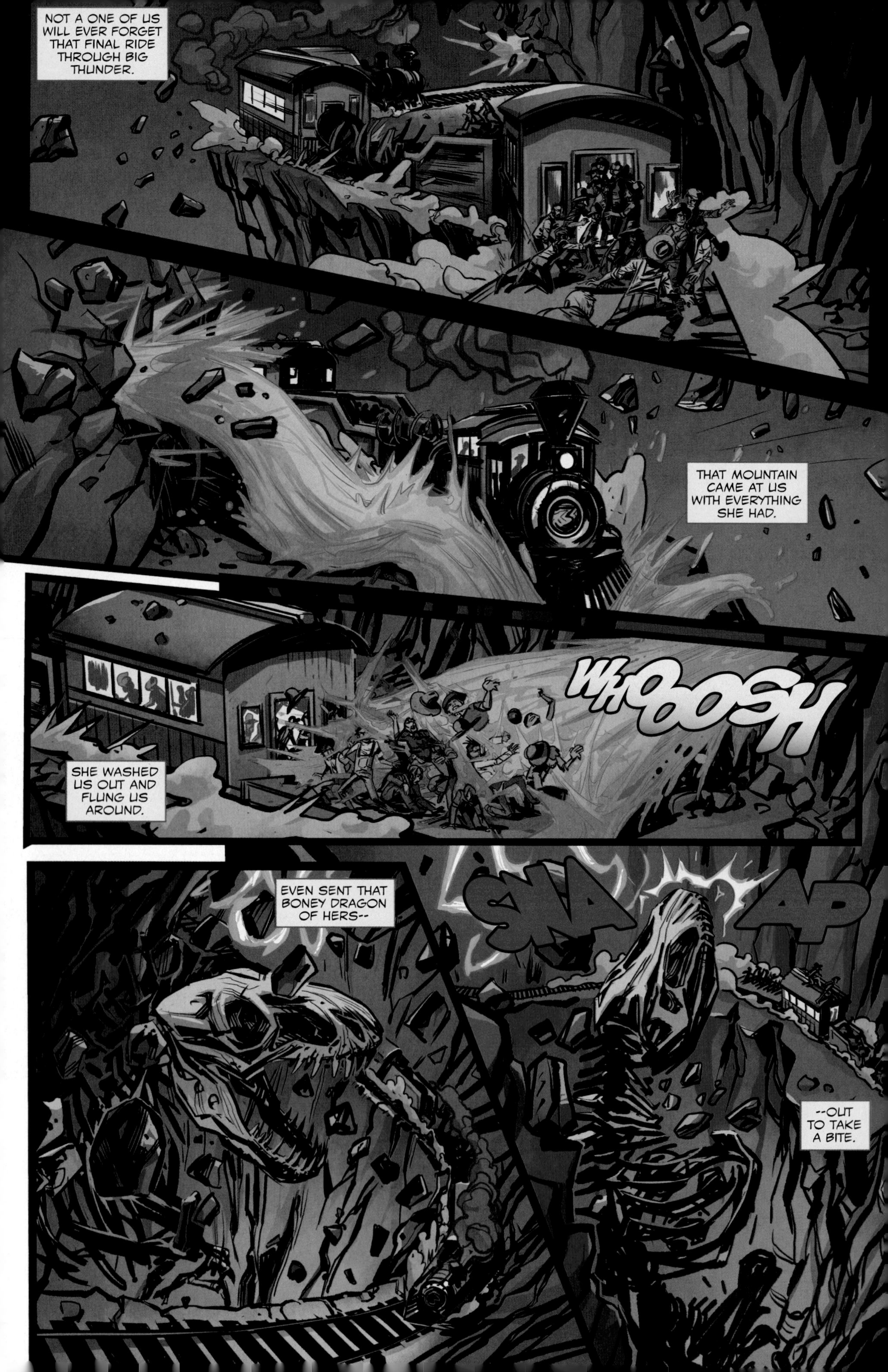
NOT A ONE OF US WILL EVER FORGET THAT FINAL RIDE THROUGH BIG THUNDER.
THAT MOUNTAIN CAME AT US WITH EVERYTHING SHE HAD.
WHOOSH
SHE WASHED US OUT AND FLUNG US AROUND.
EVEN SENT THAT BONEY DRAGON OF HERS--
SNAAP
--OUT TO TAKE A BITE.

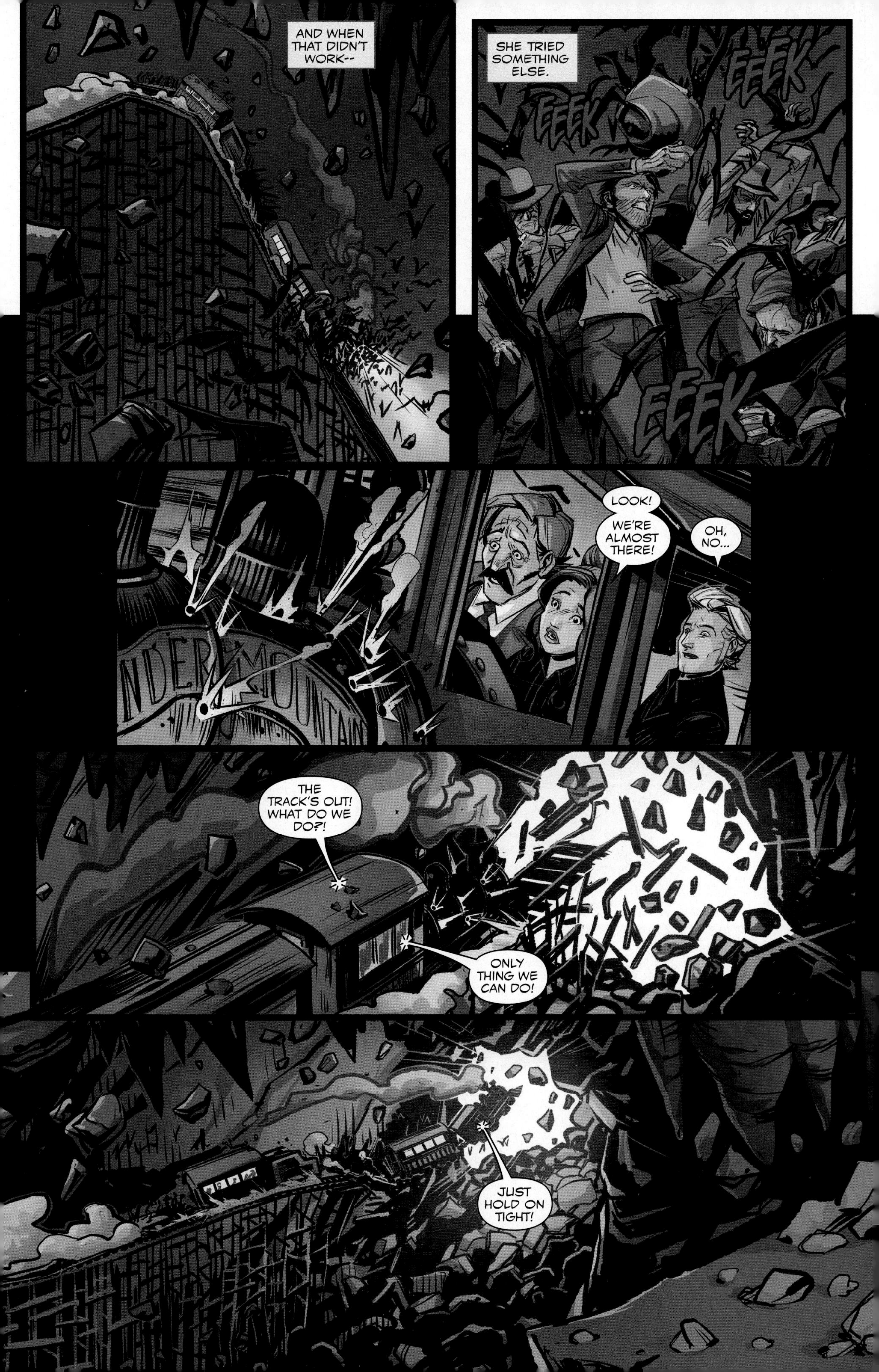
AND WHEN THAT DIDN'T WORK--
SHE TRIED SOMETHING ELSE.
EEEK
EEEK
EEEK
LOOK!
WE'RE ALMOST THERE!
OH, NO...
THE TRACK'S OUT! WHAT DO WE DO?!
ONLY THING WE CAN DO!
JUST HOLD ON TIGHT!

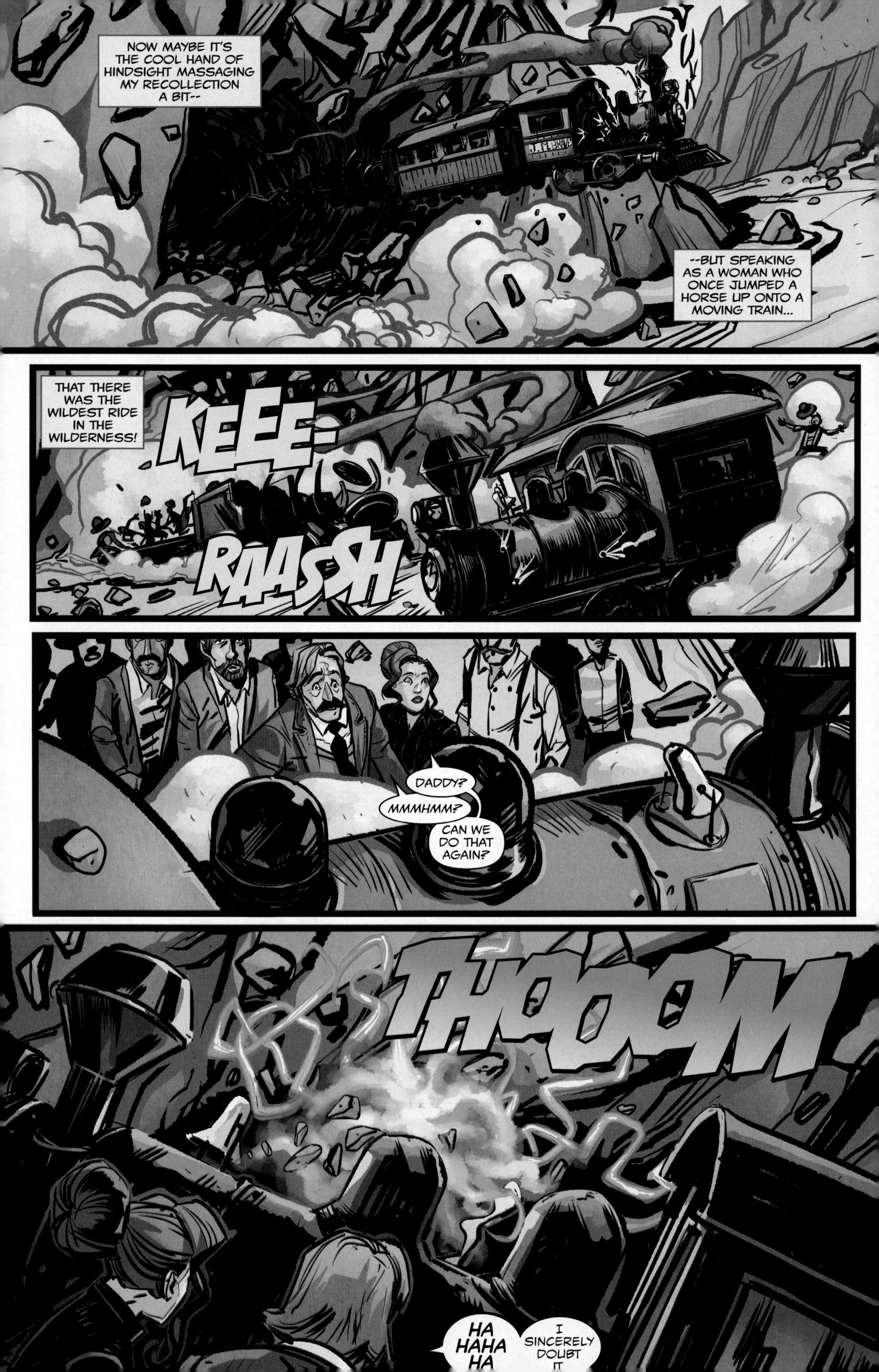
NOW MAYBE IT'S THE COOL HAND OF HINDSIGHT MASSAGING MY RECOLLECTION A BIT--
--BUT SPEAKING AS A WOMAN WHO ONCE JUMPED A HORSE UP ONTO A MOVING TRAIN...
THAT THERE WAS THE WILDEST RIDE IN THE WILDERNESS!
KEEE-
RAASSH
DADDY?
MMMHMM?
CAN WE DO THAT AGAIN?
THOOOM
HA HAHA HA
I SINCERELY DOUBT IT

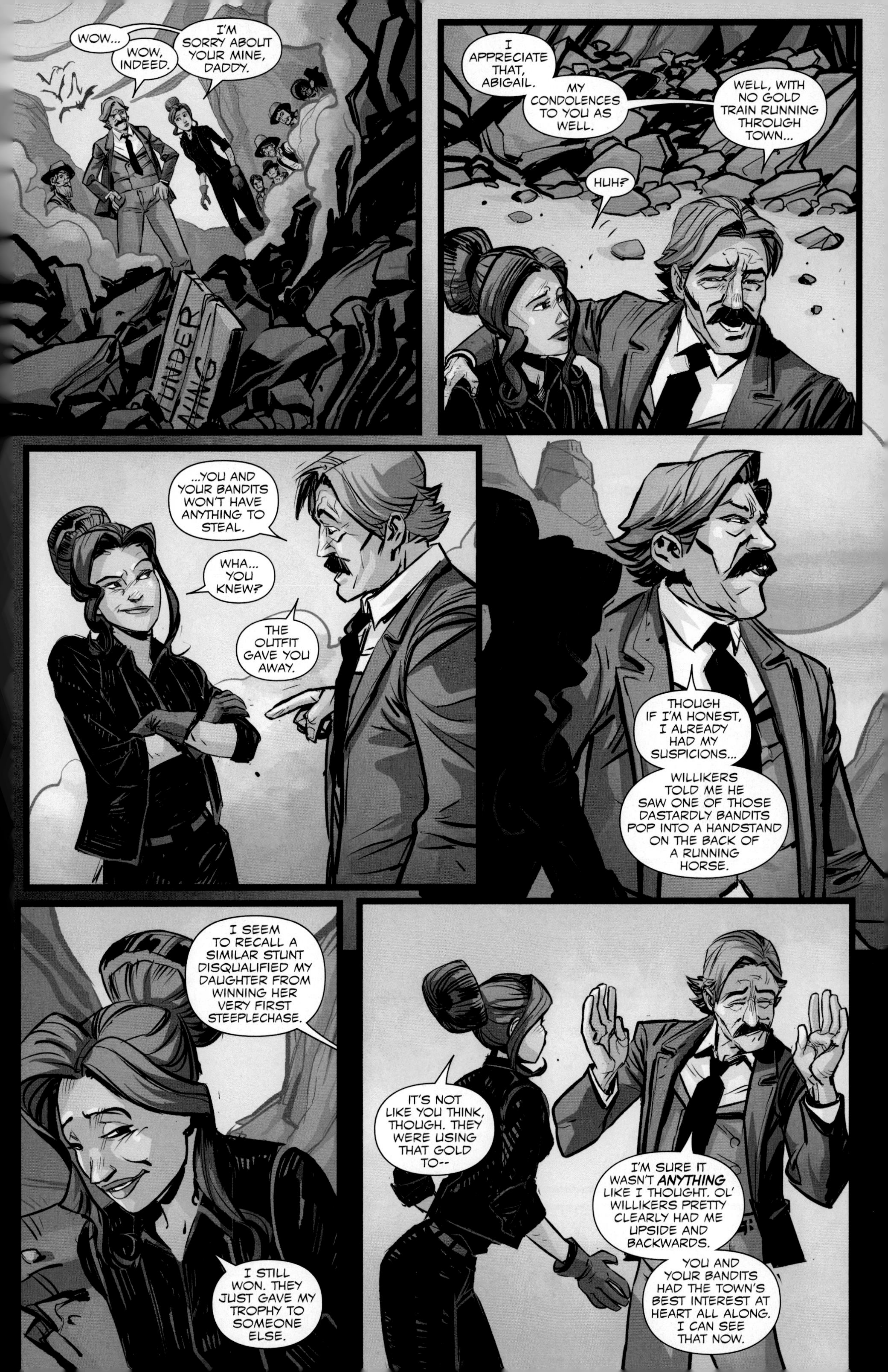

WOW...
WOW, INDEED.
I'M SORRY ABOUT YOUR MINE, DADDY.
UNDER
ING
I APPRECIATE THAT, ABIGAIL.
MY CONDOLENCES TO YOU AS WELL.
HUH?
WELL, WITH NO GOLD TRAIN RUNNING THROUGH TOWN...
...YOU AND YOUR BANDITS WON'T HAVE ANYTHING TO STEAL.
WHA... YOU KNEW?
THE OUTFIT GAVE YOU AWAY.
THOUGH IF I'M HONEST, I ALREADY HAD MY SUSPICIONS...
WILLIKERS TOLD ME HE SAW ONE OF THOSE DASTARDLY BANDITS POP INTO A HANDSTAND ON THE BACK OF A RUNNING HORSE.
I SEEM TO RECALL A SIMILAR STUNT DISQUALIFIED MY DAUGHTER FROM WINNING HER VERY FIRST STEEPLECHASE.
I STILL WON. THEY JUST GAVE MY TROPHY TO SOMEONE ELSE.
IT'S NOT LIKE YOU THINK, THOUGH. THEY WERE USING THAT GOLD TO--
I'M SURE IT WASN'T ***ANYTHING*** LIKE I THOUGHT. OL' WILLIKERS PRETTY CLEARLY HAD ME UPSIDE AND BACKWARDS.
YOU AND YOUR BANDITS HAD THE TOWN'S BEST INTEREST AT HEART ALL ALONG. I CAN SEE THAT NOW.

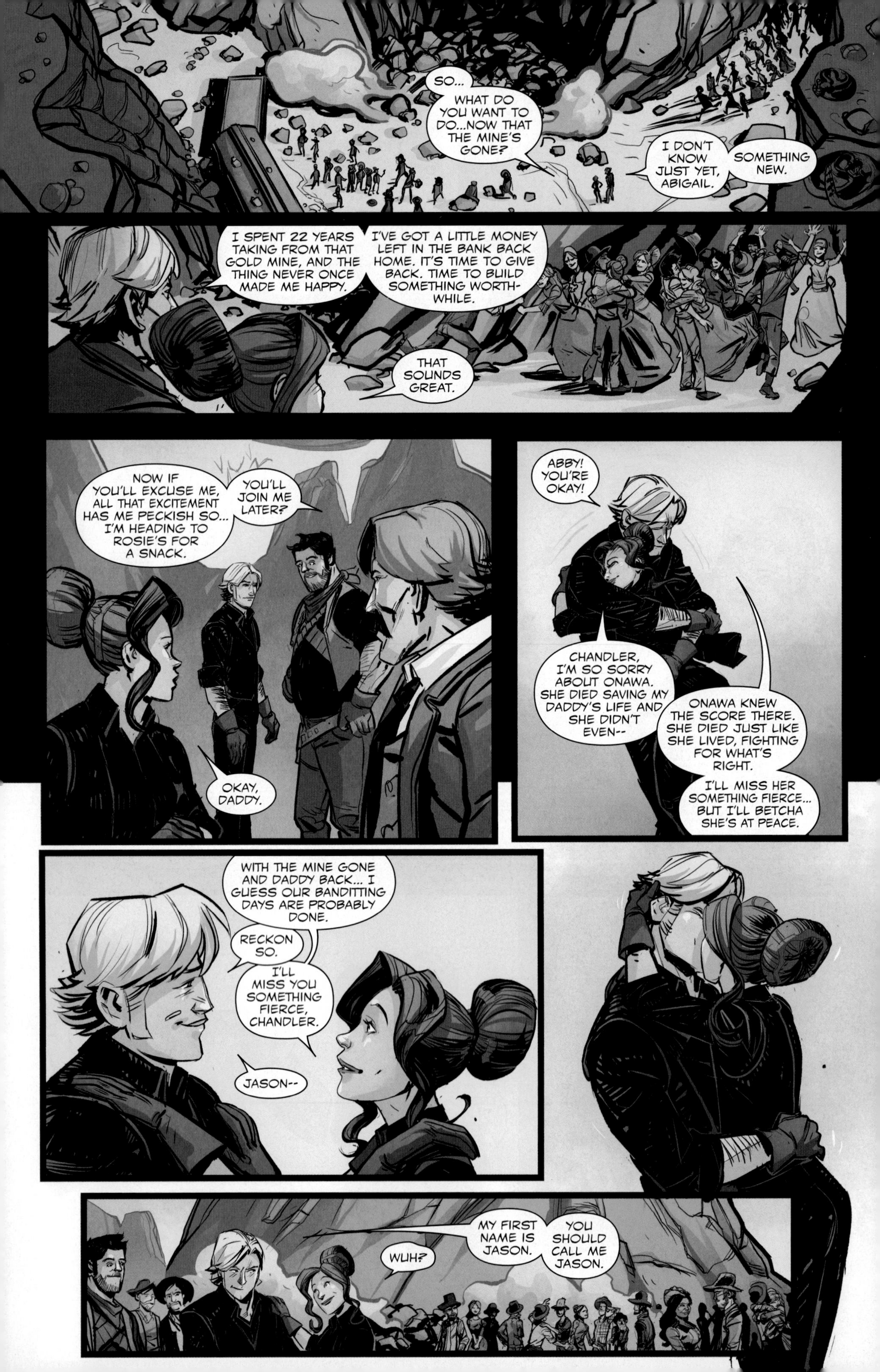
SO...
WHAT DO YOU WANT TO DO...NOW THAT THE MINE'S GONE?
I DON'T KNOW JUST YET, ABIGAIL.
SOMETHING NEW.
I SPENT 22 YEARS TAKING FROM THAT GOLD MINE, AND THE THING NEVER ONCE MADE ME HAPPY.
I'VE GOT A LITTLE MONEY LEFT IN THE BANK BACK HOME. IT'S TIME TO GIVE BACK. TIME TO BUILD SOMETHING WORTH-WHILE.
THAT SOUNDS GREAT.
NOW IF YOU'LL EXCUSE ME, ALL THAT EXCITEMENT HAS ME PECKISH SO... I'M HEADING TO ROSIE'S FOR A SNACK.
YOU'LL JOIN ME LATER?
OKAY, DADDY.
ABBY! YOU'RE OKAY!
CHANDLER, I'M SO SORRY ABOUT ONAWA. SHE DIED SAVING MY DADDY'S LIFE AND SHE DIDN'T EVEN--
ONAWA KNEW THE SCORE THERE. SHE DIED JUST LIKE SHE LIVED, FIGHTING FOR WHAT'S RIGHT.
I'LL MISS HER SOMETHING FIERCE... BUT I'LL BETCHA SHE'S AT PEACE.
WITH THE MINE GONE AND DADDY BACK... I GUESS OUR BANDITTING DAYS ARE PROBABLY DONE.
RECKON SO.
I'LL MISS YOU SOMETHING FIERCE, CHANDLER.
JASON--
WUH?
MY FIRST NAME IS JASON.
YOU SHOULD CALL ME JASON.

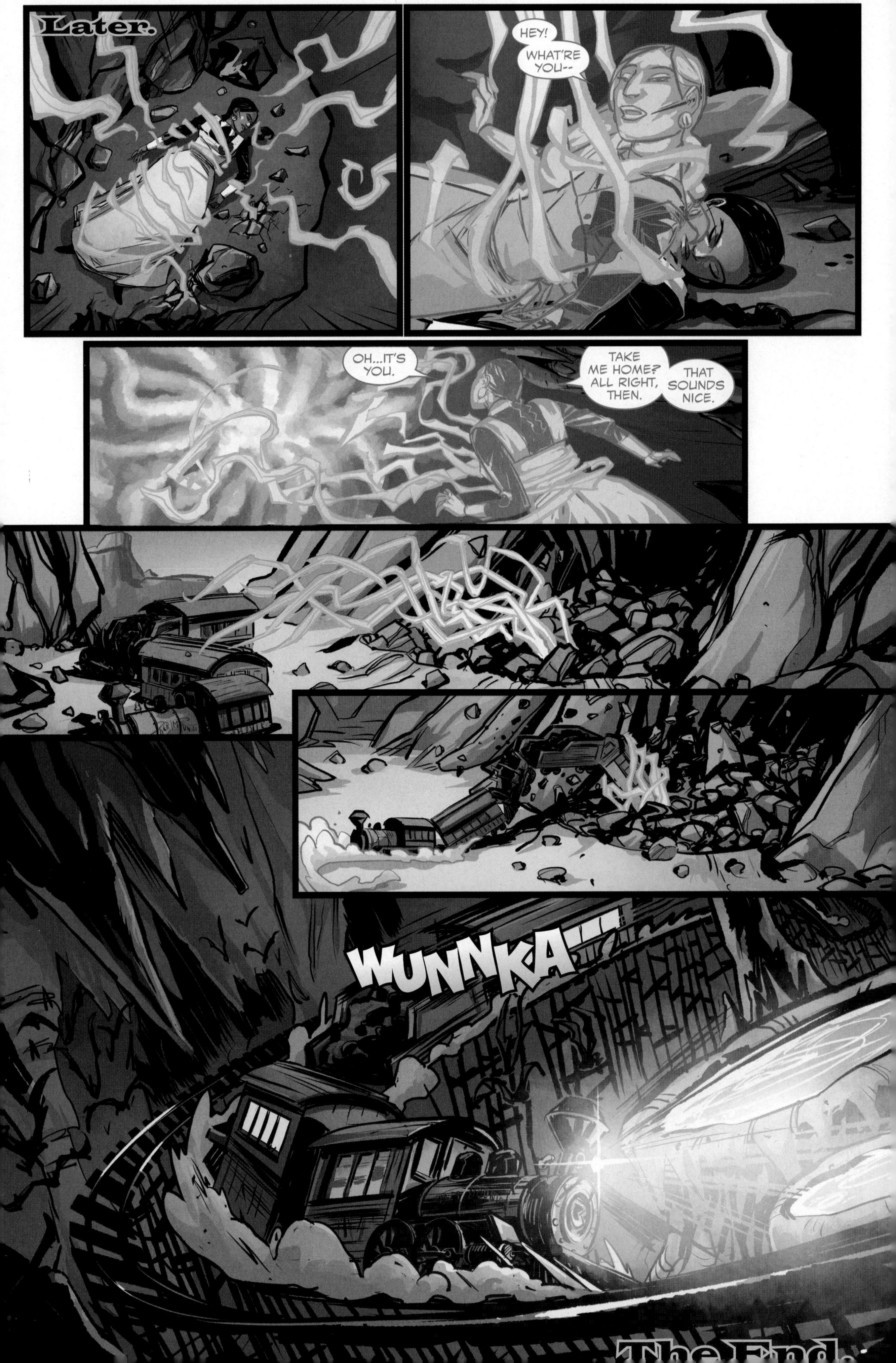
Later.
HEY!
WHAT'RE YOU--
OH...IT'S YOU.
TAKE ME HOME? ALL RIGHT, THEN.
THAT SOUNDS NICE.
WUNNKA
The End.

~ Big Thunder Mountain Railroad Designs ~

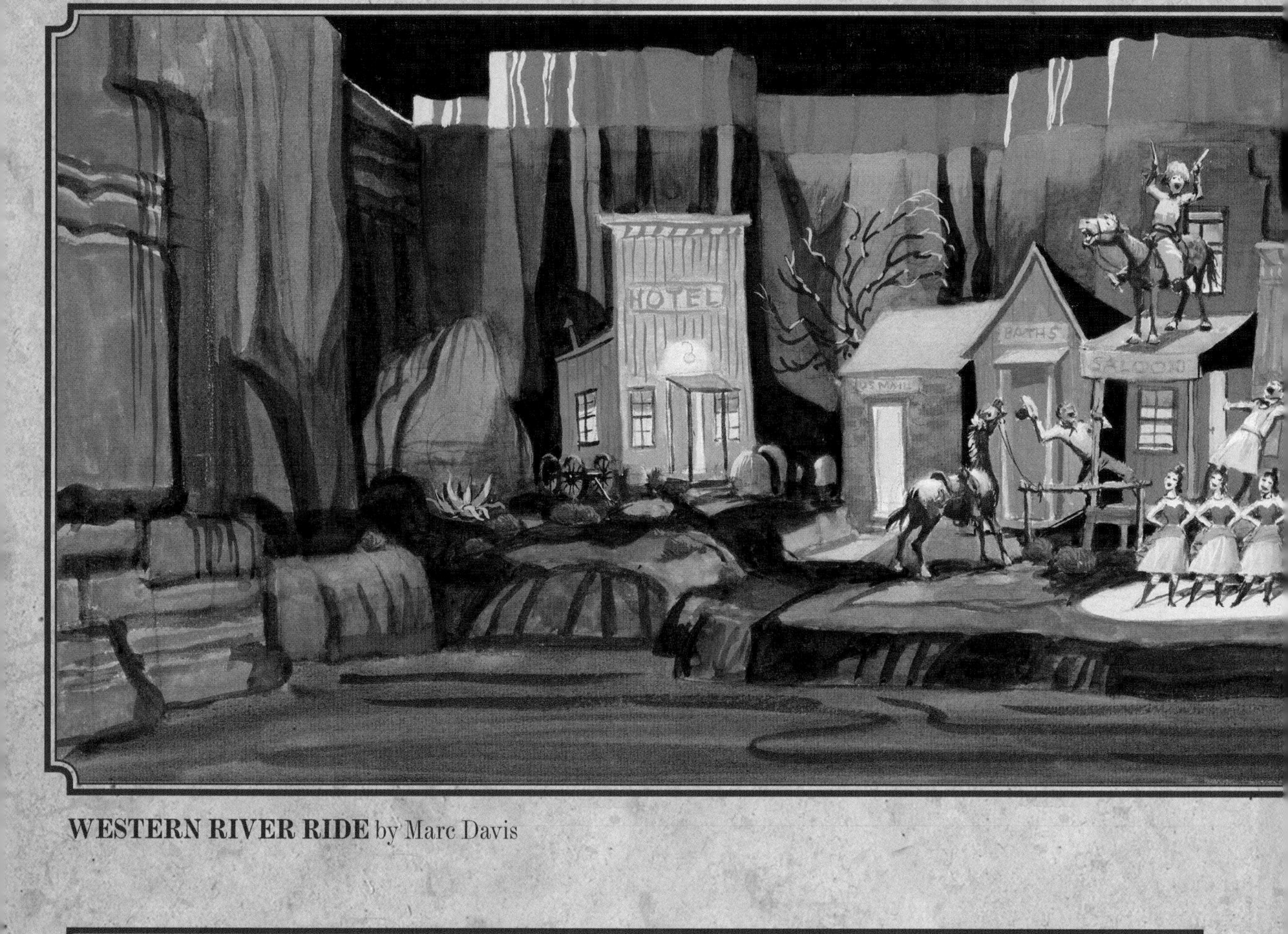
HOTEL
BATHS
SALOON

WESTERN RIVER RIDE by Marc Davis

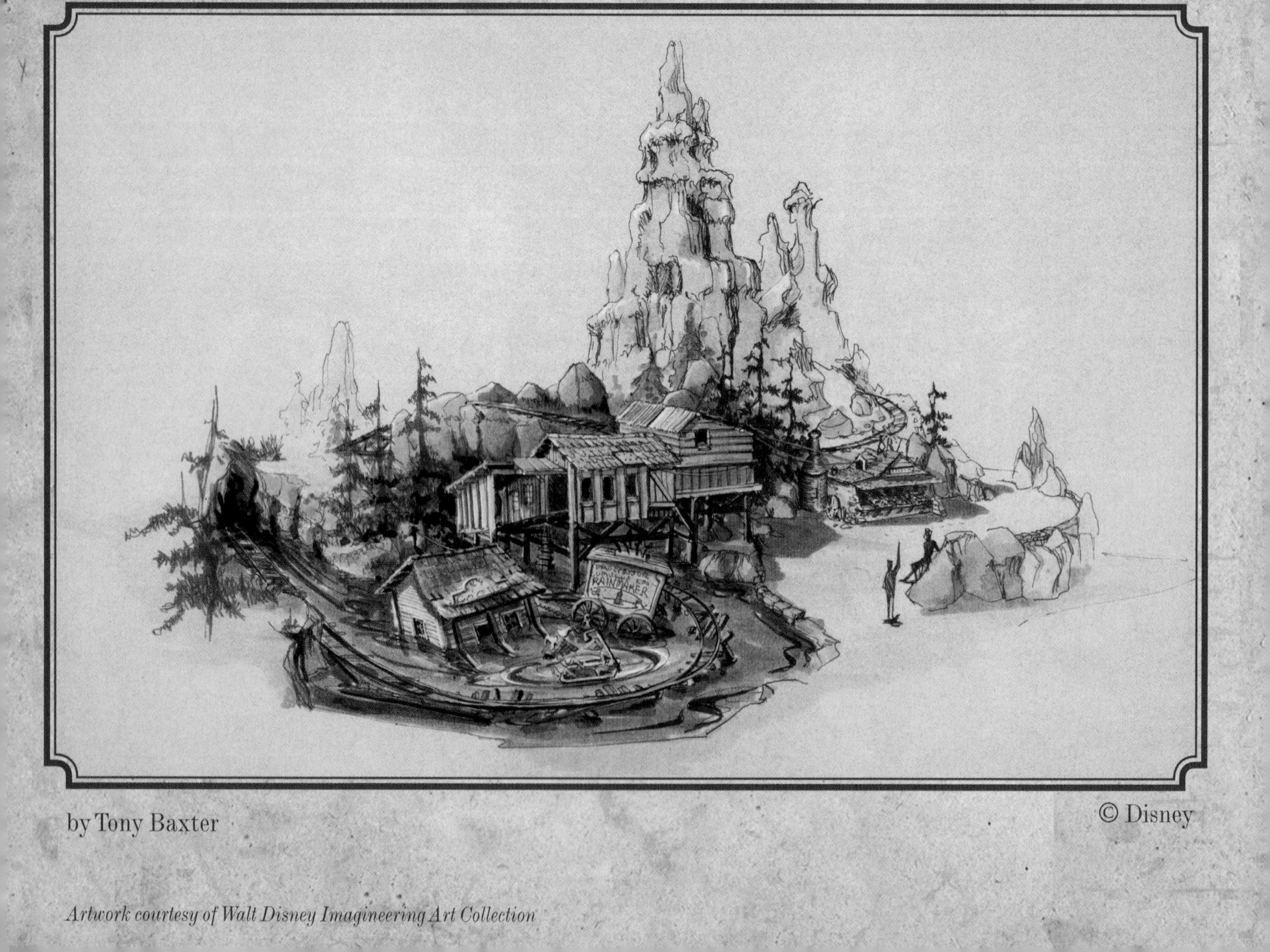

by Tony Baxter

Artwork courtesy of Walt Disney Imagineering Art Collection

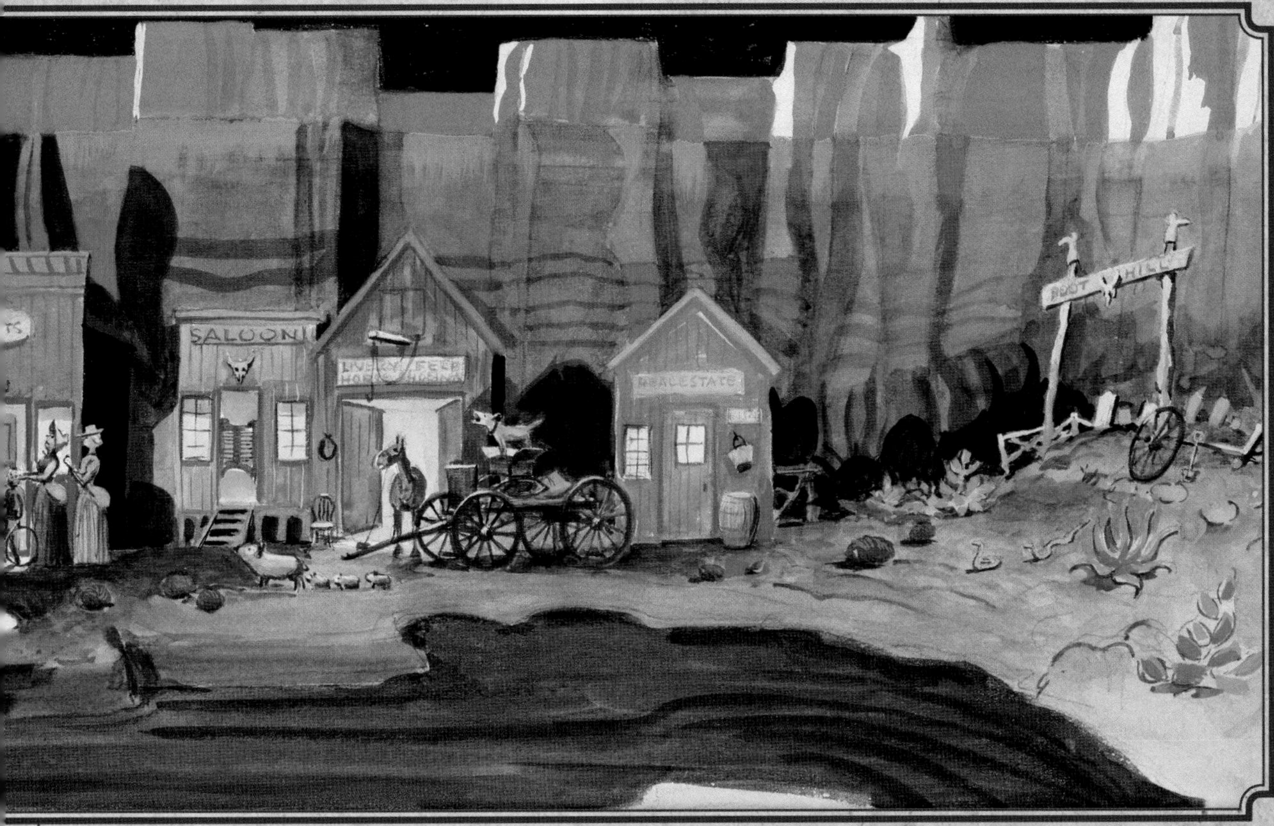
SALOON

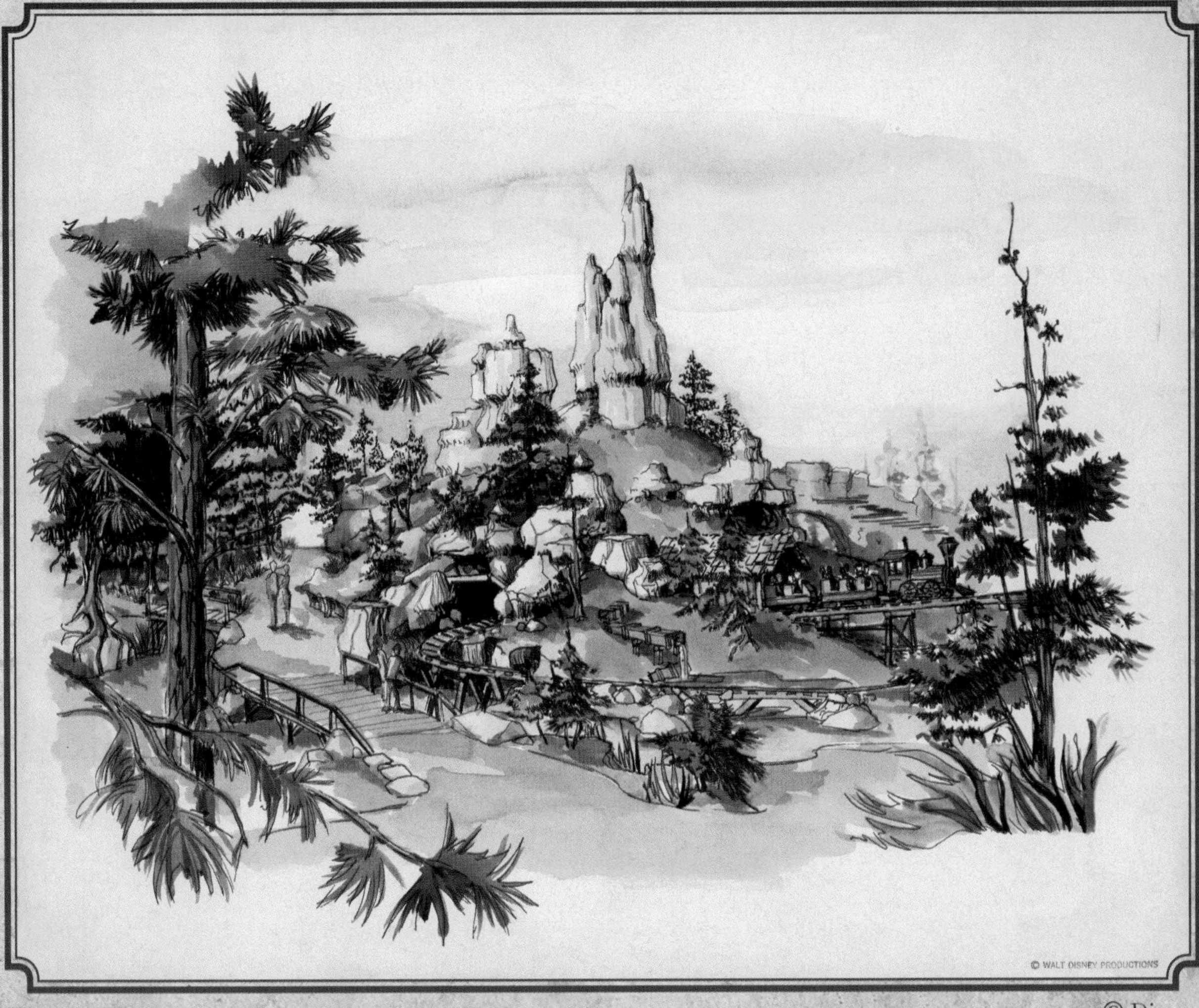
© WALT DISNEY PRODUCTIONS

by Tony Baxter

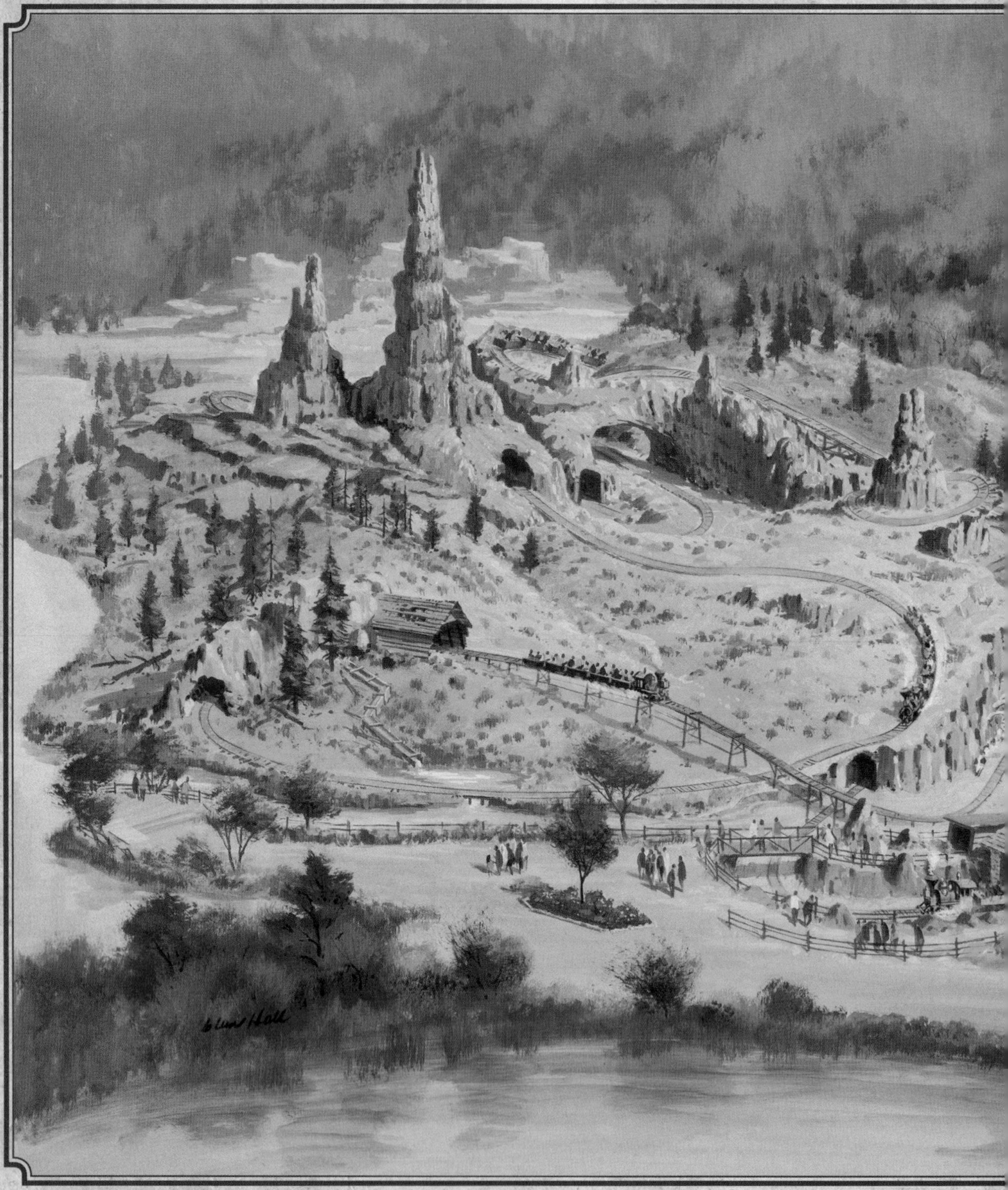
Clem Hall
by Clem Hall

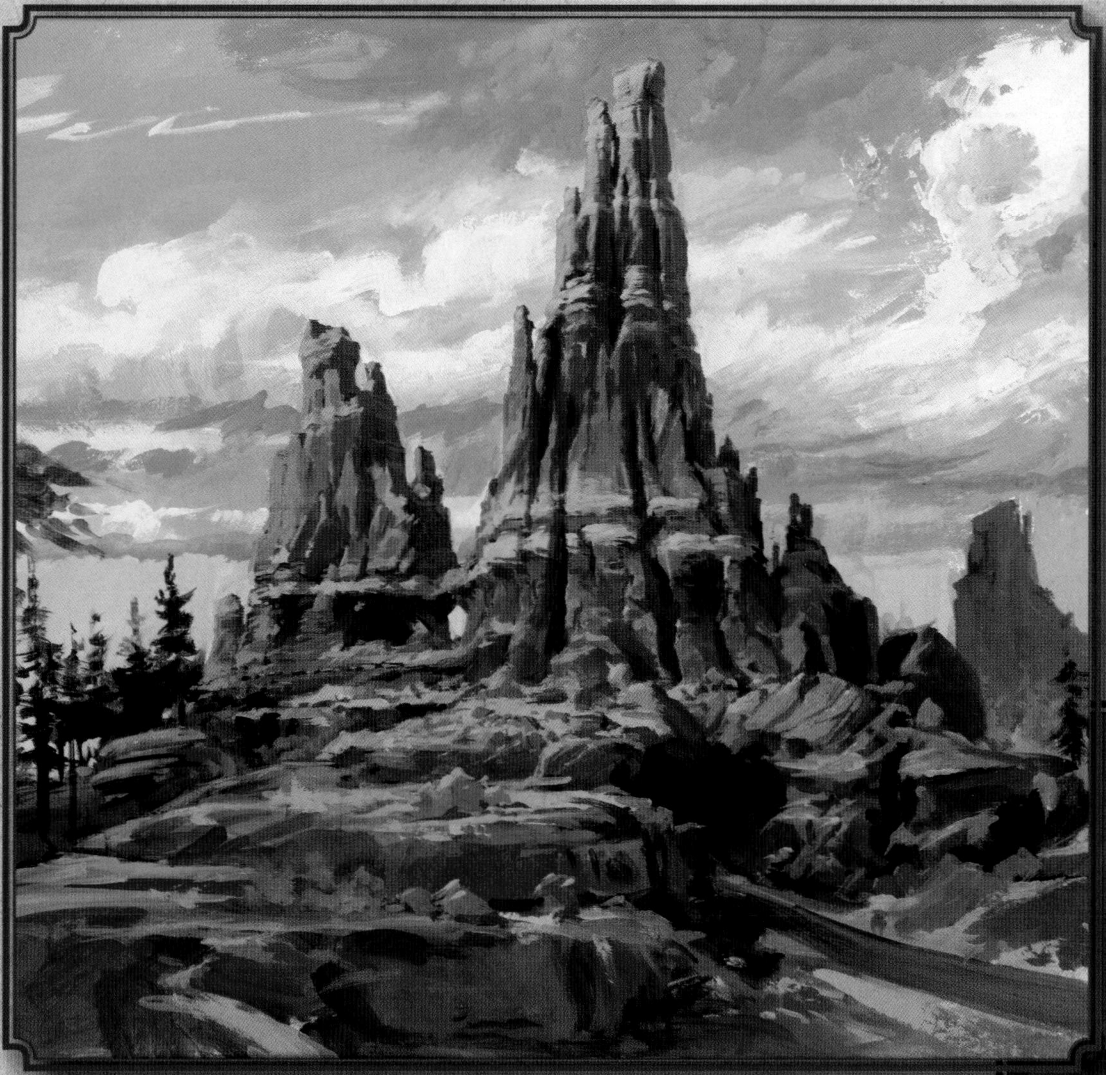

by Dan Goozee

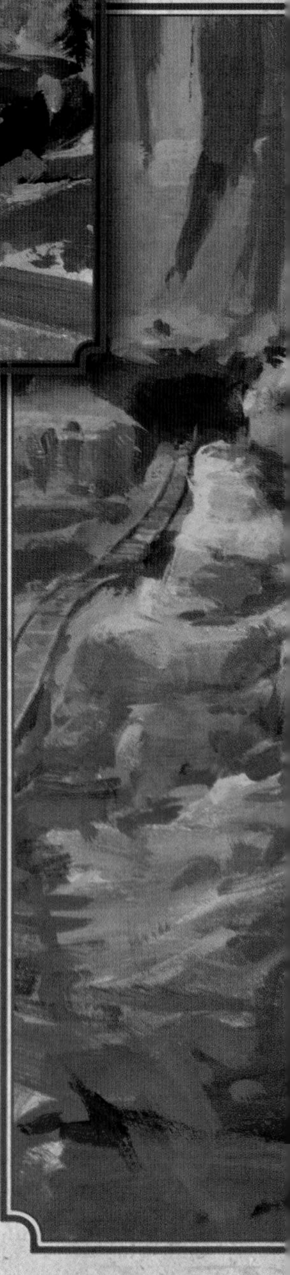

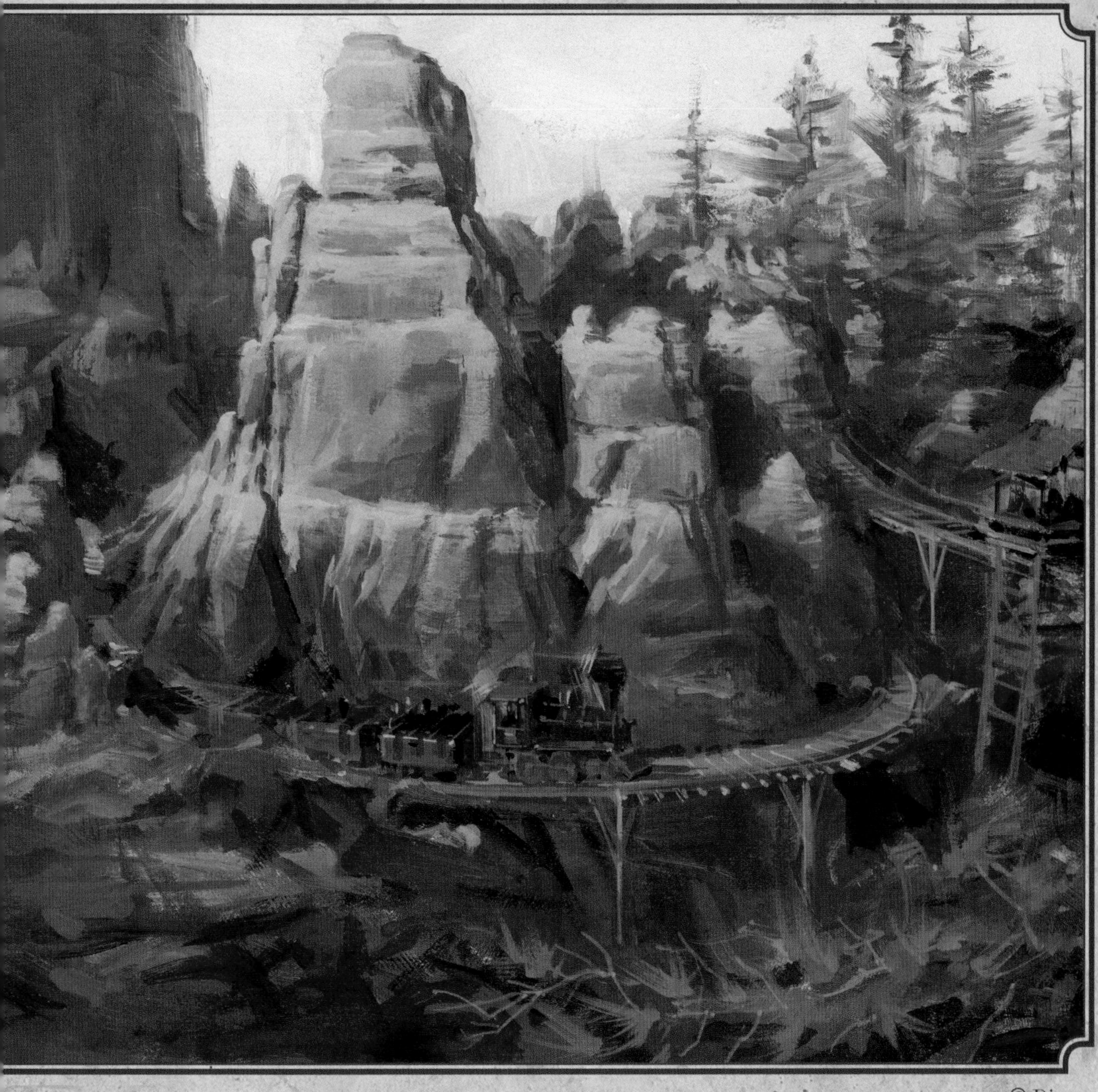

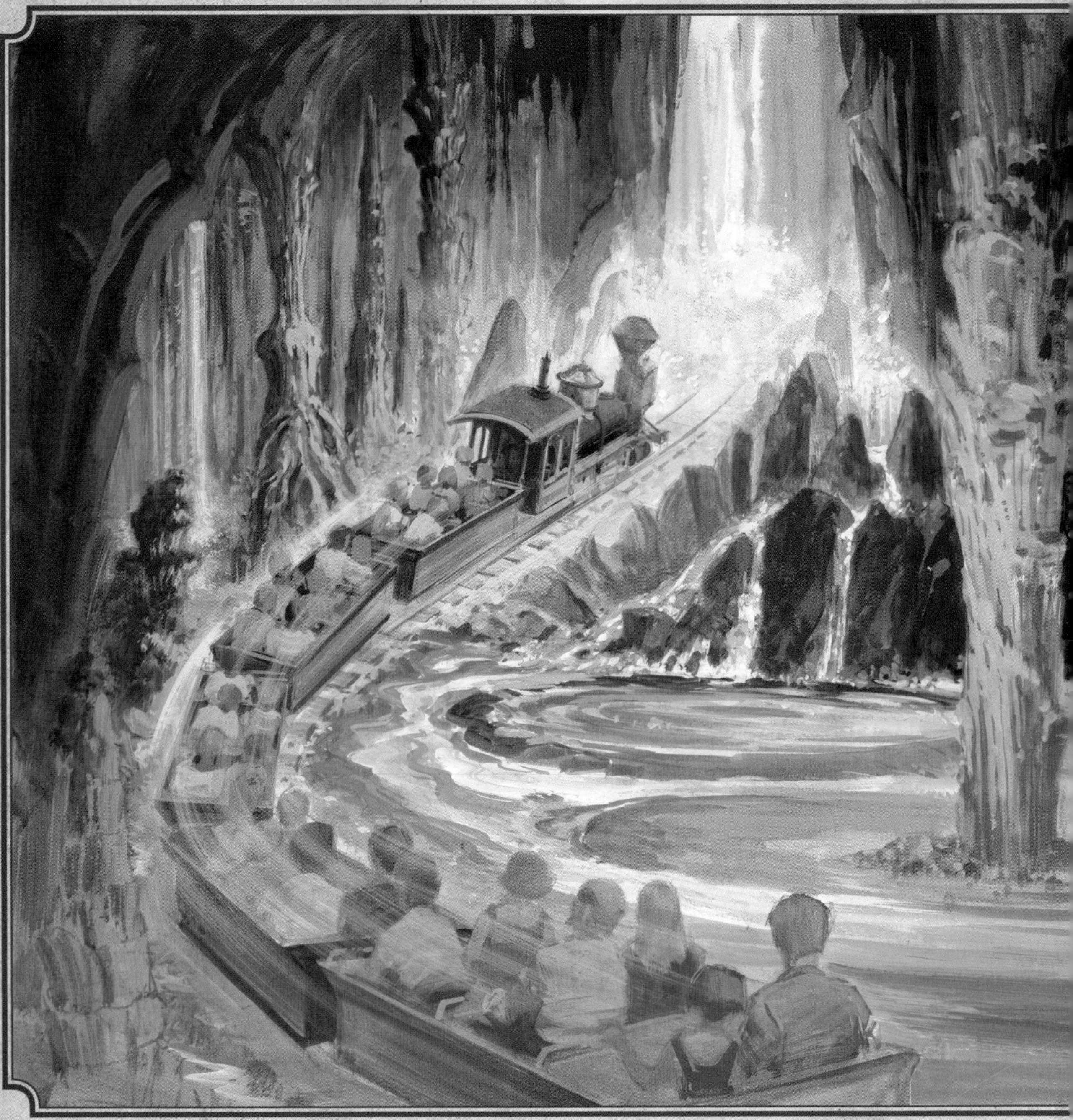

by Clem Hall

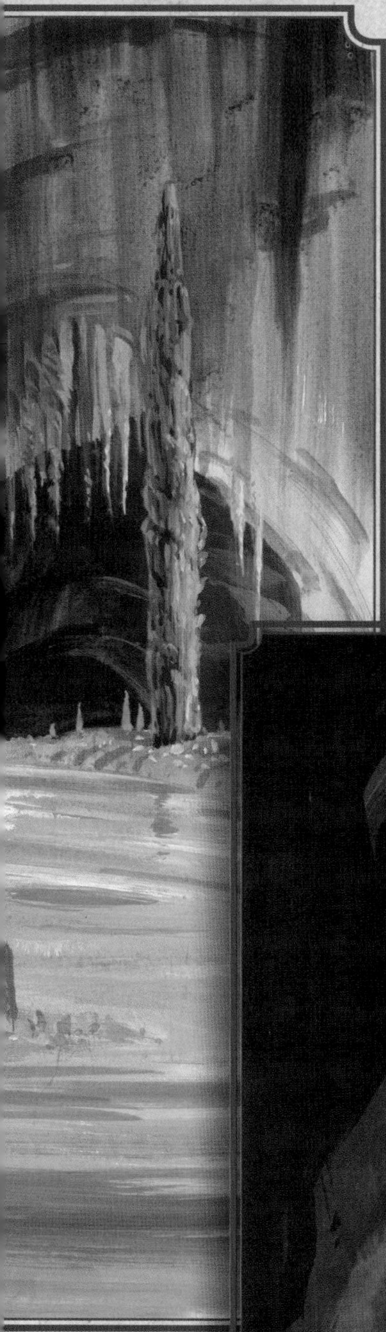

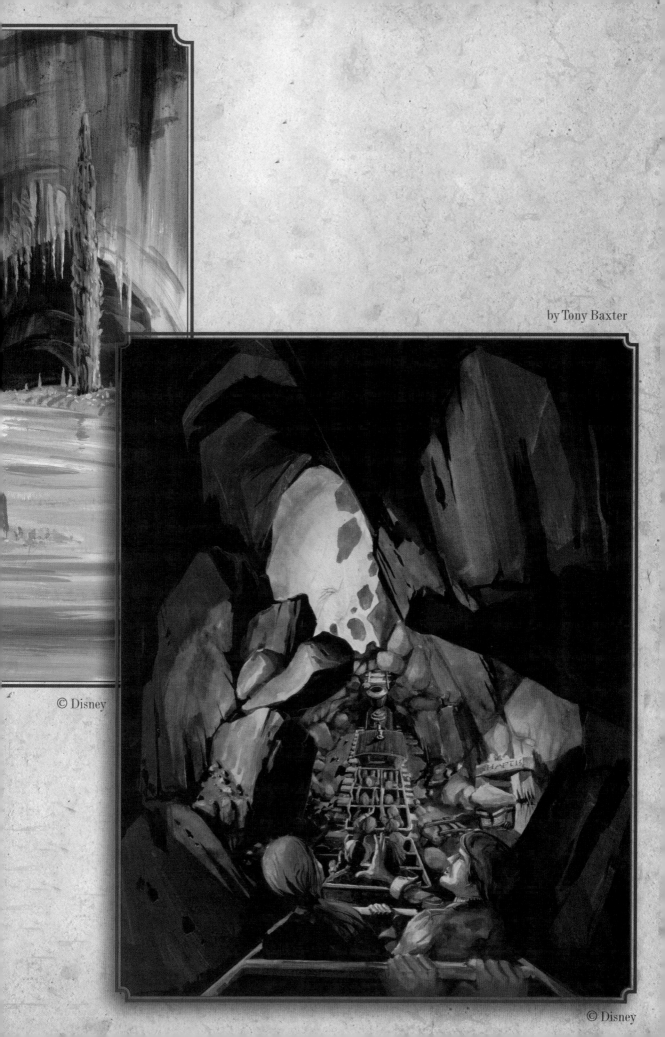

by Tony Baxter

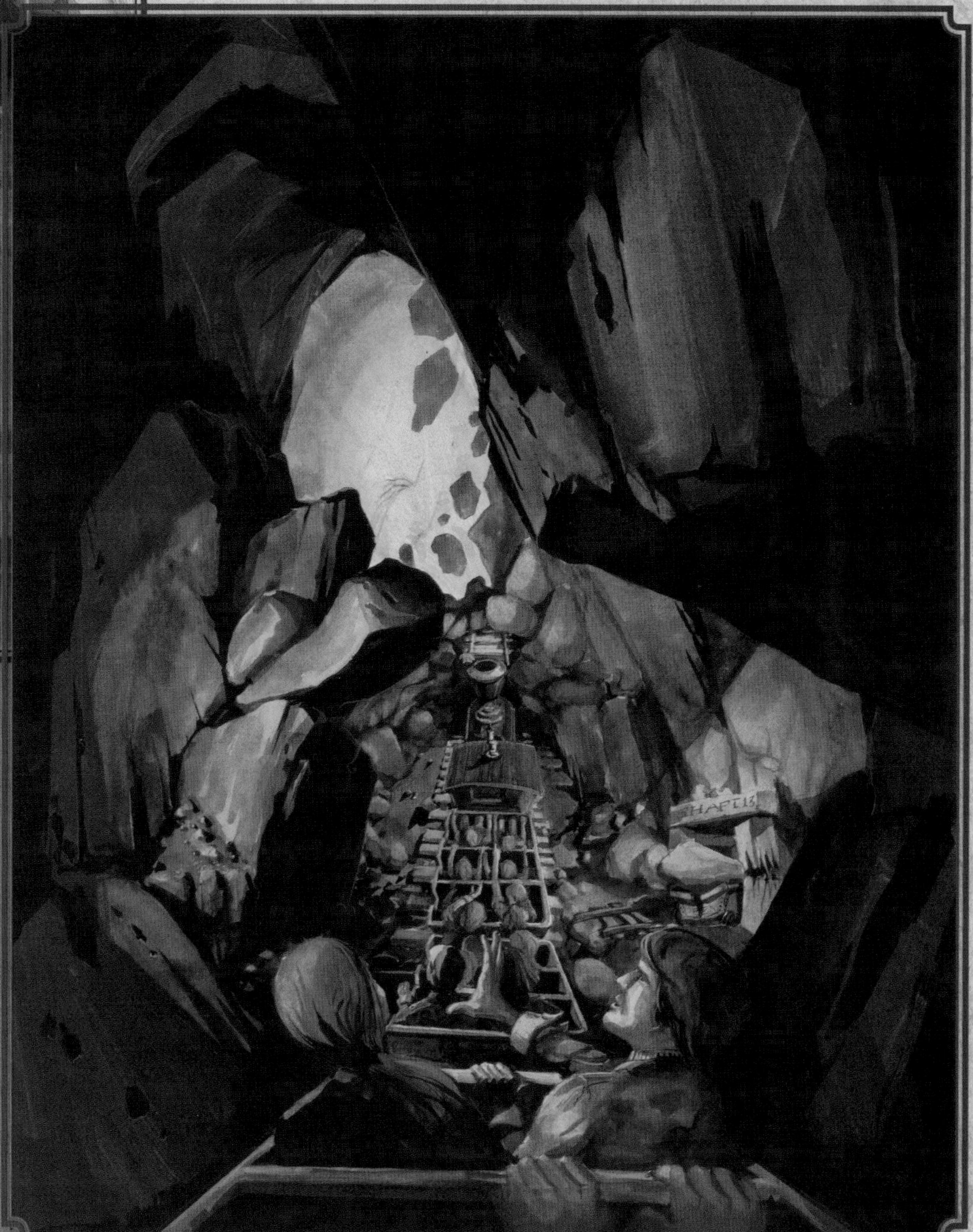

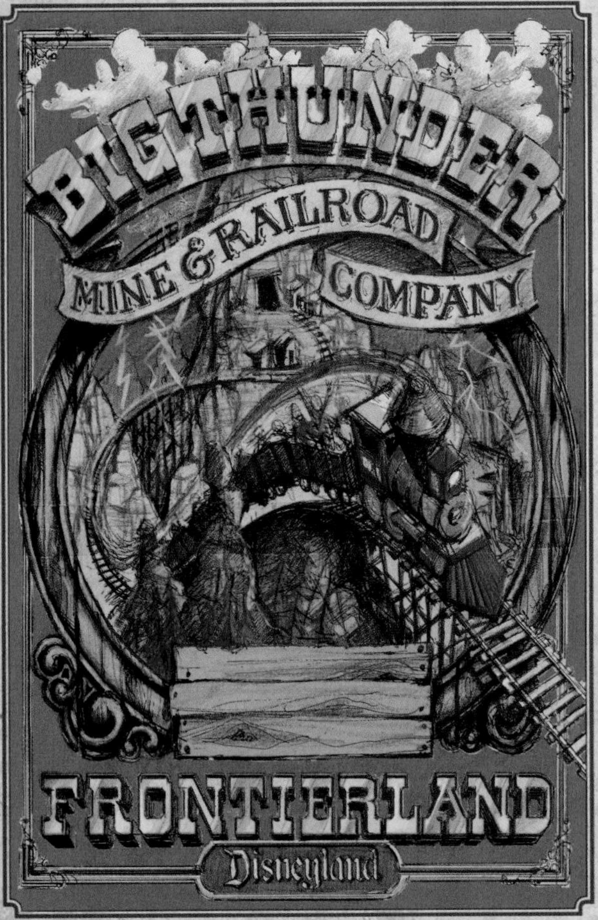
BIG THUNDER
MINE & RAILROAD COMPANY
FRONTIERLAND
Disneyland

by Jim Michaelson © Disney

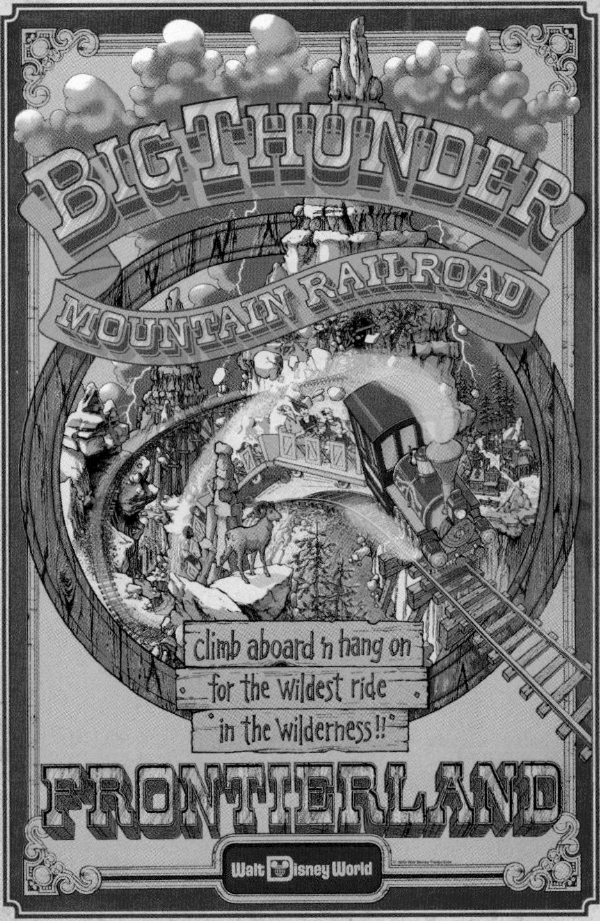
BIG THUNDER
MOUNTAIN RAILROAD
climb aboard 'n hang on
for the wildest ride
"in the wilderness!!"
FRONTIERLAND
Walt Disney World

by Jim Michaelson © Disney

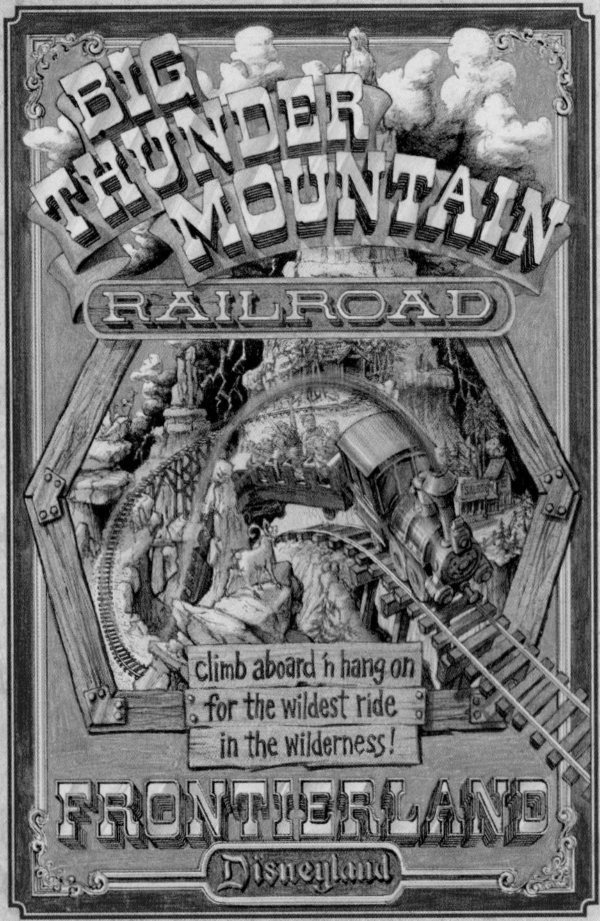
BIG THUNDER MOUNTAIN
RAILROAD
climb aboard 'n hang on
for the wildest ride
in the wilderness!
FRONTIERLAND
Disneyland

by Jim Michaelson, Rudy Lord & Greg Paul © Disney

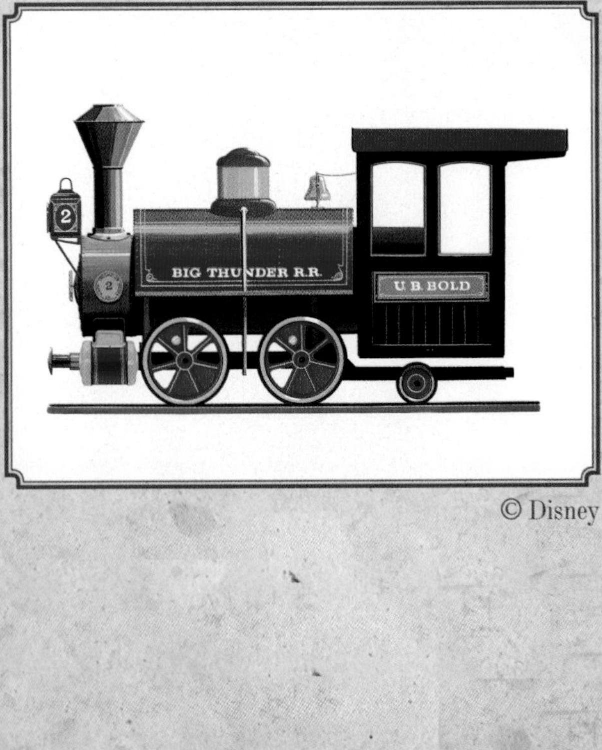
2
BIG THUNDER R.R.
U.B. BOLD

© Disney

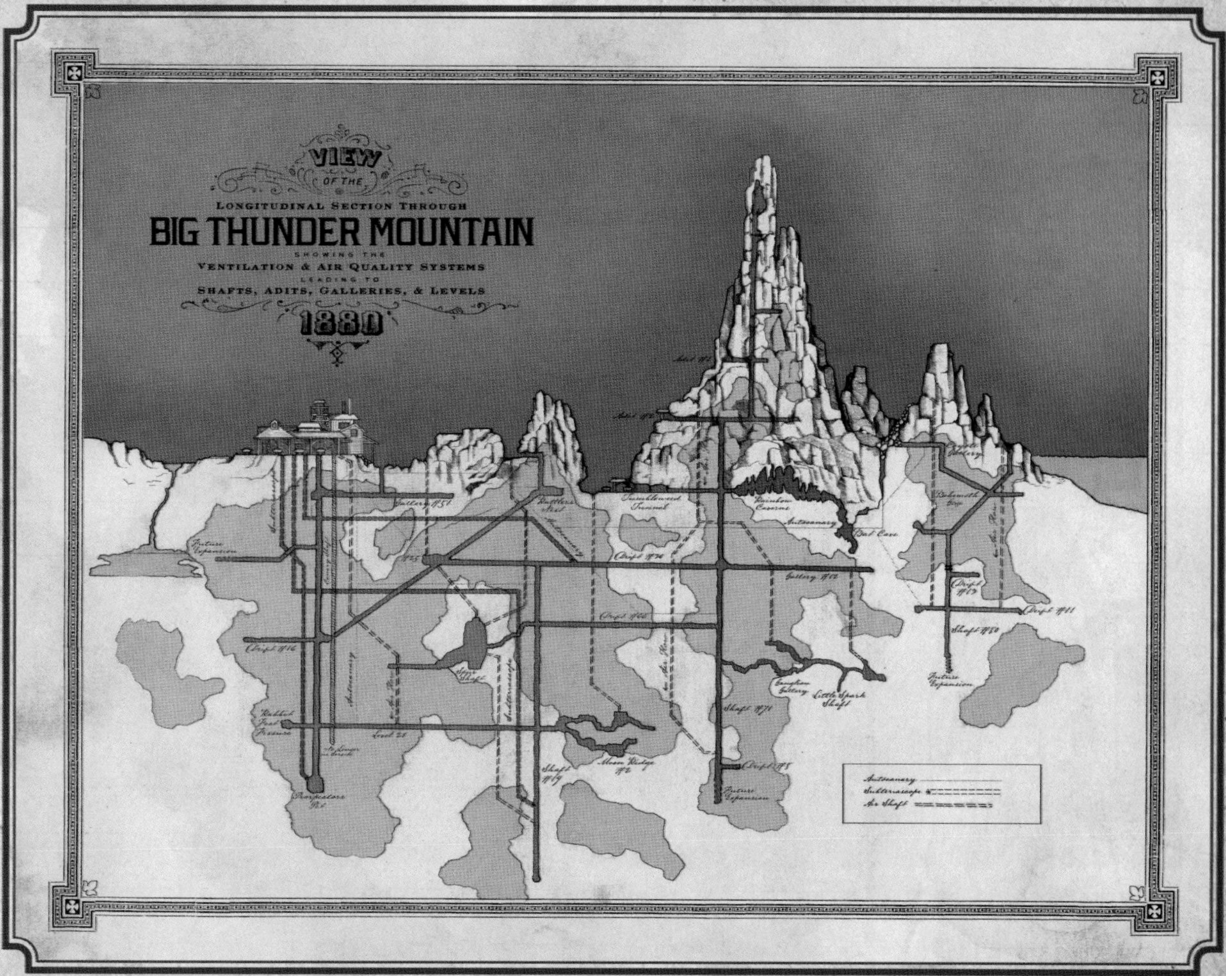
VIEW
OF THE
LONGITUDINAL SECTION THROUGH
BIG THUNDER MOUNTAIN
SHOWING THE
VENTILATION & AIR QUALITY SYSTEMS
LEADING TO
SHAFTS, ADITS, GALLERIES, & LEVELS
1880

by Jim Heffron & Carline May

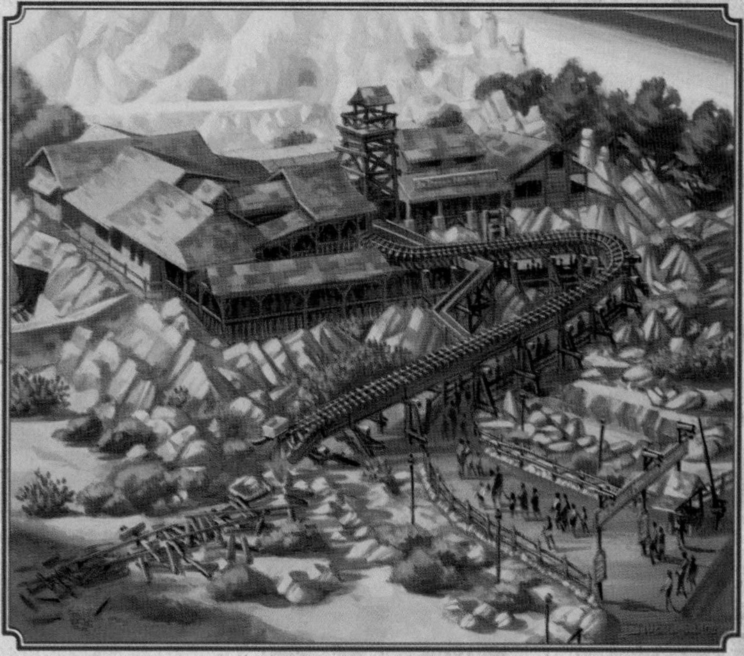

by Joe Warren

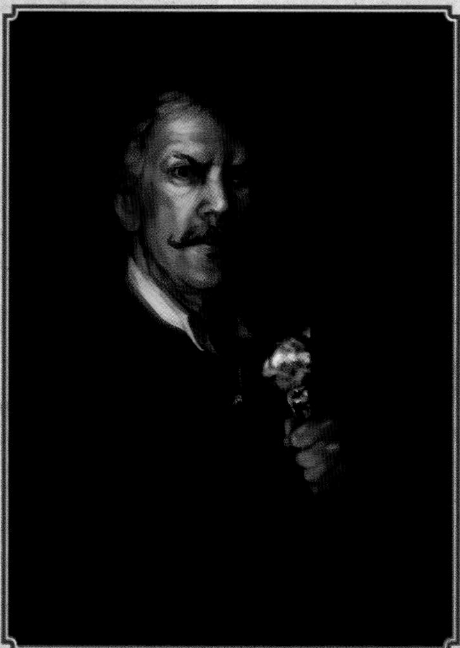

BARNABUS T. BULLION
[*Modeled after Disney Imagineer Tony Baxter*]
by Roi Horn

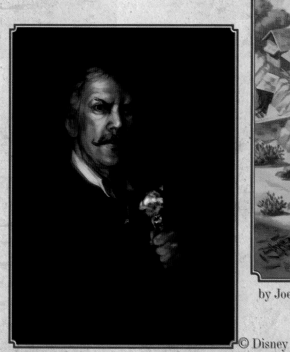

~ Character Designs by Tigh Walker ~

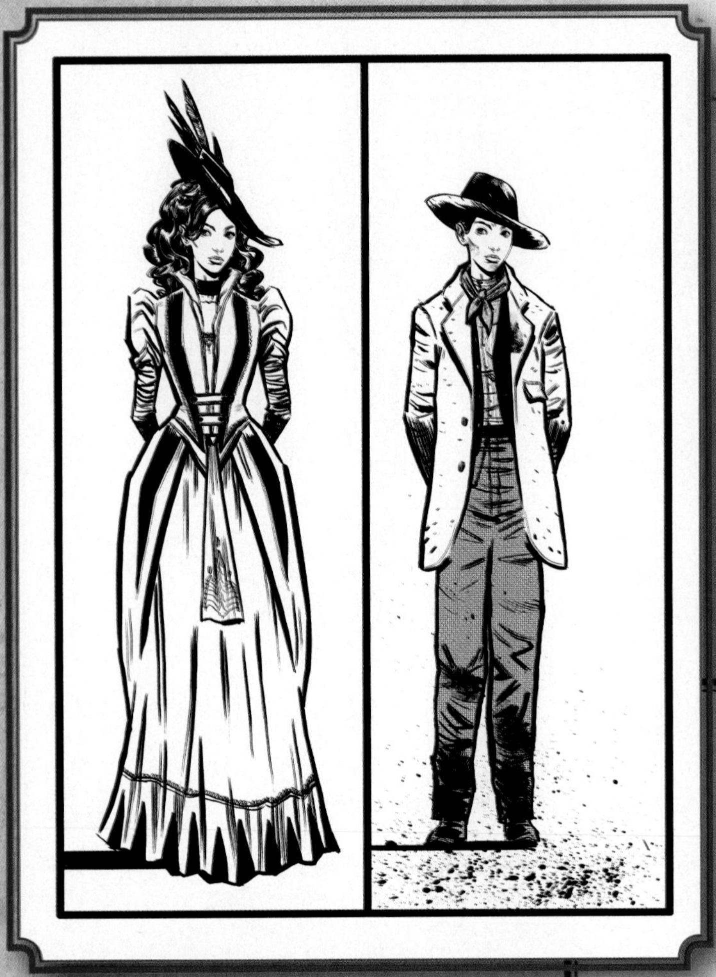

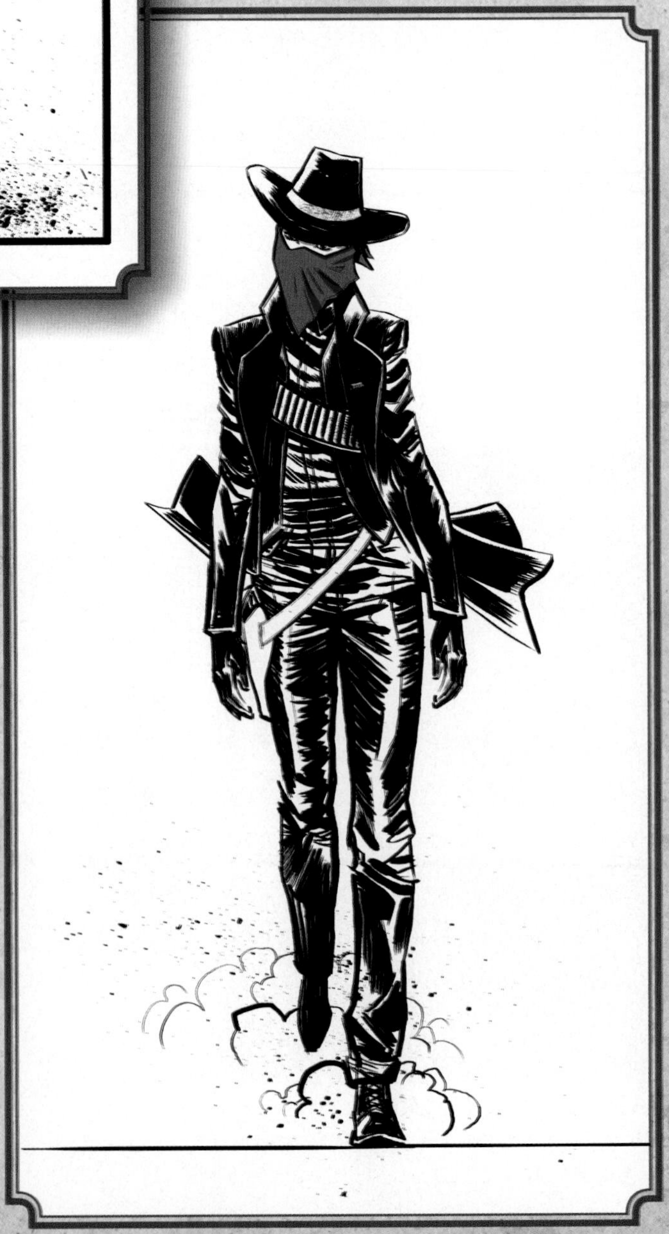

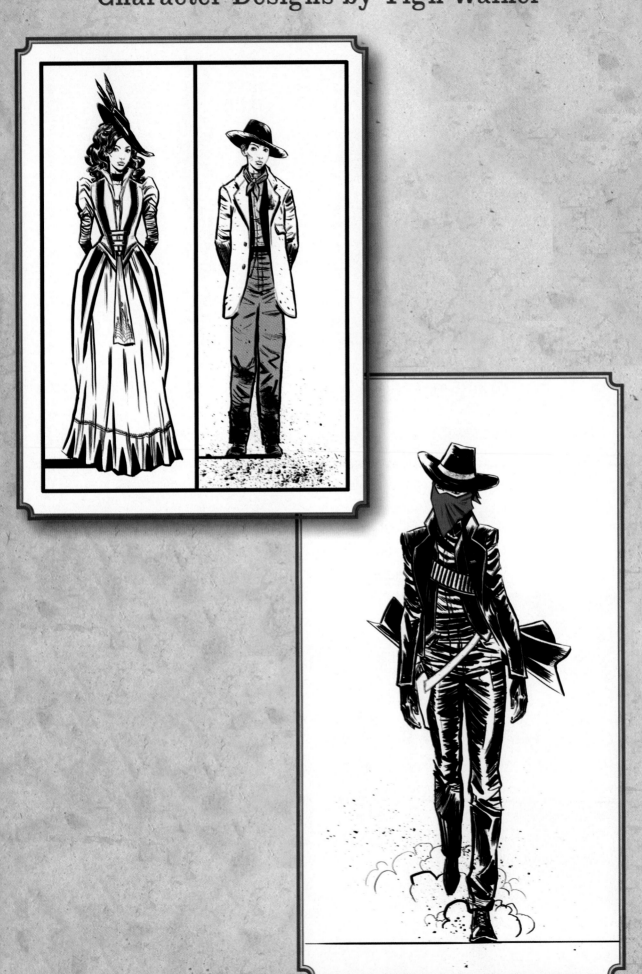

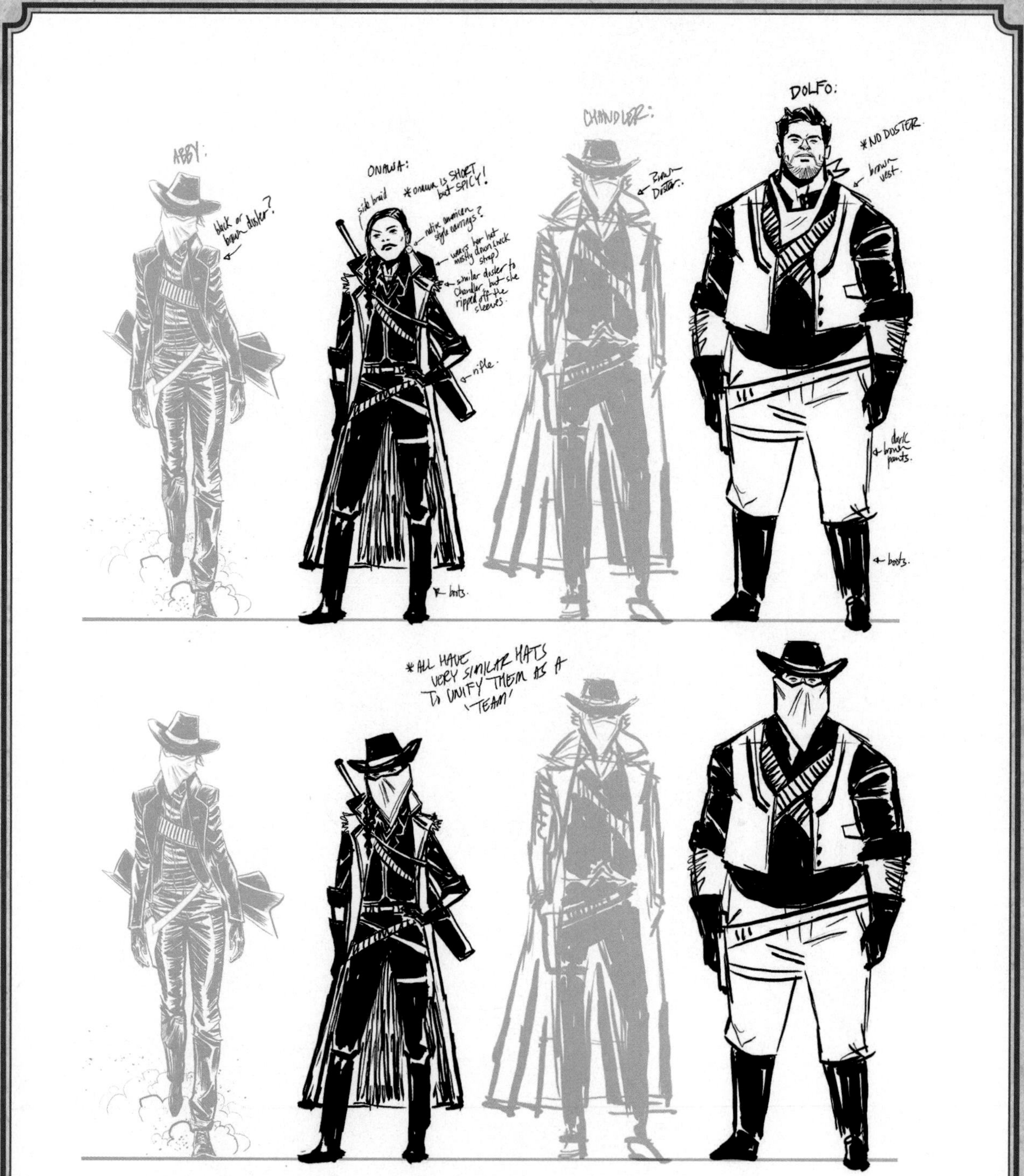
ABBY:
black or brown duster?
ONAWA:
side braid
*onawa is SHORT but SPICY!
native american style earrings?
wears her hat mostly down (neck strap)
similar duster to Chandler, but she ripped off the sleeves.
rifle.
boots.
CHANDLER:
Brown Duster.
DOLFO:
*NO DUSTER.
brown vest.
dark brown pants.
boots.
*ALL HAVE VERY SIMILAR HATS TO UNIFY THEM AS A 'TEAM'

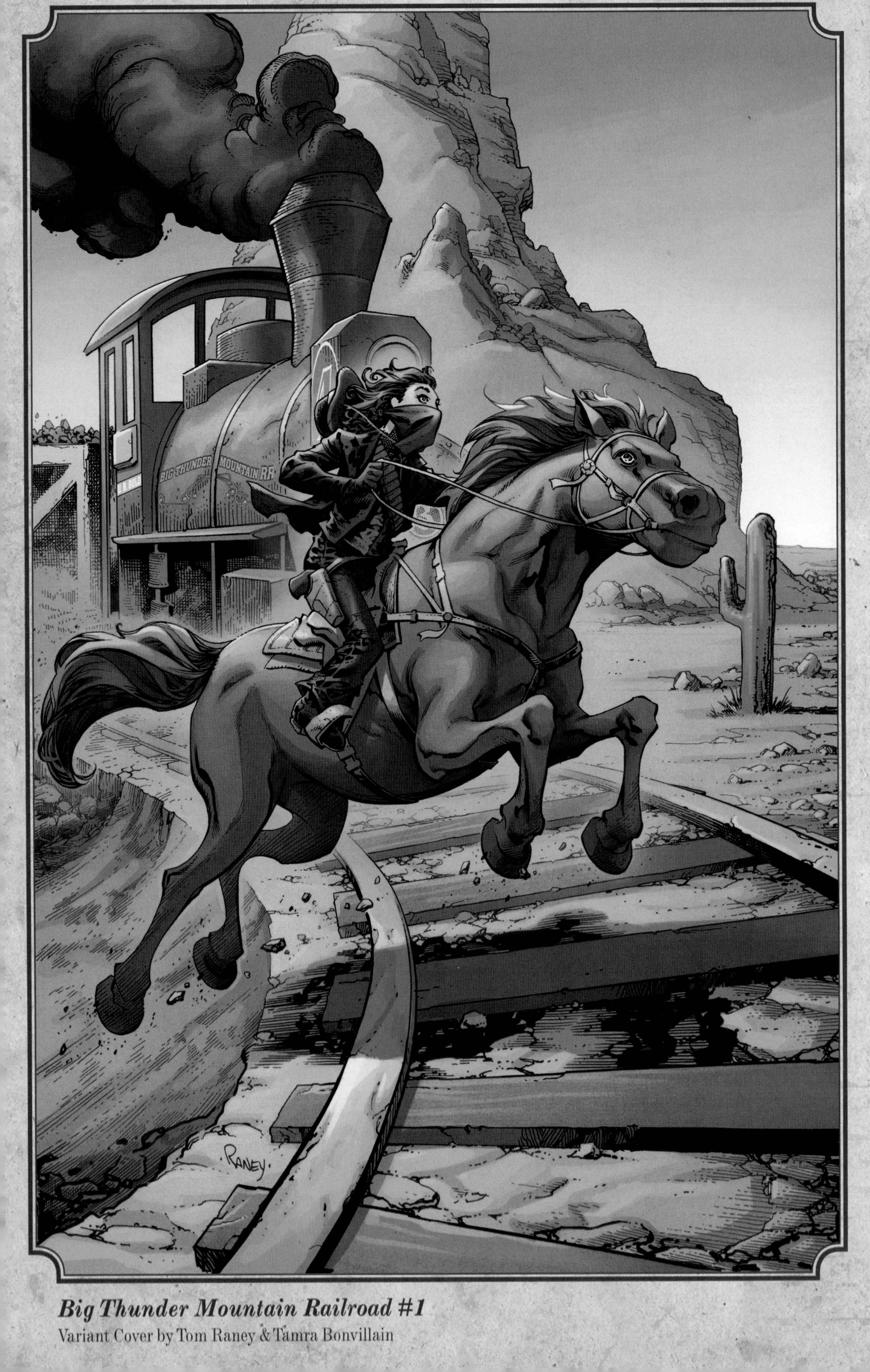
BIG THUNDER MOUNTAIN RR
RANEY

Big Thunder Mountain Railroad #1

Variant Cover by Tom Raney & Tamra Bonvillain

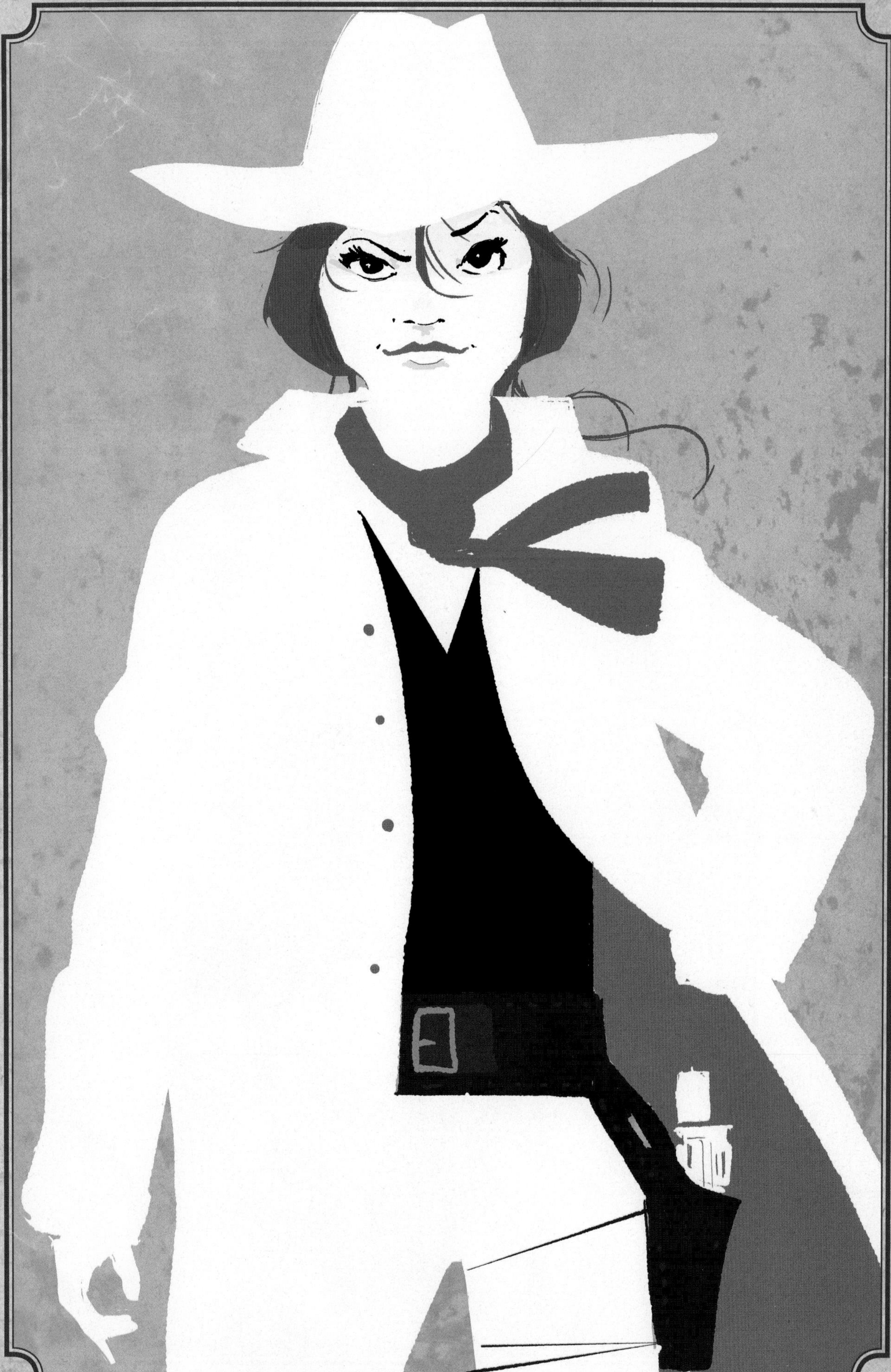

Big Thunder Mountain Railroad #1

Variant Cover by Pascal Campion

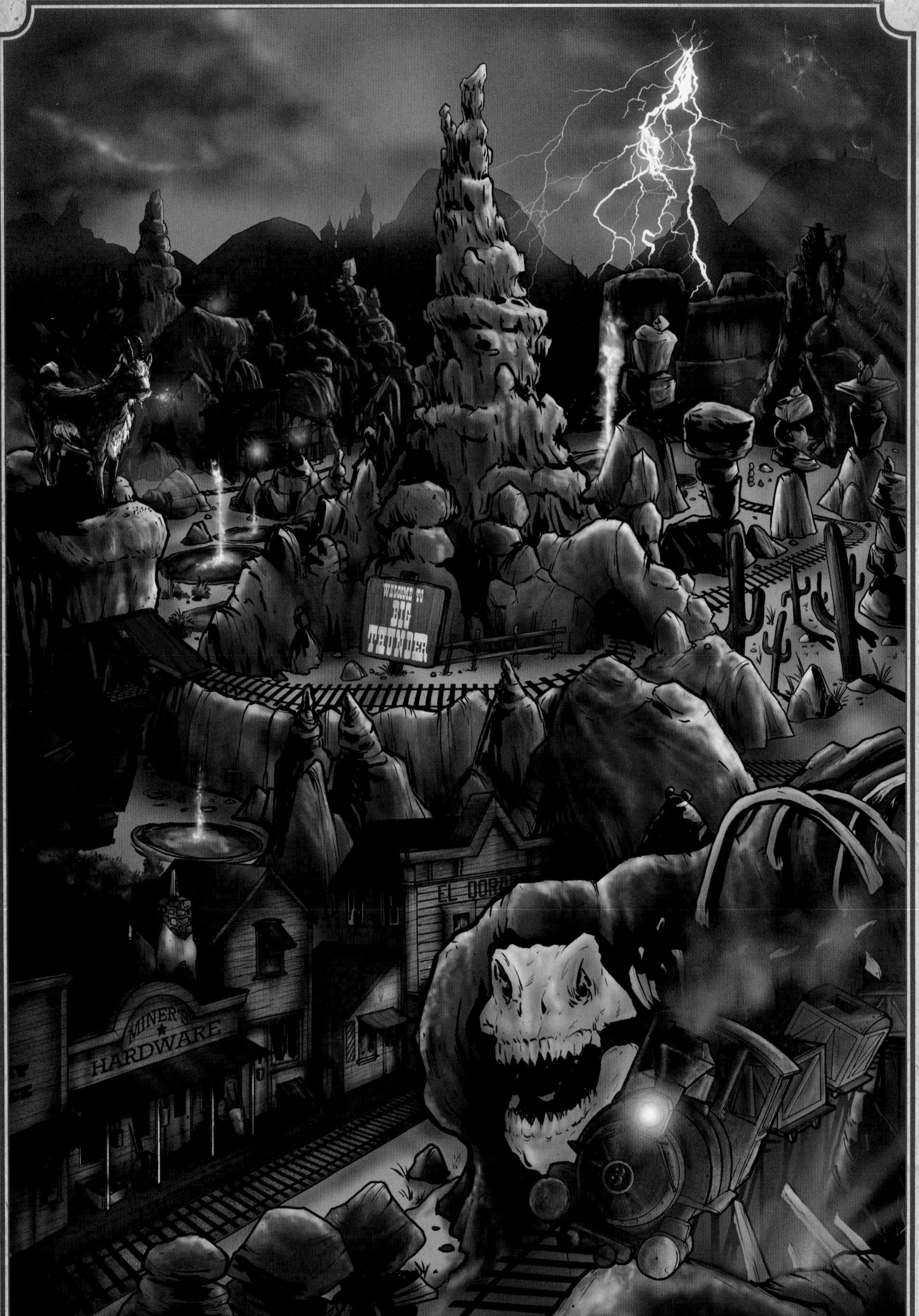
WELCOME TO
BIG
THUNDER
EL DORA
MINER'S
HARDWARE

Big Thunder Mountain Railroad #1-4
Connecting Variant Covers by Brian Crosby